UNARRESTED ARCHIVES

Case Studies in Twentieth-Century Canadian Women's Authorship

Calling upon the archives of Canadian writers E. Pauline Johnson (1861–1913), Emily Carr (1871–1945), Sheila Watson (1909–1998), Jane Rule (1931–2007), and M. NourbeSe Philip (1947–), Linda M. Morra explores the ways in which women's archives have been uniquely approached and shaped by socio-political forces. She also provides a framework for understanding the creative interventions these women staged to protect their records. Through these case studies, Morra traces the influence of institutions such as national archives and libraries, and regulatory bodies such as border service agencies on the creation, presentation, and preservation of women's archival collections.

The deliberate selection of the five literary case studies allows Morra to examine changing archival practices over time, shifting definitions of nationhood and national literary history, varying treatments of race, gender, and sexual orientation, and the ways in which these forces affected the writers' reputations and their archives. Morra also productively reflects on Jacques Derrida's *Archive Fever* and postmodern feminist scholarship related to the relationship between writing, authority, and identity to showcase the ways in which female writers in Canada have represented themselves and their careers in the public record.

LINDA M. MORRA is an associate professor in the Department of English at Bishop's University and the current president of the Quebec Writers' Federation. She edited the collected letters of Emily Carr and Ira Dilworth, published with the University of Toronto Press (2006), and edited and annotated Jane Rule's *Taking My Life* (2011).

Unarrested Archives

Case Studies in Twentieth-Century Canadian Women's Authorship

LINDA M. MORRA

UNIVERSITY OF TORONTO PRESS
Toronto Buffalo London

Toronto Buffalo London
www.utppublishing.com

ISBN 978-1-4426-4881-4 (cloth)
ISBN 978-1-4426-2642-3 (paper)

Library and Archives Canada Cataloguing in Publication

Morra, Linda M., author
Unarrested archives : case studies in twentieth-century Canadian women's authorship / Linda M. Morra.

Includes bibliographical references and index.
ISBN 978-1-4426-4881-4 (bound) – ISBN 978-1-4426-2642-3 (pbk.)

1. Canadian literature (English) – Women authors – Archives – Case studies. 2. Women – Canada – Archives – Case studies. 3. Archives – Social aspects – Canada – Case studies. I. Title.

HQ1453.M674 2014 305.40971 C2014-905018-6

University of Toronto Press acknowledges the financial assistance to its publishing program of the Canada Council for the Arts and the Ontario Arts Council, an agency of the Government of Ontario.

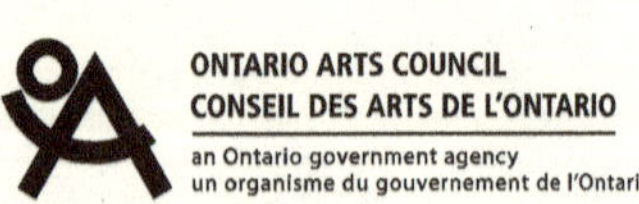

This book has been published with the help of a grant from the Canadian Federation for the Humanities and Social Sciences, through the Awards to Scholarly Publications Program, using funds provided by the Social Sciences and Humanities Research Council of Canada.

University of Toronto Press acknowledges the financial support of the Government of Canada through the Canada Book Fund for its publishing activities.

As always, for my loving parents –
and also for all those women
who are a part of my family

Contents

Acknowledgments

I am surrounded by an invaluable and supportive group of people who helped me to see this book to fruition. Several archivists gave me access to important collections and generously facilitated the research process, including Candice Bjur, Chris Hives, and Leslie Field (University of British Columbia Archives, Irving K. Barber Learning Centre); Catherine Hobbs (Library and Archives Canada); Carl Spadoni (McMaster University Archives); Kathryn Bridge (British Columbia Archives and Records Service); and Gabrielle Earnshaw and Anna St. Onge (Archives & Special Collections at the University of St Michael's College). Then there are the more formal and early readers of the book, Kel Pero and Jessica Schagerl, who provided me with useful insights and positive feedback; these readers were then followed by the two anonymous reviewers at the University of Toronto Press, to whom I am deeply grateful for their thorough and considerate assessment of the manuscript. Their meticulous reading of my work allowed me to rethink the ideas and reshape the manuscript accordingly. No less important to this process was Siobhan McMenemy, acquisitions editor at UTP, who gave essential advice and guidance as I worked through all stages of the manuscript, from its first submission to the crucial revisions in preparation for its publication. Terry Teskey, an attentive and brilliant copy editor, then took the manuscript in hand and smoothed out its clumsy bits: her conscientious work made the manuscript considerably better than it was. I am also grateful to Licia Canton for creating the book's index, and the editorial team at the University of Toronto Press, Leah Connor and Frances Mundy.

Aside from these key readers, archivists, and editors, I was surrounded by a group of colleagues, friends, and family members who were equally supportive, especially Anna Sedo, Deanna Reder, and Mercedes Watson, but also including Tunji Osinubi, Tina Trigg, Chantel Lavoie, Lynn Charpentier, Elise Moser, Graziella Forbes, Lori Schubert, Connie Guzzo-McParland, David Anderson, Janice Stewart, Gary Kuchar, Gerald Lynch, Janice Fiamengo, Teresa Petruzzo, Thomas Tapley, Paul Bayan, Carolyne Van Der Meer, Barbara Richardson, Sharon Davidson, and Wendy Roy. I am thankful to Paul Hjartarson and Gregory Betts, who answered a few inquiries related to specific chapters, and to Andrea Szilagyi for her work as my assistant in the early stages of this project. I presented some material from this book at various conferences, at which time several academics provided excellent feedback: Carole Gerson, Eva-Marie Kröller, David Bentley, Glen Lowry, Paul Hjartarson, and Dean Irvine. I am especially indebted to Tunji Osinubi, a brilliant scholar with whom I regularly exchanged and tested ideas, who read over the fifth chapter in its entirety, a segment of the first chapter, and the first five pages of the introduction. He has been an encouraging and dear friend.

I am deeply honoured that Fred Flahiff read over the chapter on Sheila Watson and provided helpful feedback and support. I am immensely grateful to M. NourbeSe Philip, who granted me access to her "unarrested archives" and read over the last draft of the fifth chapter before giving me her approval. I am also grateful to the executors of the Jane Rule Estate, who graciously allowed me to use the material from the Jane Rule Fonds for this book and then read over the chapter about Rule, at which time they endorsed it. I am thankful to L.G. Harvey, whose regular commute with me to and from Bishop's University provided the space for rich, contemplative discussions about many facets of the book. I am deeply grateful for his support and encouragement. As always, my loving parents, Anthony and Jessie, and my siblings, Sue and Mark, have consistently supported and nourished my efforts and have been quick to send me a heartening word when it was needed.

A small part of this manuscript was published elsewhere: a selection of the fourth chapter on Jane Rule was published as "'Vexed by the Crassness of Commerce': Jane Rule's Struggle for Literary Integrity and Freedom of Expression" in a special issue of *Canadian Literature* (Summer 2010). I have revisited this essay with the kind permission of *Canadian Literature*. About five pages of the chapter on Jane Rule also appear in an essay titled "Autobiographical Text, Archives, and Activism: The Jane Rule Fonds and Her Unpublished Memoir, 'Taking My

Life,'" which is to appear in *Out of the Closet, Into the Archives: Researching Sexual Histories*, edited by Jaime Cantrell and Amy Stone (SUNY Press).

Doing archival research is extremely costly. I therefore deeply appreciate the Social Sciences and Humanities Research Council for awarding me a Standard Research Grant, which enabled me to lay the foundations for this book. Thereafter, I was awarded the FQRSC Établissement de nouveaux professeurs-chercheurs grant, with which I completed the research in the archives. Throughout this process, Bishop's University also awarded me two Senate Research grants, which facilitated extra research trips. I am thankful to the university for its support as I worked through the manuscript from beginning to end.

UNARRESTED ARCHIVES

Case Studies in Twentieth-Century Canadian Women's Authorship

Introduction

"The Law of What Can Be Said"

Unarrested Archives is in part about archives, specifically Canadian women authors' literary records housed both in and beyond official institutions; at times, it is also about the institutions themselves. Studying twentieth-century Canadian female authors and investigating why some of their records disappeared or were released from, refused by, or eventually housed in state-sanctioned establishments highlights the autonomy these women achieved, first, by virtue of how they approached or avoided official institutions and, second, as manifested in the nature and range of materials preserved in either personal or official archives. The visibility of female citizens is dependent upon the preservation of their socio-political and cultural traces. Since there are multiple ways of connecting with the state, these traces determine the kind of visibility a citizen might assume. It is common knowledge that a woman's authorship might have been curtailed prior to the early twentieth century because of her gender.[1] When institutional archives refused her records, as they often did, that refusal threw her legibility as a citizen and her status as an author into question, if it did not entirely erase her. The twentieth century thus offers a critical moment when women could increasingly appear as citizens, as public figures, and, as is pertinent to this book, as authors.

As Michel Foucault suggests in *The Archaeology of Knowledge and the Discourse on Language*, an author's own contributions are provisional, dependent upon the discourses of the period that inform one's texts: he argued that archives were not "the sum of all texts that a culture has kept upon its person as documents attesting to its own past," but rather "the law of what can be said, the system that governs the appearance of statements as unique events" (1972, 128–9). An archive defines "at the outset *the system of its* enunciability" (129). What is included within a repository determines and limits potential enunciations of personhood. A woman could only uneasily make claims to authorship if discourses of a given period or the "law of what can be said" did not recognize her as such. Still, over the course of the twentieth century, women's contributions slowly came to inform the statements of female authors that followed and allowed for their greater visibility: this book deals with that transitional period when women were increasingly represented in institutional archives. Although Foucault's definition of archives has broader reach, extending to the totality of residual discourses of a particular cultural period, this work focuses on archives of a more specific order: not the sum of all texts, but rather the literal establishments that hold material traces of an author's contributions, the mediating spaces that showcase who was able to articulate publicly and what was articulable in a given period; the very cache of papers that a female author deposits in or withholds from a literal institution; and, finally, what else may be approached as an archive when institutions either refuse to preserve or mislay the literary records of a female author.

Foucault's *The Archaeology of Knowledge and the Discourse on Language* and Jacques Derrida's *Archive Fever: A Freudian Impression* set up the terms of this book. They are inevitable starting points when grappling with the subject of archives: they provide the framework of the discourse in the field, the "law of what can be said" on the subject. As Antoinette Burton observes, the "work of Michel Foucault, with its focus on archives as 'documents of exclusion' and 'monuments to particular configurations of power,' is responsible for the shifting fortunes of archival discourse in the academy" (2005, 6). Most critics whose work engages with archives, therefore, begin by calling upon or critiquing these two theorists as foundational to their own work, in fields ranging from postcolonial studies, to gender and sexuality theory, to history and literature. A number of scholars of postcolonial theory and imperial history have turned to both Foucault and Derrida to characterize the power of the archive, the "symbolic weight" it carries in relation to "broader cultural and political projects of colonialism" (Ballantyne 76). Tony Ballantyne, for example, argues that the "archive has been reimagined as a site saturated by power, a dense but uneven body of knowledge scarred by the cultural struggles and violence of the colonial past" (75).

Other scholars are more focused in their application of theories of the archive: Anjali Arondekar's *For the Record: On Sexuality and the Colonial Archive in India* and Ann Cvetkovich's *An Archive of Feelings: Trauma, Sexuality, and Lesbian Public Cultures*, both of which I call upon in this book, simultaneously ground their assumptions in and challenge Derrida's notions of archive, and then argue for attention to representations of, respectively, sexuality and trauma. Arondekar identifies sexuality as central to the colonial record and addresses how one might yet approach archival losses: it is this latter concern that informs my theoretical approach in chapter 1 on Pauline Johnson. Similarly, Cvetkovich identifies how "publics are formed in and through cultural archives," with the result that the experiences of queer and female agents have often remained unrecognized because "the cultural traces they leave are frequently inadequate to the task of documentation" (9). She reminds us that "gathering even a history of the present" is further taxing when documenting emotional lives; yet, she notes, incorporating "affective life into our conceptions of citizenship" is imperative when traditional archives are insufficient and when such "affective forms of citizenship may fall outside the institutional practices that we customarily associate with the concept of citizen" (11).[2] She argues that trauma thus "raises questions about what counts as an archive" (10). It is the raising of such questions that leads not only Cvetkovich but also Burton to insist upon expansion of what is traditionally understood as an archive, a critical attitude that informs my own. In *Archive Stories*, Burton observes that what Derrida has called "archive fever" may apply more broadly, "to denizens of the street or the Internet" (3). Indeed, she adds, the "availability of archival sources of all kinds online arguably makes us all archivists now" (4).

Although I do not invite such radical breadth in my readings of what constitutes an archive or an archivist, I do follow the examples set by Helen Buss and Marlene Kadar in *Working in Women's Archives* (2001), JoAnn McCaig's *Reading In: Alice Munro's Archives* (2002), and the contributors to *Basements and Attics, Closets and Cyberspace: Explorations in Canadian Women's Archives* (2012), extending their crucial foundational work on how to approach women's archives. I also call upon Carolyn Kay Steedman in *Dust: The Archive and Cultural History* (2002), Diana Taylor in *The Archive and the Repertoire* (2003), Wendy W. Walters in *Archives of the Black Atlantic* (2013), and Ann Laura Stoler in *Along the Archival Grain* (2010) in expanding our understanding of what constitutes the historical record and how to approach it. Steedman refers to Foucault's *The Order of Things* to suggest how citizens were arranged and codified by government systems, and to argue that the archive obscures as much as it reveals. In chapter 5, I develop the former idea by demonstrating how M. NourbeSe Philip complicates such codification in her cultivation of what I refer to as a "minor archive." Drawing upon Françoise Lionnet and Shu-mei Shih's concept of "minor transnationalism," I argue that she offers an alternative space, a private cache deliberately withheld from formal institutions, by which to critique the existing national arrangements of archives and to expand her engagement with others beyond national borders. Constructing such a "counter-archive" is "an aspiration," as Walters notes, as much as it is a form of "recollection" (138). In this instance, a scholar's reading practices extend from the archival records themselves to the institutions and the context in which they appear.

An expert in performance studies, Taylor offers another means by which to assess such arrangements. She suggests that approaching traditional archives as the sole repositories of cultural material in fact privileges certain epistemologies, and shows how alternative practices such as performances are integral to the transmission of knowledge. Embodied practices, she argues, are vital to an understanding of the history of the Americas and as a counterbalance to the written archive. Following her, in chapter 1 I consider how Pauline Johnson's embodied performance might be read alongside and against the grain of available print material about her literary career. Stoler also demonstrates how reading "along the archival grain" offers opportunities to study archival production as an expression of imperial governance. It is not merely the content of archives that matters; the very shape they assume and the sociological epistemologies that undergird them must be properly apprehended. I also take this approach in chapter 4 on Jane Rule, in which I assess the papers she left behind for future researchers as part of her activist commitments, and the reasons for where and why she deposited her literary materials.

In addition to engaging with such theorists of the archive, I locate my work within an impressive trajectory of archival scholarship with respect to women writers in Canada. The resurgence of such scholarship is evidenced in the volume of publications that have grown out of various forms of archival research: Lorraine York's *Canadian Literary Celebrity* (2007) and *Margaret Atwood and the Labour of Literary Celebrity* (2013) both rely heavily upon the archive, as did the book York co-edited with Jennifer Blair, Daniel Coleman, and Kate Higginson, *ReCalling Early Canada* (2005); Ruth Panofsky's extensive study *The Literary Legacy of the Macmillan Company of Canada* (2012) examines the key personalities, such as John Gray and Hugh Eayrs, who shaped the press, but also the women who served as readers and whose editing lives were previously sidelined or marginalized; and Carole Gerson's painstakingly detailed and award-winning study on eighteenth- to early-twentieth-century women writers, *Canadian Women in Print* (2010), is informed by extensive archival research that is indispensible to the fields of Canadian literature, women's writing in Canada, and book history. These are only a few among many examples.

My study differs from the ones cited above in its focus upon individual cases in the twentieth century to showcase how women writers were regulated and contained, and how at times they existed in or negotiated both personal and professional antagonist relationships – often asymmetrical relationships that were further vexed by questions of class, race, and sexual orientation. Such antagonisms generated the very divisions, the complex set of relations that in turn resulted in women's productive disruptions. *Unarrested Archives* interrogates and reframes research conducted by other scholars in the fields of archives, Canadian literature, and women's authorship, and then extends that research to reformulate and expand the definition of the archive, to reanimate approaches to its materials, and to remap the means by which women writers' agencies were enacted through their publications or their archives – or both. This book thus recalibrates current scholarly perspectives on Canadian archives and Canadian women writers' agencies in relationship to the archive in the twentieth century.[3]

Arrested and Unarrested Archives

This scholarly lineage into which my work fits does not provide the underpinnings for the formulation of "arrested" and "unarrested" that I establish and explore in this book and that give rise to its title; instead, a definition offered by Derrida provides the starting point. The "meaning of 'archive,'" he notes, emerges from "the Greek *arkheion*: initially a house, a domicile, an address, the residence of the superior magistrates, the *archons*, those who commanded" (2). There is, therefore, a fundamental association between those who held and "signified political power" and had the "right to make or to represent the law" (2), a power and right that emerged from the magistrate's dwelling place:

> It is thus, in this domiciliation, in this house arrest, that archives take place. The dwelling, this place where they dwell permanently, marks

> this institutional passage from the private to the public, which does not always mean from the secret to the nonsecret ... [The] documents, which are not always discursive writings, are only kept and classified under the title of the archive by virtue of a privileged topology. They inhabit this unusual place, this place of election where law and singularity intersect in *privilege*. (2–3)

This passage reveals a peculiar and crucial complication in Derrida's formulation of domiciliation and politicized space. The passage above appears directly after he observes that *arkhē,* the Greek for "archive," coordinates two principles: one related to *commencement* and the other to *commandment*. The authority to command and claim sovereignty issues from the authority procured through claims of origins: from the beginning, one might say, it was this way and is therefore immutable. That the *arkhē* has such a legacy, Derrida argues, is forgotten, taken for granted: the concept of "the archive *shelters* itself from this memory which it shelters" (2). The sheltering of such authority was manifested almost literally when one considers that the very place where archival papers were stored and guarded by the *archons* was the residence of the superior magistrate. These papers were thus held under "house arrest" at "their home"; their physical security in this space undergirded the magistrate's hermeneutic entitlements (2). So Derrida observes that it is "at their home, in that *place* which is their house (private house, family house, or employee's house), that official documents are filed" (2). The parenthesis he uses in this quotation suggestively represents the space bracketed from the public domain, one that was unmistakably private and yet the source of the magistrate's external power and stability.

The *Oxford English Dictionary* contains several definitions of "arrested" upon which I call in this book. The first of these is "to stop, stay, remain, rest," which bears most directly upon how authority was generated by the magistrate's safeguarding or preservation of papers – that is, to call upon another nuance of the word, papers related to the legal system were "detained" in the residence or the private space of the magistrate. Arresting archives sanction and render visible certain individuals, but also vigilantly control those records with which individuals are associated. A second meaning of the word carries negative valences and is conjured up by the first: to "capture, seize, lay hold upon, or apprehend by legal authority" either papers or persons. The contradiction embedded in this practice is related to the fact that the place of privilege from which legal power emanates was associated with confinement and even criminality; the same place that therefore empowers male subjects is also the one to which family members and servants, but particularly women, had been habitually consigned – the private sphere.

This book singles out women as the primary actors who inhabited this private space alongside, in Derrida's formulation, the legal papers in the magistrate's residence, although he himself makes no reference to women. The sphere that was habitually incapacitating for women– as well as servants and other domestic dependents – is vitally different when inhabited by materials of the civil servant or magistrate: authority was accorded only to those who guarded and had interpretive power over the papers, rather than to the papers themselves, and to the "place of election where law and singularity intersect in *privilege*" (Derrida 2). Such papers, contained within the private sphere, were registers of the power of civil officers, those who administered the laws and who determined what was preserved and safeguarded, especially because of the papers' status in relation to law. Such tendencies towards preservation also illuminate its logic: there is "no political power without the control of the archive" (4n1). Archival documents held in custody often reinscribe power structures, and are therefore sometimes much less a sign of transgression from the public to the private sphere than sites of privilege, an enunciation of both permanence and immovability. Constructs of stability, the papers also appeared as hermetically sealed entities that were guarded jealously by the *archon* to assure both his political autonomy and his historical legacy. Rather than simply material evidence of legal transactions, these "arrested papers" held within a private space became signs of the magistrate's authority. This formulation contradicts the feminist conception of space as constructed along gender lines: the private (female) and the public (male). Instead, the magistrate's power as it is invested in the archive is expressed across these two domains.

But what then of women's archives or their own personal papers? Many of these papers were apparently *unarrested*; it is at this point that I call upon three other significations associated with the word "arrested." By "unarrested" I mean, first, those records that were in fact "non-arrested": materials that were never relegated to formal institutions or within spheres of power, and that were refused a place by and in institutions. The term secondarily refers to those materials deliberately withheld from institutions by a women writer, as is the case with M. NourbeSe Philip, who used such withholding as a strategy to counter institutions that wielded control over and disciplined national subjects: when, as a woman, she was no longer ignored by the state, she could choose whether or not to deposit her papers with an official archive. These papers, when neither impeded nor contained nor apprehended within formal institutions, showcase the means by which to disrupt, undermine, and unsettle the gathering of elements that work towards expressing a homogenous and ideal configuration.

"Unarrested" might also be understood as referring to archival materials that were released from the care of a formal institutional, that is, those that were once guarded in official archives but then either misplaced or discarded altogether. Papers that are in this way unarrested may be characterized as such not simply because of their location beyond the reaches of the traditional archive, but also because of their potential to be mobilized for the purposes of critiquing the partial knowledge that perpetuates hierarchy and domination. Significantly, a fourth meaning the *OED* lists for "arrested" implies movement, an unchecked course of action. Rather than an attempt to "stop the course" or impede a "train of things in motion or progress," the act of unarresting involves mobilization: I consider how records are either freed from legal and socio-political constraint or are mobilizing in terms of their socio-political effects. While institutional archives might physically hold or "stop" papers, they also contradictorily allow for ideas to be circulated as researchers gain access to them and render them public. If the arrested documents within a formal archive suggest stasis, the act of arrest also paradoxically allows for mobility – specifically of the ideas to which a general public will have access, rather than the papers themselves.

As we shall see in chapters 3 and 5 on, respectively, Sheila Watson and Philip, house arrest is a preliminary stage – sometimes quite literally in one's private accommodations – that precedes the cultivation of an archive within an institutional repository. Watson's "imminent archive," for example, is most illuminating for how records might then be used to create such mobility. Chapter 4 on Rule complicates the notion of arrested archives by contextualizing her preserved records in other state pronouncements about papers and books it deemed illegal: arrested archives become nuanced when we consider who safeguards the materials, what purpose informs their safe-keeping, and what eventually becomes sanctioned as a legitimate fond or an archive. It is upon this paradigm that my study focuses its attention and from which it draws its methodology in its application to contemporary Canadian women writers. The title of this work, *Unarrested Archives*, derives its logic from a fifth nuance of the word "arrested": to "fix one's attention" or "keep our minds, ourselves, resting or fixed upon the consideration of a subject." Women's papers were not only exiled from the very institution that otherwise determined the power of the state, but they also escaped notice – until critical consideration began to reverse the process, to focus its attention upon and seek out these wayward papers.

What of the women who wrote these works? If their papers were exiled, languishing on the periphery of authority and experience, women themselves habitually suffered from confinement, also under the rubric of being "sheltered" – that is, they themselves suffered house arrest and were consigned to this private sphere. Since women did not carry significant ontological weight, as Judith Butler and Gayatri Chakravorty Spivak have observed, and were considered scarcely legible subjects within political networks, they would not have been regarded as registering important socio-political or cultural traces. Neither would they have been regarded as possessing materials worthy of being arrested. This omission of women and women's contributions from sites of knowledge production suggests both partial and limited ways of knowing their histories and experiences, which were otherwise mediated and governed by patriarchy and dominant culture.

Papers by women have yet survived, and how they used and preserved their records to express autonomy extends well beyond the reach and scope of institutions of power and the principles of domiciliation. Indeed, it is in the very fact that papers are sometimes located outside centralized repositories that women find sources of empowerment, beyond the reach of institutions that hold papers under house arrest. Unarrested archival materials thus come to serve as crucial articulations of women's social locations and offer an interesting vantage point from which to view sites of epistemological privilege. As the title suggests, *Unarrested Archives* in general invites rethinking of seemingly clear designations, of what the archive means, of what power structures are undergirded by papers under house arrest, and by whom and for whom archives are established. My research shows that there is no neat binarism related to papers preserved by or about men or women. However, such archives complicate the tendencies that involved the general exclusion or discarding of women's papers from centralized repositories, even as twentieth-century Canadian women's papers increasingly find their way back into national and symbolic institutions.

The methodology of this book offers the only way I can proceed, since it showcases the extraordinary range and the crucial evolution of women's agencies by locating them within a historical context; in other words, the chapters are arranged chronologically to demonstrate how women's self-empowerment is manifested differently over the course of the twentieth century and how their agencies can only assume particular forms in specific decades in response to the socio-political conditions of the time. I use a case-studies approach to examine a range of temporal periods, genres, and socio-political concerns. The five women writers selected for this study are established authors who find unique ways to express their autonomy by setting up and controlling their own archives in view of restrictions in part related to their gender; such strategies meant that they were also controlling their literary and cultural legacies. Collectively, these writers allow for a variety of issues to be considered in relation to class, race, education, and sexual orientation. As one example, M. NourbeSe Philip, who is the subject of chapter 5, decided not to deposit her papers in an official, national institution. Her refusal was her means of expressing control over how she would come to be interpreted by researchers, academics, and others. She could not have expressed power by *withholding* her papers in the early twentieth century, a gesture that can only be made by the late twentieth century when women's papers had greater cultural value and were sought after by official establishments.

I selected these five Canadian female authors because they allow me to draw a broader range of conclusions about practices related to authorship and archives, and to the national imaginings that sometimes governed and affected literary practices for women writers: Pauline Johnson (1861–1913), Emily Carr (1871–1945), Sheila Watson (1909–1998), Jane Rule (1931–2007), and M. NourbeSe Philip (1947–). In the process, I show what shaped or influenced the literary production of these Canadian women writers, assess their negotiations with the publishing industry, and demonstrate how they side-stepped the means by which their potentially incompatible loyalties might have been disciplined. Many of their interactions demonstrate that they implicitly – if not explicitly – challenged and worked against the authority of state institutions or key figures in the publishing industry, or found ways of cooperating with them to find publication. These authors are similar in that none was apologetic about her career as author, but rather assumed the importance of her writing. They differed in the reasons that they wrote: to earn money, to answer to patriotic claims, to represent local or personal concerns, to develop a distinct aesthetic, or to address issues of race, national identity, socio-cultural politics, sexuality, and morality. They equally differed in terms of the strategies by which they gained agency: among others, proximity to powerful male figures, public performances, the use of agents, and legal means. These strategies would have been variable, especially given the fact that the authors were writing in different decades in Canada and represent a range of different interests, from the late nineteenth century when authorship was an occupation considered less legitimate for a woman, to the later part of the twentieth century when their socio-political position was more secure.

There are thus five modes of unarrested and arrested archives that I explore, each of which corresponds to one author included in this study. Individual chapters offer a unique and significant instance of how we might read in, around, and against archives. The material I use to assess the authors' achievements might be found inside or beyond the reaches of a formal institution, but I also evaluate the means by which their archives were negotiated, established, displaced – and, in Johnson's case, unarrested and misplaced. These readings then extend to the writers' negotiations with others, to approaches to the work they subsequently produced, and to the archives they set up, directly or indirectly. In chapter 1, I focus upon the turn-of-the-century Mohawk poet and performer Pauline Johnson. Although she began writing and performing in the late nineteenth century, she is a pivotal figure for showcasing attitudes towards Indigenous women at the turn-of-the century and thereafter. In confronting an unexpected absence in her papers at the University of Reading, I was reminded of a larger gap related to her stage performances. Although there are surviving papers at McMaster University and elsewhere, and even newspaper reports that tell us something about these performances, this gap invites a reconsideration of her work in terms of unarrested archives, especially in this instance, concerning oral cultural forms. Her performed text is what Taylor would refer to as the "scenario" and invokes an intimate and confessional dynamic that cannot be read or accessed directly in archival materials proper. As Cvetkovich contends, matters of affect, indeed performed and embodied experiences, are "difficult to chronicle through the materials of a traditional archive" (241). Johnson's performances, therefore, are a reminder of the elusiveness of some women's archival materials and of how we may reanimate approaches to them.

The second chapter focuses on Emily Carr's attempt to create two archives, both grounded in the principle of kinship: the first related to preserving Indigenous cultural iconography, the second to her own personal aesthetic achievements, which she preserved as a result of her intimate relationship with her editor, friend, and executor, Ira Dilworth. The former archive involved a forgetting of kinship to gain access to the public sphere, which did not succeed; the latter involved a remembering of kinship for the same purpose, which was ultimately efficacious. Her intimacy with Dilworth thus allowed her the vehicle not only to find publication for her autobiography, *Growing Pains,* after her death, but also to establish extensive archival holdings at the British Columbia Archives and Records Service in Victoria. Indeed, her will identified Dilworth, rather than an official repository, as the person to whom she bequeathed her papers. This gesture is revealing about how Carr achieved agency. One may approach her increasing dependence upon him as the means by which she was reinscribed as a subject submissive to masculinist control and national governance, but these efforts also paradoxically allowed her to acquire ontological weight, to be rendered a legible subject in a national imaginary that would have otherwise excluded her. The archive of kinship reveals how she identified a means of articulating her concerns through a male agent.

Chapter 3 addresses a similar tendency: Sheila Watson entrusted her papers to a friend, Fred Flahiff, whom she charged with the responsibility of setting up her archive, or to seeing it done. Her decision to leave her literary records and, more specifically, her handwritten journals in the hands of another might be read as a strategy of *displacement*, a particular manifestation of unarresting archives that registers power by virtue of collaboration. That strategy finds its complement in another dynamic she invoked, of *imminence*. The setting up of her fonds at St Michael's College and the telling of the story she expressly wanted told were purposely contingent upon others for their formation, and extend the process of imminence: her gestures simultaneously ensured that others would be involved in disseminating her narrative – indeed, multiple versions thereof – well after she was no longer able to tell her own story.

The papers of Jane Rule afford us an entirely different perspective because she scrupulously retained all her papers; over fifty boxes of material were amassed and preserved as part of the first and subsequent accessions at the University of British Columbia Special Collections and Archives. In chapter 4 I explore how two legal cases set the precedent and showcase the reasons for Rule's decision to leave her archive with the University of British Columbia. That decision, in conjunction with the materials she selected to deposit with the university, demonstrate her activist commitments; contextualized within these legal cases, her decisions display the importance of considering who preserves archival records, what justifies their preservation, and what are deemed legitimate fonds or archives. The papers Rule preserved are consistent with other decisions she made in her lifetime: to assert the value of her life, her work, and her papers, and to challenge literary spaces in Canada and abroad that until then had been governed by heteronormative structures and practices. She offers us an example of how women writers might actually seek house arrest for their papers, but as a means of expanding the "law of what might be said" about women. The challenge for researchers in such instances relates not to lack of papers but to how to approach the voluminous materials preserved. It is no surprise, then, that this chapter is the longest in this book: the sheer wealth of archival material meant that I was able to conduct a much more detailed study of how Rule negotiated her professional career and expanded aesthetic and imaginative spaces for the articulation of the queer community's concerns. These papers, taken together, are also significant in demonstrating her activist tendencies, how she consistently challenged the parameters of the literary market through the figure of the agent. The papers are essential to understanding the cultural and political milieu out of which Rule worked and that profoundly shaped her literary consciousness, but they are also essential as a reminder to women of the importance of preserving their own papers for posterity.

Chapter 5 focuses on two distinct archives, the "minor archive" and the "media archive." M. NourbeSe Philip preserved a significant cache of papers in her basement, the clearest example of the unarrested archive. At the time of writing this book, that cache remains "uncaptured" by mainstream Canadian repositories and yet is mobilizing in its effects. Indeed, at the time of writing she was continuing to withhold her papers from Canadian institutions. In effect, Philip creates what I call the "minor archive," as a means of activating power and resisting domiciliation, for good reason: she works against a political imaginary that would construct Black Canadians as "outsiders," whose presence in and contributions to Canada have been often contested. The very need for the construction of her minor archive identifies the social location and subjectivity to which Philip might have been consigned had she not refused, as it also highlights the failures of an imagined multicultural community in Canada. This consignment was exacerbated by a particular media incident, produced by a media archive, which characterized her interactions as a political activist and those of the African

Canadian community in demeaning ways. As I argue in this chapter, women are critiqued primarily for their "category membership – as females first and foremost" because femaleness carries a "devalued status" (Schur 6–7); but this process of devaluation is intensified as the result of Philip's race. Her safeguarding of these papers thus needs to be viewed as part of the agencies and political strategies she used to represent herself and to critique discourses that were detrimental to her career as an author in Canada.

This book, then, explores not only the reformulation of archives, but also how researchers can approach the different kinds of archives that have developed around women writers, consider what they reveal about those writers, and assess the forms of self-agency those writers assumed in twentieth-century Canada. How women writers express such agencies and how such agencies are mediated, governed, or impeded is a direct function of the temporal conditions and contexts from which they worked. Those conditions offer the most prominent reason for the means by which they eventually create particular archives, secure publication, or engage with an audience. This book examines how women writers interacted with public figures and negotiated their presence in the public sphere; it then draws conclusions about and clarifies the modes of agency they adopted or were implicated in through their negotiations. How they expressed autonomy is also directly related to the political apparatus that gives permission, mediates, disciplines, and sometimes even silences their literary efforts. How they negotiated their status in relation to the publishing industry suggests how they located themselves within the body politic and laid claim to authorship. This book ultimately illuminates not only how women writers were interpellated in twentieth-century Canada and the different modes of agency women adopted to secure and valorize their aesthetic achievements, but also sheds light on the imaginative ways we might define and approach women's archives.

1 The Archive of Embodiment: Pauline Johnson's "A Cry from an Indian Wife"

What if the recuperative gesture returns us to a space of absence? How then does one restore absence to itself? Put simply, can an empty archive also be full?

– Anjali Arondekar, *For the Record*

I am a Redskin, but I am something else, too – I am a woman.

– Pauline Johnson, "As It Was in the Beginning"

The Recuperative Gesture: The Spectacle as Embodied Archive

Upon deciding to include Pauline Johnson (1861–1913) as the subject of a chapter in this book, I sought out those archival deposits in Canada and abroad related to her literary and dramatic performances, as a means of laying the foundation for my research. I found considerable material housed at McMaster University and Queen's University, among other institutions, before I approached the Random House Group Archive and Library at the University of Reading in England, into which the Bodley Head Papers had been enfolded. Bodley Head , the publishing company set up by John Lane, produced only Johnson's first collection, *The White Wampum*, and was at the time renowned for its erotic and risqué books.[1] The promise of an enriching record of how her first book came to be negotiated was tantalizing. Unfortunately, the Bodley Head papers preserved *before* the year 1929 had been transferred to the Harry Ransom Centre at the University of Texas at Austin (the papers *after* 1929 remained at the University of Reading), and at some point in their transferral Johnson's papers went missing or were simply not retained.

Thus, when I approached the University of Reading, I was told that "we have no material from this period because it all went to the University of Texas many years ago."[2] The University of Texas responded in similar terms: they regretted that they were "unable to locate any correspondence by Johnson in the Lane holdings."[3] Since Stephen Leacock's papers had been relocated to and preserved in Texas, I assumed those of Johnson would have been treated in a similar fashion. In fact, papers from this facet of her life did not surface anywhere.[4] As I explained in the introduction, her papers might be seen to be unarrested in terms of the third meaning I identify: released from institutional care and either completely dispensed with or misplaced.[5]

The logic that might have informed the preservation of Leacock's papers but engendered the loss of Johnson's in at least one formal archive and by one publishing house certainly relates to the fact that her "life on the road was not conducive to saving papers" (Gerson 2004, 433), but also to the fact of her gender.[6] The loss might also be interpreted within another, larger context involving the collection and preservation of papers at the turn of the century in Canada. A woman's papers did not have as much currency as those of a man, to be sure, but Indigenous persons were also subject to a different interpretive lens and value system. Arresting the papers of women – Indigenous women, no less – was not a common occurrence, since their papers would have been seen to have little value. Since Johnson was part Mohawk, some of her materials would also likely have been subject to ethnographic collecting practices of the period, for which Canada was regarded as a central site in the early twentieth century (Nurse 42). Canada was seen as a source of "authentic" cultural artefacts, practices, and traditions, less susceptible to outside influences or "contamination" from Europe. The belief that such authentic and traditional Aboriginal cultures in Canada were in decline fuelled collecting practices of anthropologists in Canada, Britain, and America. As a result, Canada implemented a series of reforms that modernized cultural collecting, to shift it from amateur to professional and scientific practices (43). Of utmost concern to most professional ethnographic collectors was the preservation of what was viewed as the "moribund First Peoples," and the materials collected therefore included "oral traditions, songs, legends, recipes, family genealogies, histories, cultural practices related to education and totemism, and religious views and languages" (44). As critic Andrew Nurse notes, the Anthropology Division of the National Museum endorsed certain cultural forms and sanctioned those who could speak authoritatively about and collect legitimately from cultural collections: in other words, "a new system of authority supported by the state ... recognized the voice of the professional as the legitimate spokesperson for culture" (45).[7] As we shall see in chapter 2, where I discuss Emily Carr's attempts to capture Indigenous iconography in her canvases, such professionals eventually determined whose materials were worthy of house arrest, that is, worthy of preservation, and whose were jettisoned. As the Bodley Head incident suggests, past practices continue to inform current decisions about what papers should be preserved in and sanctioned by official institutions, albeit to a lesser degree.

Material archives, of course, were – and to some extent still are – more explicitly valued over oral forms of transmission, a Western perspective that does not find its equivalent in Indigenous nations and that cannot capture the cultural and temporal dimensions of Johnson's public appearance on the stage. Yet, as Diana Taylor notes, orality and embodied performances are key to the production of knowledge in Indigenous cultures because they play a vital role in "conserving memory and consolidating identities" (xviii). This understanding is especially important for a poet and performer like Johnson, since there is little (if any) evidence that such ethnographic professionals actively solicited Johnson's work, nor are her artefacts part of, for example, the Canadian Museum of Civilization's archive.[8] Most of her materials, literary in nature, were in fact acquired by McMaster University, by Queen's University in the Edith and Lorne Pierce Collection of Canadiana, by Trent University, by Chiefswood, and by the City of Vancouver, where I was subsequently able to do much of my research. Certainly, enough archival material has been preserved in these and other institutions that critics Carole Gerson and Veronica Strong-Boag and cultural biographer Charlotte Gray, as examples, have been able to produce their extraordinary research about Johnson's life and work. Indeed, selected materials from the McMaster University collection of Johnson's paper were being digitized in the mid-1990s, one of the first such initiatives undertaken in Canada.[9]

The gap I encountered, however, occasioned the questions that inform this chapter and the crucial argument being made: why Johnson's own work was at times also unarrested, how a critic might interpret or approach such gaps, and what alternatives there are to paper-based archives. Of course, no archive is ever absolutely complete: absences in archives exist for all manner of reasons that might extend from the record-keeping practices of institutions to decisions made about privacy by individual writers and executors. Certainly family interventions sometimes play a vital role in the preservation or destruction of crucial papers, as was the case for Johnson, whose sister reputedly destroyed some of Johnson's personal materials after her death. In Johnson's case, one must also consider the role played by *both* literary and anthropological institutions of the period, for which her material might have occasionally fallen outside the purview of their collecting practices, such as Bodley Head or the Canadian Museum of Civilization. Sometimes, her work did not fit into existing categories that would have determined what was legitimate or worthy of preservation.[10] From the point of view of ethnographic collectors, for example, her literary work and public performances would have been regarded as either inappropriate in terms of acceptable genres, or "impure" and "inauthentic" rather than properly informed by Indigenous orality; from the point of view of formal, national institutions, her work would have been seen as "contaminated" by popular European influences and she as a popular Indigenous writer rather than a serious (male) author contributing to high culture. To examine her work – or that of other women – inevitably means dealing with related limitations or gaps in the available archival materials. When we cannot locate such unarrested archives, we might approach the absence by measuring its contours, determining its character and dimensions, by virtue of those material traces that consistently point to and take shape around an event or a significant moment. The "recuperative gesture" to which Anjali Arondekar refers involves working productively against such absences, while also allowing critics to read their contours and depths as part of a larger political framework and agenda of the period. Put another way, an empty archive might be read as "full" in terms of its suggestive and interpretive possibilities.

One such interpretive possibility and meaningful alternative to arrested archives, or to traditional institutional repositories, serves as the focus of this chapter: that possibility is related to Johnson's embodied performances and performance practices, especially given their proximity to Indigenous orality. As Taylor (2003) observes, these embodied performances have been habitually caught in a "double critical move," when they are both highlighted and then negated as a form of non-Western cultural production (11); to that end, attempts to encompass such a performance within a Western epistemological system involve either characterizing it as disruptive or downplaying and ignoring those elements that elude an "explanatory grasp" (11). The Western tendency to privilege written texts over embodied performances engenders a loss that is critically duplicated when such performances are not seen as part of what Taylor calls the "ephemeral *repertoire* of embodied practice/ knowledge" (19). Her definition of the repertoire, "all those acts usually thought of as ephemeral, non-reproducible knowledge," is useful here in that it also permits individual agency to be recognized as integral to the deployment of repertoire. The repertoire, moreover, also requires another "presence" – that is, it is only deployed as other individuals bear witness to and "participate in the production and reproduction of knowledge by 'being there'" and by recognizing and responding to its elements (20). It thus offers an alternative system of knowledge and preservation that expands the traditional, material archive. Calling upon the repertoire to some extent circumvents the reduplication of ideologies that also informed past ethnographic collecting practices.

In particular, Johnson's performance of "A Cry from an Indian Wife," the focus of this chapter, might be seen as an articulation of a more specific form of the repertoire, what Taylor refers to as the "scenario." The "portable framework" of the scenario might be approached as the unarrested archive: in fact, it offers itself as the most radical form of the unarrested archive, by virtue of how it is implicated in the mobilization of ideas. The scenario is repeatable and thereby renders visible the socio-cultural fabric of the period, or rather, some of its ideological formulations that sometimes resemble stereotype – in Johnson's instance, not only "wronged wife" but also "savage" and "native princess" (28). Indeed, in this period, the "Indian princess" stereotype was in vogue, involving depictions of "beautiful, innocent maidens, uncorrupted by the modern world but eager to be at the service of white men" (Sonneborn 101). In forging such roles and in erotically displaying her physical self, Johnson risked reinvoking the colonial violence wrought upon the Indigenous female body. She ultimately evaded the reinscription of this stereotype by invoking the scenario. Johnson intervened in the cultural construction of Indigenous woman as fantasy object to demonstrate the real legacy of colonial violence, even as she ultimately sidestepped outright contravention of political orthodoxies of the period. The resulting performances may have appeared to draw upon stereotype but, in fact, derived their kinetic charge by virtue of repetition.

Calling upon performance theory, Taylor attributes another four characteristics to the scenario, all of which are relevant to approaching Johnson's dramatic performance of her poem. First, the scenario is set in motion by the physical location of the performance, both the material stage and the "highly codified environment," and by the social construction of bodies within particular contexts (28). Johnson's considered use of her own body, the costumes she wore, the venues she deliberately selected for her performances, and the intimate dynamic she consequently invoked between her and audience members were strategies by which she harnessed affective power and engaged her audiences. Her embodied performance in "A Cry from an Indian Wife" called upon intimacy to great effect, a strategy she extended to her public negotiations with those who could further her career on the stage. Second, although one may draw from the archive and the repertoire to understand a scenario, the scenario itself may call upon multiple forms of transmission for its expression. The latter may not only render visible "an entire spectrum of attitudes and values" but also exceed the limitations of verbal description – in Johnson's case, the "cry" that expresses the embodied experience of an Indigenous woman whose husband will most assuredly become a casualty of war (49). Third, the scenario requires the participant or audience as witness, to be engaged in "the act of transfer" of affect in a manner that precludes a disengaged posture or attitude. The participant is inducted by the performance into its imaginative context and thereby implicated within its ethical and political frame. The audience's relationship to the performer is therefore crucial (32). Here a link may be made more generally with theories of performance, which, like the scenario, allow for the transfer of embodied knowledge and for approaching women's experiences and lives in a more nuanced fashion in the absence of material archives.[11] As Jeanie Forte notes, reconsidering the material body and a woman's "body in representation" offers strategies not only for feminist performance, but also for the means by which to approach them (249). Such a reading allows for greater imaginative latitude, "whereby the emotive and cognitive, the popular and the esoteric, the local and the global can come into play," as it also allows for the audience "to be interrogated as to its role in the production of meaning" (Reinelt and Roach 2007, 1, 5). The audience thus becomes a key participant in the transfer of embodied knowledge. Finally, a scenario invokes a sense of immediacy that refuses "duplication," but rather reanimates a past situation that has been so internalized by a society that its precedent cannot be recalled (Taylor 32). The scenario is thus positioned against Western systems of interpretation and valuation that worked to discredit or dismiss outright Indigenous performance and narrative and that both "repudiat[e] and foreclos[e] the very embodiedness it claims to describe" (36). In effect, it offers another rich source for the preservation of cultural knowledge and draws attention to the hierarchy of knowledges and knowledge formation, while urging a return to embodied knowledge as a proper counterbalance to the privileging of material archives.

The absence I encountered in Johnson's material archives might thus serve as a reminder that there are other, more creative approaches to recovery. This point is especially important when her individual performances are contextualized within federal bans against Indigenous ritual forms of performance, such as the potlatch, as one example, or elements of the Sun Dance, as another: these latter absences are a reminder of how she and other Indigenous persons were sanctioned in the period. The scenario she draws upon in "A Cry from an Indian Wife," moreover, offered a recognizable and legitimate means of invoking cultural memory that cannot be contained within the archive but that is integral to elucidating an Indigenous attitude and perspective. Her performance of trauma demands an engaged audience, reminds that audience of what had been and was being repressed, and suggests that she was endeavouring to rouse and shift socio-cultural memory. The framework of "A Cry from an Indian Wife" restages a crucial historical event that offers an enlightening personal and Indigenous perspective, as it also engages in the transmission of traumatic memory and socio-political crisis.

Still, a critical repositioning of her embodied performance as scenario means not only drawing upon these theories and discourses but also returning to the material, arrested archives. Other archival research might be conducted laterally, to call up other sources as a means of contextualizing and reorienting the dramatic and oral permutations of her performance. Research and criticism about Johnson have to some extent worked laterally, and indeed, focused on her performances, in part by using archival research to analyse media reception.[12] One might also read *against* or alongside such reception, for received models of understanding would have been circumscribed by, if they did not curtail, other more productive forms of reading and of understanding the imaginative space Johnson was trying to cultivate as an Indigenous woman. In one instance, the reviewer invoked conventional discourse about the "vanishing race" as he commented that her voice "was like the voice of the nations who once possessed this country who have wasted away before our civilization."[13] In another instance, however, a journalist for the *Chicago Tribune* was confounded by her embodied performance of a grieving Indian wife; he quipped that "she does pretty much everything that a real Indian would not be expected to do, and leaves undone everything that one would expect from a child of the Iroquois" (qtd. in Gerson 2004, 436). As Gerson and Strong-Boag note, the "meaning of empire was so alien to the usual terms of distinction between Native and white that several journalists ran short of words" (2005, 53). However, as the opening line to Johnson's "As It Was in the Beginning" ("I am a Redskin, but I am something else, too – I am a woman") underscores, this undoing of distinctions was to animate an important part of her literary production; that is, she repudiated the limitations inherent in being both a Mohawk and a woman in early twentieth-century Canada, when neither were allowed political autonomy or agency.[14]

Yet these attitudes would still affect her, and extend their effects well beyond her lifetime to the very archival safeguarding of her papers (or the lack thereof), as they also render it expedient for critics to adopt renewed approaches to her embodied performances. Although critical inquiry and focus upon Johnson has not been lacking, the critical formulations that currently exist extend from constructions of racial identity and gender (Gerson and Strong-Boag), to media reception (Leighton), to rhetorical strategies Johnson employed (Fiamengo), to her accumulation – and loss – of cultural capital (York 2002).[15] I do not propose to challenge these studies, but rather to extend these debates by approaching her public performances as examples of the scenario, as a form of the unarrested archive. The focus of this chapter will be on Johnson's "A Cry from an Indian Wife" to show how the scenario is set in a zone of familiarity and comfort – a domestic scene – which she disrupts by recontextualizing it within the North-West Rebellion. The scenario generates stability and instability, an ambivalence that would have compelled and catalysed her audiences. Her political posturing, these strategies related to dramatic intimacy, came together perhaps most successfully as she repeated the scenario. Therein, she used forms of dramatic intimacy as a means of protesting countervailing images and perspectives of Indigenous women, yet still engaged her audience and their faculty for imaginative sympathy. But in also reading "A Cry from an Indian Wife" alongside other discursive patterns related to Indigenous legalities and oral culture, one gains an appreciable understanding of the politicized affect (and effects) she likely and strategically generated during her embodied performances. The implications for such reconsiderations extend to how we approach archives, arrested and unarrested – that is, renewed approaches to her performances suggest how to confront the limitations of Indigenous women's archives, to reanimate approaches to existing material, and to sidestep the fetishization of material objects or documents.

The Codified Environment and the Material Stage

However uneven the materials available about Johnson are, it is known that she became Canada's most renowned Indigenous writer in the period. Born in 1861 on the Six Nations Reserve near Brantford, Ontario, she was both Mohawk and British. This lineage meant that she inherited and then later strategically shifted between at least two different ideological systems that engendered the complexities and contradictions of her identity. Her father, George Martin Johnson, was the "son of an elite Mohawk family which had long resisted European sovereignty" (Gerson and Strong-Boag 2002, xv). His ancestry reached back to the original founders of the Iroquois Confederacy, a league of Indigenous nations that included the Mohawk (33). Emily Howells Johnson, her mother, was an Englishwoman related to William Dean Howells, a renowned American novelist. Educated by English governesses at home, exposed to the "refinements and privileges of being British in Canada," and trained in a British literary tradition, her daughter Pauline was also exposed to the Mohawk oral storytelling of her grandfather, John Smoke Johnson (Sakayengwaraton) (Lukens 47). Her grandfather, while clearly holding to his Indigenous origins, "anticipated finding an advantageous accommodation with the Euro-Canadian power structure" (Gerson and Strong-Boag 2002, xv). In his ambivalent approach to nationality, he would set an example for Pauline's public performance of self: she would call upon Indigenous forms of storytelling and she, too, would seek to promote a sense of Iroquois autonomy and integrity within a framework of Canadian nationalism.

When her father died in 1884 from injuries he sustained at the hands of White liquor traders, Johnson and her sisters alike were obliged to turn to other means to support themselves and their mother (Keller 43).[16] Johnson turned immediately to writing. She was motivated both by financial need and by her strong commitment to Indigenous issues, especially to the Iroquois.[17] So she observed to a friend, Archibald Kains, in 1890 that "I have a double motive in all my work and all my strivings – one is to upset the Indian Extermination and non-education theory – in fact to stand by my blood and my race. The other is that I am not a millionairess" (as qtd. in Gerson and Strong-Boag 2002, xvi).[18] To these primary reasons she added that she would "consent to anything legitimate, that will mean success in the end" (xvi). To fulfil her ambitions, she initially turned to publishing in magazines and newspapers, although the earnings were paltry. By the mid-1890s, "two-thirds of her lifetime output of about 165 poems had appeared in print," many of which were about nature and love, or accounts of her adventures in the outdoors, rather than her Mohawk background (Gerson and Strong-Boag 2002, xix). Two of these poems were also included in W.D. Lighthall's anthology *Songs of the Great Dominion* (1889), a significant gesture, since it "signalled her inclusion in the pantheon of the country's most significant English-language writers" (Strong-Boag and Gerson 101). Thereafter, her poetry production began to decline, possibly because the reviews were less effusive after *Canadian Born* emerged in 1903, but also because publishing poetry was not a lucrative endeavour. She turned to writing prose pieces or performing her work on the stage, only retiring from the latter in 1909, so that in total she produced approximately "160 poems and 200 pieces of prose, selections of which were issued in three volumes of poetry and three books of stories" (Gerson 2010, 184). These works included *The White Wampum* (1895), *Flint and Feather* (1911), *Legends of Vancouver* (1911), and *The Moccasin Maker* (1913).[19] Her performances, however, were the most profitable of all her endeavours.

During her negotiations on and off the stage, Johnson used her dual racial heritage to call upon and mediate her concerns, and to register the political dimensions of her literary and performative pieces. It is clear that she "always sought a broad English-speaking audience in Canada and abroad" to whom she would profess her adoration for Canada: "I cannot tell you how I love my Canada or how infinitely dearer my native soil is to me," she wrote in a letter to a friend (Gerson 2010, 183; qtd. in Strong-Boag and Gerson 213). But that professed love did not allow her to turn a blind eye towards the legal restrictions the state imposed upon Indigenous nations or to the exclusions that followed such impositions. As her literary corpus shows, on the one hand she proclaimed her identity as a "Canadian" writer, but on the other hand she protested against a national imaginary that viewed Indigenous persons as illegible subjects. That is, citizenship for Johnson was complicated, since she would have been formally excluded as a woman and an Indigenous person from the political rights conferred upon others. Lauren Berlant notes that the practices of citizenship encompass "public-sphere narratives" and "concrete experiences of quotidian life" (1997, 10); so Johnson experienced first-hand the disjunction between public narratives and her daily life and the repercussions of that disharmony. She thus used her work to draw attention to the discrepancies and to identify the complex codification of daily life for Indigenous women.

Such discrepancies – and not only the complications of her dual citizenship – account for why Johnson seemed to vacillate between or be ambivalent about her claims of citizenship. At times, she asserted or argued for an Indigenous presence that would be equal to that of her imperial counterparts; at other times, she was fiercely proud of her participation in imperial Canada. In her 1903 collection of poems, *Canadian Born*, for example, Johnson seems to appeal to an encompassing notion of citizenship:

> Let him who is Canadian born regard these poems as written to himself – whether he be my paleface compatriot who has given to me his right hand of good fellowship, in the years I have appealed to him by pen and platform, or whether he be that dear Red brother of whatsoever tribe or Province, it matters not – White Race and Red are one if they are but Canadian born.

This passage makes clear that she was drawing a fine distinction. The seemingly democratic evocation of nation she espouses here is modified by an important conditional – *only* those White Canadians who have "given" a hand in "good fellowship" are included in her apparently sweeping vision. The same qualification is not made for the "Red brother." Her invocations of citizenship or claims to participation, especially troubling for a woman, still allowed her the space to work against and even decry those injustices against Indigenous nations; to enunciate a vision of "fair Canada"; and to develop the autonomy that as an Indigenous woman she could not have otherwise enjoyed.[20] In fact, her use of the word "nationality" very specifically pointed to her own Indigenous heritage. Strong-Boag and Gerson observe that this word was interchangeable for Johnson with "Indian" rather than "Canadian," as exchanges with the anthologizer Lighthall showed: she was thus "unique [in her] self-placement within the country's emergent national literature" (101–2). Her literary work demonstrates that she envisioned herself, on the one hand, as "national" in terms of her Indigenous background, but on the other hand, as also entitled to full participation in another national – that is, Canadian – imaginary that legally excluded her. She took to task the country that had visited such abuses on Indigenous nations and struggled to subvert a dominant colonial discourse that insisted upon characterizing her as part of a "vanishing race." She thus used "A Cry from an Indian Wife" to protest against political exclusions and forge a sense of "national" belonging on the stage.

Before turning my full attention to the scenario generated by "A Cry from an Indian Wife," I will explore the material stage and the social construction of her body, on and off the stage; in doing so, I will showcase how she deployed the scenario to mobilize her audiences. That social construction was elaborated in her use of costume, in her personal engagement with patrons and publishers, in the venues in which she chose to perform, and in the content of her literary work that often focused on family life "to articulate the intimate and complicated dynamics of national belonging and reconciliation" (Fiamengo 108). Several critics, including Gerson and Strong-Boag, have already addressed how she adopted different costumes, in part as a means to resolve her dual heritage and her racial tensions during her performances. Her father was Mohawk and held "one of the nine Mohawk hereditary titles on the Iroquois Grand Council," but inheritance of these titles was matrilineal (Marshall 20). Her mother was British, but at a time when Canadian law decreed that it was the father who determined the racial identity of his children. By Canadian law, therefore, Johnson would not have been defined as white; however, by Mohawk law she would not have been able to inherit a Mohawk title. Whatever the legal or political imperatives may have been, Johnson made personal and moral claims to both traditions,[21] as is evidenced by her "staged embodiment of contradictory identities" (see Gerson and Strong-Boag 2005, 49)[22] – she used a costume based on Indigenous images in currency in the period to suggest the Mohawk Princess, as well as a fashionable European-style dress that suggested her position as an imperial lady.[23] As Cecilia Morgan observes, her resplendent gowns and hairstyles were "as much a part of Johnson's public appearances as her loosely-cut, fringed buckskin dresses with their feather and beads" (330). In fact, she purchased her first dress at "John Barker's in Kensington, part of the West End's 'elegant and modern shopping centres,'" a decision that strategically aligned her with the "late-Victorian and Edwardian milieu identified as the 'locus of middle- and upper-class women's amusement, social life, and politics'" (330). Her Indigenous costume was a "collage of various artefacts that represented Aboriginal identity": she included "a necklace of bears' teeth and ornamented her asymmetrical buckskin dress with evocative objects, including Iroquois silverwork, a Sioux scalp, and her father's hunting knife" (Gerson 2010, 185). Some contemporary critics suggested that this attire likely "called to mind Anglo fantasies about the scantily clad Native woman" (Carpenter 66). Still others have interpreted the conservative evening gown as a means by which she managed the potential disruptiveness of her Indigenous representations (Gerson 2010, 185).

There are other ways, however, of approaching the apparent facility with which Johnson could transform her stage persona. The scenario involves the risk of invoking stereotypes, in this instance the possibility of pandering to a white construction of the Indigenous woman, even as it relies upon the repetition of an image or event for its kinetic potential. Johnson likely appreciated the attraction her persona would have had for her often-male audiences.[24] In adopting the persona of the chaste "Indian poetess," Morgan notes, she still risked being perceived as the "promiscuous 'squaw'" (336). She was in danger, in other words, of reinscribing stereotypes that would render her exotic, a form of social deviancy that yet appealed to imperial fantasies and desires. Her individual, self-conscious, and embodied performances, however, were far more complex, at once conforming to and deviating from accepted cultural identifications. Even if her dress reinforced stereotypes, the content of her work expressed a contradiction. Johnson may have known "how to play to settler audiences' expectations of stage Indians by adopting costumes that connoted the noble savage, and Indigenous cultural artifacts that suggest[ed] the primitive warrior" (Strong-Boag and Gerson 2000, 111);[25] however, she manipulated those codes of culture about Indigenous women, first, by adopting a costume informed by popular conceptions of what constituted Indigenous dress, and second, by expressing difference within the framework of the scenario. Indeed, to look at her use of costume as a form of reinvoking colonial violence or participation in the "vanishing race" is to belie the content of her literary texts. Aspects of her stage persona, moreover, suggest her transgressive gender performance: Marshall observes that scalps were "badges of merit in battle," mostly likely worn only by men, and the writing name she adopted, Tekahionwake, was that of her grandfather (35). This kind of staged, gender-transgressive posturing was used to great effect. Johnson used such self-display to work within and then against the available lexicon of a cultural and political system that would have oppressed her and denied her self-agency, as a means of gaining intimacy with her audiences rather than conceding to their preconceived notions of Indigenous nations. She would therein both capitalize on and dislodge stereotypical images of Indigenous nations to move beyond the confining and "potentially degrading" view of herself in stereotypical terms, to work upon and against the idiom and images in circulation of "'the savage' and 'the civilized,'" and to construct a more complex identity than the limited options with which she had been presented (Aigner-Varoz viii; Fiamengo 90).

She was transgressive not only in terms of race and gender but also in terms of class. Indeed, she adopted two roles masterfully for this purpose, a fact that showcases how Johnson could locate a sense of autonomy during her performances, in spite of her lack of political weight. Even as she was consigned to the margins of her culture, she could "return to the centre" in her forays to Britain, Morgan observes, where she instead "gaz[ed] upon and comment[ed] about those to whom [Indigenous persons] were supposedly subjected" (319). Critics such as Mary Elizabeth Leighton suggest that her change from Indian to late-Victorian dress may be read as her participation in the foreclosure of an Indigenous presence in Canada (7).[26] The contingencies of imperialism, however, would have set limitations and would not have been so easily navigated in her writing and stage productions. We might thus read her use of costumes as a means of insinuating herself into the aristocracy of the period, while also suggesting her closeness to her Indigenous heritage. Such proximity to both the aristocracy and her Indigenous heritage created the conditions necessary for greater and more intimate exchanges, and allowed her greater mobility and agency in relation to conceptions of nationhood. Her self-presentation was a subtle and complex strategy to place her in close relationship with those who were empowered, to locate a sense of autonomy, and to find greater political and ontological weight.[27]

The material stage that she and her manager chose for Johnson's performances in England also suggest that she was working against the grain of imperial and gender expectation, while endeavouring to generate greater political weight and social intimacy with her audience. Johnson had initially given exclusive and private recitals in aristocratic homes, frequently by invitation from women patrons.[28] When she performed in more public venues in England, Morgan observes, she did not appear in the mass commercial music halls, which would have risked the sexual propriety and earnestness of her performances, but on concert-hall platforms (331). Nor did she partake in colonial exhibitions' displays of Canadian Aboriginal peoples, but rather held herself apart from them (331). In so doing, she was involved in "the manipulation of a range of cultural symbols expressed in gendered and racialised bodily display," which had the effect of mocking "the imperial power's ignorance of Iroquois religion's complexity" (320, 330). The fact that she had embarked on such a career, moreover, in itself contradicted the stereotypical passivity ascribed to the "Indian princess" or the "unlearned children" who required enlightenment. Instead, she actively endeavoured to enlighten her audiences and to assert Indigenous political autonomy.[29]

These kinds of tensions even registered themselves with those with whom she negotiated, that is, those who sanctioned her performances, or with whom she allied herself during her public career as writer and performer. Johnson aligned herself with patrons to secure their support and, at other times, to delight her audiences, even as she simultaneously denounced imperial devastation wrought upon Indigenous nations in Canada. As with any writer or artist dependent upon a patron for stability of income or support, Johnson had to navigate her connections with great attention. Appeals were judiciously made to wealthy patrons, including the Lord and Lady Strathcona and the Duke of Connaught, who began serving as the governor general of Canada in 1911, to whom she dedicated *Flint and Feather*, and who visited her in the hospital before she died (Foster 145). When she sought publication for her first book of poetry in 1894, she travelled to London with letters of introduction from, for example, the governor general, the lieutenant governor of Ontario, and the minister of justice. She also forged an alliance with Theodore Watts-Dunton, the preeminent literary critic and reviewer for *The Athenaeum*. Watts-Dunton had been called upon by the *Athenaeum*'s editor, Norman Maccoll, to review *Songs of the Great Dominion*, and later was asked, apparently at Johnson's own request, to write the introduction to *Flint and Feather*. That she apparently made this request may seem to contradict her purpose, since it was Maccoll who focused upon her exotic Indigenousness while privileging his European and imperialist background (Gerson 2010, xx; Marshall 52). As he clearly positioned himself in the introduction as a part of the "mother country," he characterized her as part of "Red Man's Canada" (x). He also reiterated her expressed "indebtedness" to him for her success. It may be perplexing that she would appoint such a patronizing figure as the author of the introduction to her book – unless it is contextualized in her need to seek such alliances to gain support and access to a sphere from which she would have otherwise been excluded.[30]

Perhaps the most important example of her navigation of this codified environment manifests itself in her interactions with the prime minister, Sir Wilfrid Laurier. She had written to ask him for letters of introduction to those who might show her support in London. In the process, she called upon national intimacies to remind him of how a cooperative Indigenous presence had allowed Canada to become the country it was. A letter dated 4 February 1904 demonstrates how she exercised control over her identity: signing her name as both "E. Pauline Johnson" and "Tekahionwake," she expressed her gratitude for his "allusions to [her] Indian ancestors' loyalty to the British crown." That she used her grandfather's name to sign her letters is a significant gesture, since it had not been clearly conferred upon her through the Mohawk ceremony of name giving. As Strong-Boag and Gerson note, "presenting herself as Indian could accommodate and even mitigate embarrassing situations, such as indebtedness, that would otherwise be regarded as transgressive for a lady of her class" (2000, 117). In addition, identifying and locating herself within a larger national framework entitled her to make larger claims. In another letter regarding a meeting between Sir Wilfrid Laurier and West Coast citizens, she commented upon how "the Indians are to join these citizens in welcoming you and those coast tribes are anticipating with the most loyal hearts the pleasure of greeting you" (7 July 1910). "Loyalty," a key feature of intimate relationships, is strikingly repeated in her ostensibly deferential letters to Laurier.[31] It is a strategy she uses elsewhere: in, for example, her refusal to condemn the monarch outright, since "like many Six Nations," Johnson also used "historic loyalty [as] a critical justification for fair treatment" (Strong-Boag and Gerson 2000, 204).

It was also a strategy by which she could develop space for Indigenous women, who could be empowered, and who could invoke and respond to calls for action.[32] The various relationships of affect that Johnson managed in her personal life and investigated in her literary and performance lives showcase the range of concerns and complications that issued forth from them, and specifically, the means by which political realities had a direct bearing on the personal – her own life as a woman and a Mohawk and, collectively, Indigenous nations. But these relationships were also vital to the embodied performances that were used to rescript the strict gender and racial roles that had been thrust upon her, and allowed her to remap and perform against the grain of imperial culture.

The Embodied Performance of an "Indian Wife": The Confession, the Witness, and the Act of Transfer

Perhaps one of Johnson's more popular texts is the one that is seen to have launched her career, "A Cry from an Indian Wife." The scenario provocatively addresses the 1885 North-West Rebellion. Centred in what is now Saskatchewan, the Rebellion was the second uprising in support of Métis land rights. Although it was directed by Métis leaders Gabriel Dumont and Louis Riel, it also involved groups of Assiniboine and Plains Cree led by Poundmaker and Big Bear. Johnson focuses on a member of one of these First Nations groups involved in the Rebellion to illuminate how a public and highly inflammatory event expressed the tensions between the Métis and Anglo-Canada and had a bearing on even exceedingly personal interactions, in this instance a relationship of conjugal intimacy. Strong-Boag and Gerson see that this work's strength resides in her "first public positioning of herself as woman/ Native/other" and also in its depiction of Canada as "a site of conflict between two founding peoples" (149).[33] The archival legacy in relation to the poem reveals that it was first published in the intellectual periodical *The Week* on 18 June 1885; however, its tremendous power was registered when she performed it on 16 January 1892 at a Canadian Literature Evening organized by Frank Yeigh and arranged by the Young Men's Liberal Club of Toronto. At the time, this embodied performance attracted considerable notice, and is seen as launching Johnson on a touring career spanning fifteen years. The unfolding of this scenario had an extraordinary impact on some of its audience members and reviewers: at that first performance, apparently, she "received the honor of the only recall by the audience."[34] In one review, she was characterized as possessing "an unusual gift of expression."[35] It seems that they were responding to the emotional outcry of an "Indian wife," whose husband was about to leave for the Rebellion and whose sharp pain revolves around, as the narrator notes in the poem, what he might "suffer from the white man's hand" (l. 4). The power of devotion to her husband and their loss of rights as Indigenous persons occasion her vacillations: she is aware that she may lose her husband (as the audience would have fully appreciated), but that there is a greater cause for which the Métis needed to fight, that of indifference to the injustices inflicted upon them. So she argues about the wives of those soldiers representing Anglo-Canada:

> They never think how they would feel to-day,
> If some great nation came from far away,
> Wresting their country from their hapless braves,
> Giving what they gave us – but wars and graves. (ll. 25–8)

The emotional intensity of the wife's outcry on the evening of her first performance evidently made an impact, as the audience was sufficiently roused to demand a second performance. Indeed, the fact that W.D. Lighthall refused this poem for his anthology *Songs of the Great Dominion* (1889) suggests its inflammatory potential. A review that followed some years after her performance indicated that what Johnson had accomplished continued to resonate. In "Elocutionary Entertainment. By Miss E. Pauline Johnson," which appeared in the *Emerson Journal* on 17 December 1897, the reviewer noted that "the train of thought" awakened by such a performance was striking. The "hardships" endured by Indigenous nations at the "hands of the white man" had become clear: "Such is the train of thought that the poems arouse in the minds of the audience, and when the anger of an Indian maiden, feeling from experience the sufferings of her race, is depicted in every line; dull indeed is the man that cannot be aroused by Miss Johnson's recitations."[36] Bearing witness to the scenario brought results: the reviewer concluded that an obtuse person alone would be oblivious to the highly wrought emotional state Johnson embodied.[37] This response makes clear that she was successful in her deployment of trauma and intimacy as the primary means to diminish the relational gap between her and her audience, to evoke sympathy, and to render a perspective that had been otherwise excluded.

In her performances and literary texts, Johnson was quite consistent in developing the figure of a strong female heroine who, through affect, engendered change.[38] This figure underlies the seeming stereotypes she would have otherwise invoked – from "Indian wife" to "Mohawk princess." In "A Strong Race Opinion: On the Indian Girl in Modern Fiction," which first appeared in *The Toronto World* in 1892, she examined the Indigenous heroine – at that point in Canadian literary history, a virtually non-existent character. She explored the failings of a national literature that predetermined that a heroine could not be Indigenous and that, when represented, an Indigenous woman would be approached as representative rather than as individual, with distinctive characteristics arising from distinctive nations, not persons. She was stereotypically depicted as a "surnameless creation ... possessed with a suicidal mania":

> her unhappy, self-sacrificing life becomes such a burden to both herself and the author that this is the only means by which they can extricate themselves from a lamentable tangle, though, as a matter of fact suicide is an evil positively unknown among Indians. (Gerson and Strong-Boag 2002, 179)

If Indigenous women were depicted as "fawn-eyed, unnatural, unmaidenly idiots," their male White lovers were unresponsive, presumably in order to abide by the conventions of an "appropriate" romance: "Alas, for all the other pale-faced lovers, they are indifferent, almost brutal creations" (182). It followed, therefore, that the presence of Indigenous women simply facilitated the romance between a white male hero and "his fair lady" (180).

Johnson asks for what purpose Indigenous women were so depicted, and notably, questions whether or not writers who were complicit in such depictions truly "loved" the nation that they "endeavour[ed] successfully or unsuccessfully to describe" (Gerson and Strong-Boag 2002, 180). In response, she suggested that to participate in or contribute to such imaginings (or the lack thereof) about Indigenous women was to reinscribe discursively the injuries that had already been wrought upon Indigenous nations. So she observed that "surely the Redman has lost enough, has suffered enough without additional losses and sorrows being heaped upon him in romance" (183). Indirectly, therefore, she critiqued and even questioned the purported "love" one held for one's nation, the kind of love she had professed to hold for her own "native soil." Johnson saw participation in national discourse as being undergirded by love and esteem for one's country and *all* its inhabitants. It followed that one's production of literature ought to reflect such love and esteem. To know the country was to know it beyond stereotype – and that was a way of loving it well.

To move past stereotype, however, Johnson needed to compel and arouse the imagination of her audience in order to see beyond received ideas, to unsettle their assumptions. She effectively did so by conjuring up the scenario in which she developed the strong heroine, an "Indian wife," who was able to rearticulate the traumas induced by the North-West Rebellion. She thereby drew upon, first, affect as the primary catalyzing mode; second, the spectacle of the eroticized Indigenous woman that was in currency in the period;[39] and, third, the autobiographical and confessional mode to implicate her audience within the ethical and political frame of the scenario. As addressed earlier in this chapter, she carefully selected her manner of dress because being on stage meant negotiating tensions involved in drawing upon the eroticized Indigenous woman while asserting her independence and conducting herself as a "proper woman" in a decidedly public sphere. The unmarried female stage performer was especially under duress to "maintain social propriety" and "to perform as a 'lady'" (Strong-Boag and Gerson 2000, 104). She was therefore careful not to identify herself as an "actress," which had associations of moral laxity.[40] Part of her protective gesture was to have performed alongside male performers, including Owen Smiley and, the most lasting of these partners, Walter McRaye, a married man about fifteen years her junior.[41]

By refusing to conform to the "vision of tractable female desire" that was seen as appropriate conduct for "the proper lady," Johnson certainly assumed some performative and personal risks (Poovey 3).[42] By this point in history, British women – and, by extension, women of the empire – had been socialized to conduct themselves such that they maintained the moral strongholds of domestic life and strove for the height of femininity. As Mary Poovey notes about the latter, however, they "harness[ed] the appetites men feared" for their own purposes (6).[43] To embark upon a public, literary life was to jeopardize the modesty that was central to such propriety because it assumed and directed attention towards the woman as the catalyst for action; to express desire and to give expression to her emotions was to endanger her chastity (Poovey 23). Johnson undid this formulation by, on the one hand, creating an imaginative context that seemed safely to revolve around a domestic space and by asserting the moral rightness of her husband's participation in the war. On the other hand, as Indian wife she gave expression to her desires and urged her husband to fight: "Go; rise and strike, no matter what the cost" (l. 10). She thus subverted the paradigm by which a man would be articulate and active and she silent and passive. By rendering the intimate conversation publicly and assuming this role, Johnson may also be seen to sidestep being viewed as the "private property" of her husband. The scenario allowed her to express statements of desire, explore her situation, and revise past histories, while not explicitly taking on responsibility for those desires, explorations, or revisions. Johnson also used what Patricia Spacks calls "acts of incorporation" (qtd. in Poovey 45): this strategy involved foregrounding and directing attention towards her relationship to her male counterpart in order to be able to make statements about herself (45). She could thus "call attention to her contribution and her value without having to confront masculine authority directly" (46). So Johnson might be seen as strategically adopting the role of "wife" to direct attention towards her husband but as a means of redirecting attention back to the political situation for Indigenous women.[44]

The staging of this scenario showcases Johnson's masterly control over her medium – both the embodied performance and content – as she worked through the complexities of an exclusive national (i.e., Canadian) imaginary. In particular, Johnson's debut performance of "A Cry from an Indian Wife" may be seen as an expression of how the gendered and racialized body embodied a vital contradiction. On the one hand, it revealed how, as an Indigenous woman, she was subject to both the authority of state power and the male gaze and was discounted as a legitimate national subject both materially and imaginatively. On the other hand, in rendering herself in spectacular terms, she converted the subjection of her body to state authority and to the male gaze into a feminist strategy, first, to speak against those forms of institutional control and governance; second, to shift that gaze, to induce new insights into the predicament of being an Indigenous woman; and third, to gain agency as a legitimate author and performer, with a view even to becoming a citizen. If she seemingly and arguably participated in both the racialization and sexualization of her body to do so, what she had to say was obviously quite different – she may have "*engage[d] with* the colonizer's own terms," but she also conjured up the violence of colonization in the demarcation from those terms (Pratt 7). That she was *saying* at all, that she was expressing her desires, demonstrates that she was able to achieve some sense of self-agency and give Indigenous women greater ontological weight.[45]

Another part of her strategy is related to the kind of "saying" Johnson engaged, that is, the literary form Johnson adopts. Strong-Boag and Gerson aptly refer to her performance as a "monologue" (139), but Johnson may be seen to draw upon another two traditions: the oral narrative in performance and elements of European poetic forms on the page. Johnson often used popular narrative forms, and this sometimes included the ballad metre for her "Indian poems" (see Strong-Boag and

Gerson 149). "A Cry from an Indian Wife" used heroic couplets rather than the metre associated with the ballad, although it is the case that ballad rhyme and structure can vary considerably. The poem's content, however, suggests this poem's relation to the ballad: mostly oral in nature, this genre often contains stories and relies on imagery to convey tragic, romantic, or historical narratives (Head and Ousby 66). In a romantic context, it calls upon an entirely different scenario, one that sometimes involves the recuperation of a female subject as a result of male, heroic interventions. The content of this poem (and others, such as "Ojistoh"), however, would contradict its form and generate irony by virtue of contrast. The "hero" here does not speak at all, not even against the injustices to which he is being subjected, and is off to a battle that he will most assuredly not survive. Conversely, the female subject articulates her pain, uses reason to do so, and argues persuasively about the injustices they are enduring. Some criticism has read Johnson's "oral performances" as "'mere' popular entertainment" rather than a "contribution to Canadian literature" (Milz 134). Yet Johnson was likely calling upon the power of oral Indigenous storytelling, as she would have learned from her grandfather. Its purportedly autobiographical inflections when she performed the piece invited her audience to perceive her as "Indian wife." As Forte observes, this kind of representational practice involves "a blurring of distinctions between reality and representation and invites audiences to 'read' their actions in the wider context of their lives outside of performance" (250). As importantly, the body's materiality is undeniable in live performance, as it is in relation to pain: these offer two instances when "the body must be acknowledged, when it becomes visible/palpable through inhabiting temporally a process that depends fundamentally on its presence" (251). It is a moment that obliges the audience to become participant by serving as witness to the trauma induced by the scenario. Johnson thus uses the body and her "cry" of pain in order to "communicate" to those not in pain, to engage their empathy, and to compel them into action. The verbal performance indeed would have exceeded the limitations of verbal description, as is characteristic of the scenario. In this manner, Johnson was trying to get her audience to listen, to foreground the very reports that had been shunted to the margins.[46]

The cry of pain and her embodied performance itself are especially effective in her deployment of an intimate, confessional mode, one that is implicated in relations of power and domination (Gerson and Strong-Boag 2002, xvii; see also Garman). Her mode of speaking is particularly important if identified in relation to confession, which requires a witness to be engaged in the act of transfer. Largely understood as the "excavation of truth" with the expectation of "being unburdened" (Garman 323), confessions are often understood as introspective statements that are revealing of the dynamics of power at work; that is, confessions unfold within power relationships, are made either in response to repression or in spite of repression, and entail disclosing a matter of a private nature that involves either having done a wrong or having been wronged (Taylor 22). As Foucault notes, the presence of an "other" "requires the confession, imposes it, weights it, and intervenes to judge, punish, pardon, console, reconcile" (qtd. in Taylor 22).[47] Confession may be deployed for the purposes of subverting power, even if it initially seems to support its existing structures. The public nature of protest would therefore elicit conflicted responses: a sense of vulnerability about the feminist body and the desire to expose the government's brutality. Yet Johnson would thereby gain a sense of empowerment. Her embodied performance is a seemingly introspective and private response to the speaker's husband's "revolting against the Union Jack" and an admission of the sufferings endured from his hand "against this stripling pack / Of white faced warriors" (ll. 11, 12–13). The repression of this perspective, which is related to her status as an Indigenous woman, is given fuller treatment as a result of the scenario she invokes. Whatever her deep agitation about the land rights, she herself cannot go off to battle but can only work upon her husband to do so. When she enacts a confession and gives full vent to the range of her well-grounded anxieties and fears about his participation in that battle, she also works through, justifies, and demands his participation in the uprising. Implicitly, moreover, she invites her audience to consider their complicity within the ethical framework constructed: they are compelled to consider who is responsible for the ravages of war and Indigenous suffering. She denounces the legacy of colonization, which has brought them nothing "but wars and graves" – she thus urges her husband to retaliate against those who have treated them unjustly (l. 28).

The use of the first-person voice was sometimes conflated with Johnson herself, as the reviews indicate.[48] Its use is a key device in registering the power of embodied femininity. Rather than producing a detached subject, she turns the otherwise "isolated and vulnerable voice," the plight of someone who was both participant in and victim of the North-West Rebellion, into a means of rallying support and eliciting sympathy for Indigenous nations: her autobiographical performance becomes a critique, opens itself to what Barbara Green would refer to as "a discussion of the concept of experience, and to the possibility of resistance within spectacularity" (8). Her staging of the "Indian wife" is key as a form of simultaneously public and yet intimate protest because, even though she employed a first-person narrative technique to convey the individual life of an Indigenous woman, she also rendered herself an unnamed subject – "an Indian wife," not "*the* Indian wife." Johnson did not always opt for this strategy, as another poem, "Ojistoh," renders clear. This strategy of namelessness, however, allowed her to operate in a singular, autobiographical, and confessional mode, while also accommodating the generality of the experience of being an Indigenous woman. At one point in the poem, that experience resonates even more largely, to encompass the condition of being a woman on either side of the cultural divide. Her individual public performance might be seen to represent a silenced and marginalized collective, for whom little representation had been made and little sympathy evinced: Euro-Canadians "never think how they would feel" if the situation had been reversed (l. 25). In so doing, she creates agency for women by forging an audience for their concerns – especially for Indigenous women, whose material, emotional, and political losses had been compounded by such silencing.

As wife, she would seemingly be relegated to a position of greater marginality. When the distinctions between status and non-status Natives were legally introduced in 1850–51 in relation to property acts, Indigenous women were stripped of their "Indian status" if they married a man who was non-Indigenous. Disenfranchised as subjects and regarded as the property of the men to whom they were married, they lost their right to make legal claims of entitlement to their cultural and racial heritage. If contextualized within imperial law, this Indian wife, then, would have been regarded as the possession of someone rather than an autonomous subject. That her embodied grief could be articulated with such precise logic might have been understood as a contradiction. However, Johnson was deliberate in her choice of "Indian wife" because she would have been contextualized within Indigenous law: she therefore invokes her *right* to speak by calling upon a different law, of which she clearly approved and envisioned in, for example, "A Red Girl's Reasoning." Whereas feminists have argued that being relegated to the domestic sphere undermined the legal rights they would have otherwise possessed in the public sphere, Johnson appropriates that space as context for change: she takes an intimate and domestic moment and renders it public for calculated effect. The use of empathy becomes strategic, a means by which to generate an act of emotional transfer in order to create an engaged audience who must be compelled by emotion *and* reason to appreciate a situation for which there would have otherwise been limited understanding.[49]

Johnson, moreover, intensifies the effect of her embodied performance by building in a strategy that is key to the mode of confession and to the scenario – the presence of an "other." As is obvious in the first four lines, the poem begins with an address by an Indian wife *to her Indian husband*. Her opening address therefore significantly positions the audience in an imaginatively familiar relationship with the speaker: the audience of the time would have been enjoined to participate in a compelling dynamic, in a form of intimacy, to listen to a confession to which they would not have otherwise been privy. The audience becomes part of the partnership between husband and wife. In so doing, Johnson also fosters empathy for an Indigenous presence, to facilitate cross-cultural understanding between Indigenous nations and a primarily Anglo-Canadian audience, as she invites them to imagine themselves as her Indian husband.

Evidently, however, an Indian wife would not need to remind her Indian husband of, or articulate a confession about, the "wars and graves" that were the legacy of colonized Canada and about which her husband would presumably have known. Indeed, the dynamic of the confession built into the scenario Johnson develops is one that discursively contains an asymmetrical relationship – one that might not have been engendered by Indian wife and Indian husband. This is the part of the scenario that critical attention neglects, the deliberately ambiguous and certainly intimate relationship between the audience and the performance. She takes the asymmetrical relationship she has with her white, Anglo-Canadian audience and invites them to insert themselves imaginatively into this relationship. As such, her audience would have been increasingly ill at ease when obliged to consider further the repercussions of the North-West Rebellion, to see themselves as part of the larger majority whose sense of nationalism was not inclusive of an Indigenous presence, and to reflect upon their complicity in the separation of wife from husband. What occurs in this performance, then, is a heightened emotional state engendered initially by the scenario of a traumatized victim of the North-West Rebellion and then by a confessional mode that is permitted not only as Johnson reconfigures herself as "Indian wife" but also as she reconfigures her audience as "Indian husband." Yet – and this point is key – this confession could not have been made to an Indian husband, even though she ostensibly addresses her audience as such, for surely such a husband would have known all that the Indian wife had to say. She deploys the dynamic of that relationship, of the scenario itself, in that moment to open up space and allow for the intimacy necessary to make the confessional disclosures that are remarkable, powerful, and compelling. Perhaps the most uncanny feature of Johnson's performance is the fact that that which her persona bears witness to is an impossibility, temporally and emotionally: she conjures up a past moment before the certain death of the Indian husband and speaks openly about injustices that would most certainly not have been heeded by her Euro-Canadian audience in the period she draws upon for the scenario. These two features heighten the scenario's affective power.

This performance might be seen, therefore, as embodying cultural memory, a means by which to make visible the unacknowledged perspective of a traumatic event and thus to work beyond the traditional material, arrested archive. Indeed, the scenario's potential to mobilize her audiences suggests its position as an unarrested archive. The mobilization of ideas, of affect, is transmitted through the performance and not the materials safeguarded in an official institution. As it unfolds within the scenario, her representation of the trauma and loss becomes transmittable through the "re-experienced shudder, the retelling, the repeat" (Taylor 208). Johnson invokes this complex strategy as a means to find space to rearticulate her identity and sense of autonomy, and to register protest against a political economy that provided limited options at the time of the Rebellion and in her own time. The scenario became a means by which she could repudiate hegemonic cultural assumptions about the place of an Indigenous woman. In so doing, Johnson also locates a way of creating self-agency that would have otherwise been refused her, while evading an oppositional framework that might have been invoked by such protestations. Her use of intimate protestations is politically inflected, as they create leverage; they allow her to assert her authorship, demonstrate the limits to citizenship, mediate the impact of colonial violence, unsettle the easy configuration of Indigenous nations as "enemy" to the state, and challenge the restrictive national imaginary espoused in the period.

Johnson's embodied cultural memory thus works against arrested archival materials that mediate Indigenous experience through a Western colonizing gaze, and undermines a traditional form of knowledge that denies Indigenous women proper representation. In Johnson's case, an initial archival absence invites us to consider unarrested archives, to read her performance in terms of the scenario, and to view the latter as part of a larger political framework of the period. Doing so reminds us, as Arondeker would suggest, of how an empty archive can still be full. We can see, first, how Johnson ultimately subverted the male, colonizing gaze by recontextualizing her performance within discursive fields of the period; by re-examining how she used intimacy and confession to forge powerful connections with her audience; by analysing how she reconstructs the eroticized body as a body of violence; and finally, by recognizing how the cultivation of the scenario and embodied performance were vital to the production of a counter-narrative that contested a pervasive national imaginary. Emily Carr, the subject of the next chapter, would also use intimacy to forge powerful connections, albeit with a single person rather than directly engaging with an audience, and like Johnson, she would do so to challenge the national imaginary. Through such intimacy, Johnson, like Carr, masterfully located a sense of self-agency, even as she was to demonstrate the limits to both authorship and citizenship at turn of the century in English Canada.

2 Her "Eye" Was Her "I": Emily Carr, Autobiography, and the Archive of Kinship

The Archive of Kinship

Modern writer and artist Emily Carr confronted several challenges to achieving literary and artistic success and securing her credibility and longevity as an artist, including the establishing of her archive; that success hinged upon the complex relationships she established between herself, her subject matter, and her closest allies. To grasp such complexity, I call upon Judith Butler's *Antigone's Claim: Kinship between Life and Death* and her exploration of the figure of Antigone. On the one hand, Antigone is expressive of political defiance, and on the other, she represents the principle of kinship – however unusual the manifestation of the latter given that incest informs most critical readings of Antigone's familial relations. In fact, these relations need not be circumscribed by blood ties nor occupy "any specific form" (5). Antigone's defiance is related to being positioned "outside the polis" because of her gender: that which becomes excluded from the polis is the "remaindered," the feminine, a necessary exclusion by which an authoritarian state secures its dominance (4). Political participation thus involves the "violent forgetting of primary kin relations in the inauguration of symbolic masculine authority" (4). Yet, she is "an outside without which the polis could not be" (4), since, as Butler notes, the two spheres are mutually constitutive: "*kinship* [*is*] *the sphere that conditions the possibility of politics without ever entering into it*" (2; italics in original).

Antigone's public protest about her brother's improper burial both demarcates and then violates the boundary between kinship and the political. I read her decision to speak publicly as transgressive in that she forgoes the private domain and publicly adopts the "very language of the state against which she rebels": "hers becomes a politics not of oppositional purity but of the scandalously impure" (5). She occupies "exemplary political status as a feminine figure who defies the state through a powerful set of physical and linguistic acts" (2). Antigone enters and ruptures the homogeneity of the symbolic, not only in terms of her gender but also in terms of her articulation of kinship within the symbolic – the result is the intermingling of these two seemingly distinct domains.

Although Carr's life might be seen to offer another such instance of political defiance, the applicability of the principle of kinship may seem a little less clear. The former is at first more apparent: she was regarded and, indeed, often represented herself as flouting conventions and traditional pathways associated with women. As Diane Gillespie observes, it was highly unusual for women in early twentieth-century Canada to devote their lives to formal artistic training – as Carr did in San Francisco, Paris, and London – to exhibit publicly, and to join professional artistic associations as part of their objective to be taken seriously as artists (768). In addition, Carr was a prolific writer over approximately the last ten years of her life; although most other female artists focused on journals or letters, and rarely wrote for a public audience, she wrote stories for which she eventually sought publication (768). In other words, rather than follow a trajectory that ran along strict gender lines of expectation, she devoted her life to building a career as a writer and an artist and, most unusually, to cultivating a visual iconography that she regarded as representing national concerns. The latter gesture was especially significant, since women in the period were urged to paint subject matter that was regarded as appropriate to their gender, such as portraits of children or floral arrangements – and certainly not subject matter that was national in scope (see Tippett 1992).

Instead, a substantial number of Carr's canvases focused on iconography derived from Indigenous communities and, particularly, Indigenous totem poles, because she believed that they could be used to represent a Canadian national identity still in its infancy, even if Indigenous cultures were perceived as in decline. She thereby also participated in the discourse of the "vanishing race," which rehearsed their certain demise: her aesthetic practices were implicated in "salvaging" what she perceived as on the brink of total loss. Although these practices might be read as politically defiant, because she chose subject matter that would have been deemed untraditional for women, they are in fact more problematic because, as Gayle Rubin observes, women themselves were often the objects of exchange by which men reinforced their political and economic relationships.[1] Women were not able to participate in such interactions when they themselves were the objects of trade. In deploying Indigenous iconography, Carr seemed to bypass this principle and, in her place, offered Indigenous representation as a means of participating in these relationships of exchange. In some ways, this gesture was less about political defiance than about political impersonation to gain access to the public sphere: by assuming such an attitude towards Indigenous nations, she was invoking attitudes associated with, and situating herself alongside, her male counterparts, who were aligned with the imperial patriarchy. As such, Carr was complicit in the artistic construction of an arrested archive of First Nations cultural goods: that is, she problematically endeavoured to capture the cultural artefacts of Indigenous nations in her canvases as a means of promoting her own career and locating a sense of agency and visibility as Canadian artist.

But this gesture also relied upon the terms of kinship, as manifested in her expressions of familial proximity to Indigenous persons who were regarded as "outside the polis." Specifically, Carr claimed that the honorary title "Klee Wyck," the "Laughing One," was bestowed upon her during her forays through Ucluelet, and that this renaming bore witness to her acceptance among the Nuu-chah-nulth (*Klee Wyck* 1941,[2] 36; Tippett 32). This particular form of kinship was to have particular use for Carr when she later drew upon it in her attempt to donate the fruits of her labour to British Columbia and, to that end, argued that her paintings arrested, or preserved, the history of peoples on the verge of extinction – an archive of sorts, in which she characterized her paintings as faithfully recording the totem poles and symbols associated with Indigenous nations for posterity. In exchange, Carr would have received validation as an artist of provincial and even national proportions. In this sense, she participated in the processes of British colonialism, still an unusual strategy for a woman in the period. Her entrance into citizenship by this route, however, entailed arresting the material elements of another culture, circumscribing its agencies, and silencing its voices. In subsuming elements of another culture into her own artistic lexicon and endeavouring to create its archive on her own terms, she denied Indigenous persons the very agencies she was seeking for herself. These practices also eventually involved compromising the terms of kinship she established with Indigenous persons to secure access to their villages, because she assumed that Indigenous persons could not represent themselves in the public arena – that is, as Butler observes, these practices entailed at least a *"partial repudiation of the kinship relations that bring the [citizen] into being"* (12; italics in original).

As this chapter demonstrates, however, she eventually turned her attention towards another form of kinship that would entail not only seeing her literary work to publication and finding a means to represent her work and her "self" publicly, but also preserving the materials for what would later constitute her own archive based on her literary and artistic accomplishment. Both archives – that related to Indigenous persons and then her own – were grounded in the principle of kinship: the first was related to her proximity to Indigenous persons, which she called upon to justify capturing their cultural iconography, whereas the second was related to turning over her materials – that is, unarresting them – to be remediated and validated by a male subject. The former attempt was problematically characterized by her capitulation to the socio-politics of the day and involved a "forgetting of ... kin relations," whereas the latter was characterized by resistance to such socio-politics and by remembrance of such relations. Upon arresting the material elements of another culture, Carr confronted an impasse. She found recourse in another form of kinship, that is, her relationship with her closest friend, editor, and executor of her estate, Ira Dilworth.

Dilworth was preceded crucially by several male figures, notably the painter Lawren Harris, whom Carr regarded as an important figure to the development of her career. Indeed, Harris would play a key role in relation to her acceptance into mainstream Canadian visual culture and her recognition as an artist of national proportions. However, it was through her close proximity with Dilworth that she would learn that releasing her own materials into his possession, rather than arresting the cultural artefacts of Indigenous nations for posterity, was the route by which to locate self-agency – and that route would not involve her own self-silencing but rather the remediation of her voice. She tested the transfer of these materials from her possession to his, beginning with the most crucial of her literary papers: the manuscript for her autobiography, *Growing Pains*. As a male subject, he was able to authorize her autobiography, then her life's work, and finally her archives, even as all were "scandalously impure" in their representation of a female subject (Butler 5). The archive of kinship thus showcases the limits to agency in this period: her association with Dilworth proved that, if she could uneasily preserve another culture in her canvases for public consumption, she could find a way to represent her "self," albeit through a male interlocutor. Through him, she would find a means to participate in the terms of exchange associated with the patriarchy that did not risk a violent intrusion of the symbolic, although it required that she initially compromise her agency in order to be represented therein. Unlike Antigone, she paradoxically gained agency by relinquishing it. She found effective representation through kinship, and located forms of agency that, first, allowed her to cultivate her writing, her art, and the materials for her archive; second, legitimated her socio-political status as Canadian artist and writer; and third, sanctioned and recognized her aesthetic achievements.

The Principle of Kinship

The terms of kinship that eventually come to inform Carr's archive, by which her life, art, and literary production might also be critically revisited, become strikingly apparent as articulated in her Last Will and Testament. As part of that document, Carr wrote a final letter to Dilworth in which she advised him not to "hesitate to burn" the "inevitable trash and leaves where one has odds & ends half-finished that they want to use for notes as long as life lasts" (Carr 2006, 301). She added, as if by way of encouragement: "It is a clean[,] satisfactory way of disposal" (301). She had already tested his ability to safeguard her literary papers by relinquishing *Growing Pains* to his care a few years prior. In her will, she would release all remaining materials that would later form part of her archive, seemingly rendering them vulnerable to obliteration had Dilworth not been so responsible towards her "odds & ends." It would appear that she relinquished considerable self-agency by allowing him to make such decisions about her estate. Yet Dilworth decided not to "burn" the "leaves" of her life, but rather held them in his private care until he was able to publish a number of manuscripts posthumously. Several years after his own death, these materials were turned into a rather impressive archival cache at the British Columbia Archives and Records Service. The Emily Carr fonds were thus established and currently hold her correspondence, diaries, notebooks, scrapbooks, manuscripts, and sketches. If he did destroy some of the "inevitable trash," he also clearly preserved a critical quantity of materials that would form her archive. From the extensive holdings, one may extrapolate that perhaps Carr herself appreciated the care and sensitivity with which Dilworth would approach the safeguarding of her materials.

She also initially assigned him the task of representing the Emily Carr Trust, a cache of paintings that she wished to leave as part of a personal and national legacy and that might be characterized as the visual equivalent to her literary archive. In July 1941 she added a clause to her will that appointed Dilworth as representative, along with artist Lawren Harris. In the process, Dilworth would come to serve as her primary confidante and would eventually replace Harris as her most intimate friend. For the purpose of the Trust, she selected eighty pictures, of which thirty-five were to be sold for the upkeep and storage of the others. Two-thirds of the cache drew upon Indigenous subjects, with the remainder focused on the West Coast forests – the later focus of her work. As Tippett notes, she characterized the Trust as a gift to the nation, and specifically "to the Vancouver Art Gallery on permanent loan" (1979, 274). The trustees were charged with the responsibility of caring for the paintings and selecting "paintings of their choice to [give to] any public gallery in British Columbia" (274). She later replaced Dilworth with Willie Newcombe, who was more adept at handling and crating canvases; Dilworth retained custody of all her manuscripts, letters, and papers. As Tippett suggests, she might have had a few "burning sessions" if Dilworth had not intervened: his "literary trusteeship meant that provision had been made for the further editing and publication of her stories after her death" (275). The principle of kinship is at work in establishing the Trust and the preservation of her manuscripts, in addition to her attempt to preserve Indigenous iconography. The results of these attempts, however, were to differ considerably.

What in part shifted by the latter part of her life was what she chose to preserve, and how she and others characterized what she chose to preserve. Earlier in her career, Carr focused on Indigenous cultural iconography. On a trip to Sitka, Alaska, in 1907, she was greatly impressed by the totem poles and resolved to "do all the totem poles & villages I can before they are a thing of the past" (Tippett 75). The terms in which she justified her painting came to revolve around preservation of Indigenous artefacts rather than her own artistic accomplishment. In November 1912, for example, Carr wrote to Henry Esson Young, minister of education and provincial secretary in British Columbia, to suggest that her collection, which she had made "for history," be placed in the art gallery in the new wing of the Parliament buildings (Tippett 109). A later exhibit and two lectures that she gave in April 1913 confirm her desire to preserve the totem poles for posterity: she spoke of how they were "fast becoming extinct" (114). The logic that undergirded this claim was related to assumptions about the "vanishing Indian": "Since the Indians were no longer carving poles, she considered her collection valuable" (Tippett 110). Indeed, she argued that they were "real treasures of a passing race."[3]

Young was overseeing the new wing of the Parliament buildings. For its development, he had already invested in collecting ethnological material for the province, for which purpose he had been in touch with Dr C.F. Newcombe. An ethnologist by training, Newcombe had already acquired "a fine collection of Indian curios and totem poles for the Provincial Museum" (110). So it was that Young appointed him to visit Carr and evaluate the value of her paintings. Young's gesture indicates that he accepted Carr's initial assessment of her work and thus approached her work for its documentary rather than aesthetic value. Dr Newcombe thereafter made his visit to Carr's studio. Although he admired her work and even bought three of her canvases for his own personal collection, and although he wrote to say that the "sketches gave a clearer interpretation than the photographs," his report about their suitability for the new library was revealing of why Young came to reject housing the paintings there (qtd. in Tippett 110). Titled "Miss Carr's Collection of Paintings of Indian Totem Poles," the report indicated that, on the one hand, the drawings had been faithful to the carvings and would be useful for identifying clan legends and the poles themselves; on the other hand, the canvases sometimes took liberties in terms of the proportions of the poles and were often "too brilliant and vivid to be true to the actual conditions of the coast villages" (qtd. in Tippett 110).

As was the case with Pauline Johnson's literary work, Carr's canvases would elude the strict categories available for artistic or ethnological achievement in the period; as was not the case with Johnson, Carr's endeavours registered less a protest against the colonizing forces at work than an acknowledgment of their deleterious effects upon the Indigenous art forms she had come to admire. That Carr would argue for the value of her work based on its documentary value suggests, in part, her gendered marginality – the fact that, as a woman painter, she was reluctant to make claims of achievement or greatness that were more easily or readily grasped by her male counterparts. Working within discourses of the period, she remained relatively open to Indigenous art forms, even as she also reinscribed particular attitudes about them. However, to focus exclusively on her marginality, as Marek Eby observes, is to ignore "the complexity of her relative position within the *multiple oppressions* and marginalities that operate within [her] work" (1). Carr was also involved in a series of "appropriative acts," including building an Indigenous archive, which implicated her in the colonizing process (1). She would not explicitly consider preserving materials for her own archive, nor would she see preserving her papers as an extension of her agency until she met Dilworth.

A few other remarks couched in her will confirm what inspired Carr's confidence in Dilworth and how he would come to play a pivotal role in the preservation of her records. In the same letter, she explained that she had appointed him her trustee because he recognized that her "work was the biggest thing in my life": "The nieces never entered into it, you did" (Carr 2006, 301). He is here identified as closer in proximity to her than those connected by blood. The principle of kinship works itself out through an intimacy that exceeds familial relations. This framing of her life's career and his vital place in it are suggested by his "entrance" into her literary and artistic oeuvre: it conveys the level of imaginative participation and commitment she ascribed to him, the importance of his role to her artistic ambitions, and the intimacy they shared even to the exclusion of her family members. Carr's seeming conferral of power upon Dilworth in her will, moreover, is not the first instance when she envisaged him thus, nor for that matter was Dilworth the first person whom she approached as a means of finding a male figure to support and sanction her work. If, however, he was preceded by a series of men with considerable public standing and socio-cultural currency, including artist Lawren Harris and Eric Brown, director of the National Gallery, no one followed him: he was the last. In terms of her interactions with Dilworth alone, her gesture in her will resonates with at least one other significant moment in the last years of her life: her decision to give him the manuscript for what was to be posthumously published as *Growing Pains*, the only one of all her books that she explicitly identified as her autobiography both in her correspondence and in its eventual subtitle. That she would give him her autobiography, which documents the achievements of her artistic life and which served as a precursor to her other papers that would form the material basis of her archive, suggests the level of intimacy they shared and the need to mediate her life through a male subject who could adequately represent her.

Growing Pains: An Autobiography

Critically, her books are often received as autobiographical en masse. These include *Klee Wyck* (1941), *The Book of Small* (1942), *The House of All Sorts* (1944), *Growing Pains* (1946), *Pause: A Sketch Book* (1953), *The Heart of a Peacock* (1953), and *Hundreds and Thousands: The Journals of Emily Carr* (1966). Helen Buss, for example, argues that "it is very difficult to speak of any of Carr's books in isolation, as each becomes an intertextual map for the others" (162). Susanna Egan also reads her texts "as expressions of Carr's ongoing and repeated narratives of experience" rather than isolating *Growing Pains* as the prototypical autobiography, which, as I will show, follows a horizontal model of development (168). In spite of how Buss, Egan, and others[4] have identified her works as autobiographical in inclination, I follow Carr's predilection to regard *Growing Pains* as "An Autobiography" and her specific identification of it as such, which she suggested to her friend, Humphrey Toms, was "very bad taste to publish ... till you're dead" (1990, 403). In March 1941 she wrote a letter to another friend, Nan Cheney, in which she suggested that "I do not feel elligible [*sic*] for a biography[.] In the first place I'm *not DEAD* & I don't think these things *should* be wrote till one is" (Walker 307). She then added that "An Autobiog. ... is the only Biog. that can truthfully be done, I think & Alice would not tollerate it & I'd feel a FOOL if I wasnt dead" (307). These letters express her sense that such a book could be the only truthful and complete rendering of her life.

Carr was, moreover, often apprehensive that she was an inadequate subject for an autobiography and that she was not equal to the task of writing it; she often turned to Dilworth to ask about its value, its shape, and its content. For verification, she inquired of him approximately four months before she died whether or not she had "to take [her manuscript] to the point where [she sat] leg-dangling over [her] grave?"[5] In light of his response, which does not survive, she insisted that *Growing Pains* not be published until after her death, which in part confirms that she believed an autobiography should capture the entirety of one's life, from the early stages to the moment of death. The writing of her autobiography was thus informed by a sense of representing the wholeness or completeness of one's life, as much as was possible. Dilworth corroborated this belief, as expressed in a letter to Carr's publisher, W.H. Clarke: "I feel that it would be very difficult to publish anything further after the autobiography had come out.

There is a finality about it which would make it impossible logically to publish anything subsequently."[6] That finality was also related to her concerns that her autobiography more accurately captured – or disclosed – aspects of her lived experience that she did not want revealed during her lifetime. Her refusal to allow its publication until after her death was the register of a practical gesture: she believed that there were elements of her life that ought not to be revealed until after her passing. She was afraid, for example, that certain admissions would elicit the ire of, among others, her sister Alice. As such, this book was distinguished from her other works in terms of its form, scope, content, and purpose.

The fact, however, that Carr would leave the one manuscript identified as autobiography with Dilworth to do with as he pleased, and as a precedent to her other papers, puts into question the self-agency for which she so vigorously struggled. Her decision to leave the autobiography for his final revisions and shaping, and her apparent acquiescence to him and his editorial interventions in the last few years of her life, have significant implications for questions of self-agency. Her self-agency would have also, of course, been affected by the socio-political conditions of the period. Participating in the national fabric of the country, if not contributing to the national imaginary, would have been difficult for women until the period in which Carr began to write. At the turn of the twentieth century, when the Canadian publishing industry began to develop, some women took up the pen yet expressed delight in national sublimation or in participating in what Benedict Anderson has called "imagined national communities." As Sunera Thobani notes, national subjects are created by the process of "exaltation," a "technique of power [that] has been central to the processes of modern national formation" (5). In seeking to be subsumed into a larger, transcendent idea of national citizenship through their writing, therefore, some women writers relinquished the very identity and autonomy they would have achieved in becoming authors. At times, that proximity suggests accommodations made on the part of the female subject so that any sense of autonomy as "writer" was forgone and sublimated into a transcendent, national ideal; at other times, that proximity suggests a relationship that is fraught. In either instance, the inequities of power compel women writers to accommodate those structures – or to challenge the structures to make room for the articulation of their own concerns.

Carr's relationship to the national ideal was ambivalent. In books such as *Klee Wyck*, for example, she protested against a national imaginary that excluded Indigenous persons and that denigrated its various nations. In *Growing Pains*, conversely, Carr expressed deep affection for a country that was often subject to critique by the imperial centre. Dilworth was instrumental to positioning her and her artistic work within a national lexicon: he himself regarded *Growing Pains* as a metaphor for national development and she as a significant cultural producer. In particular, in the articles he crafted for *Saturday Night* and *Canadian Art*, and the introductory texts he wrote for *Klee Wyck*, *Growing Pains*, and art catalogues for her exhibitions, he consistently characterized her as impassioned by the country and as representative of national development. In the foreword to *Klee Wyck*, for example, Dilworth remarked upon "this Canadian woman's vital, vivid work" (vii). Carr herself had read and approved most of these texts. National sublimation would seem to be an attitude she espoused – and he an editor to whom she increasingly acquiesced.

Her relationship with Dilworth, the means by which she involved him in the care of her papers, the Emily Carr Trust, and the publication of her autobiography and other works, might initially seem to corroborate how she forfeited the very sense of autonomy as "writer" for which she had so energetically struggled. His endorsement of her work in the form of his introductory texts might be interpreted as instructive about "the masculine authority that was brought to bear on women's writing" (Gerson 2010, 56). As Carole Gerson argues in *Canadian Women in Print*, the "allographic" or "externally authored introduction ... issued from authority figures who were usually male" and often appeared in "a landmark first volume or final publication such as an author's collected works or a posthumous memorial edition" (48). I argue, however, that her apparent deference to his "masculine authority" regarding her posthumous autobiography might also be read productively, as her attempt to integrate herself more fully into the public sphere. The principle of kinship facilitated her literary endeavours and her public representation as artist. Even as her sense of self-presentation may be complicated by Dilworth's collaboration, she also acquired greater ontological weight because she found a means to be rendered a legible subject in a national imaginary that would have otherwise excluded her. She thus paradoxically found a means of securing the very self-agency that would have been threatened or denied altogether.

The Problem of the Autobiographical Female Subject

The decision to leave her papers – both the materials for the archive and especially the manuscript for her self-identified autobiography, *Growing Pains* – in the hands of a male interlocutor is pivotal to understanding the strategy Carr employed to locate self-agency. Her very self-representation was rendered vulnerable by leaving her manuscript in Dilworth's hands. But another challenge was posed by the fact that a woman could only uncomfortably adopt the genre of autobiography: as Leigh Gilmore notes, the mark of gender has ideological implications, such that for women identity is "located provisionally in the always problematical deployment of the I" (6). In critiquing the autobiographical genre and the "hard nut" of the normative masculinity that habitually underwrites its purportedly "universal subject," Sidonie Smith explains the difficulties women face in assuming the position of that subject when, in doing so, they become entangled in its determining tendencies (3–5). So she writes:

> there are certainly histories of the subject to be negotiated in that "I" space, histories that make trouble for her as she takes up that autobiographical "I." Those histories may press her to silence or they may encourage her to cross, crisscross, doublecross that "I" in order to move from silence into self-narrative. (5)

Part of the "trouble" of moving into self-narrative is related to the emphasis on disembodiment, that is, the emphasis on "rational thinking" to the exclusion of the body and its purported association with "irrational desires." Such a requirement, however, implicitly invites a woman to forgo her identity as "Other," or paradoxically to silence herself as she tries to articulate an "I" that is not representative of her "self," since, as a woman, she has been relegated to and assumed to occupy the realm of the body (8). Her embodiment is a very contradiction of the "imperial interpreter, provocateur of totalization" that in its "teleological drift of selfhood concedes nothing to indeterminacy, to ambiguity, or to heterogeneity" (8). Smith observes that when a woman approaches the autobiographical form and "the autobiographical 'I,' she not only engages the discourses of subjectivity through which the universal human subject has been culturally secured, she also engages the complexities of her cultural assignment to an absorbing embodiment" (22). In the assumption of the autobiographical "I," women must *also* "crisscross" their own "absorbing embodiment." In so doing, however, they engender indeterminacy, ambiguity, and heterogeneity – a contradiction of the teleological drift of selfhood, of its very tendency towards determinacy, clarity, and homogeneity. As Smith and Watson note, "the dissenting subject" is thus "located in the space of paradox" (93).

Such an assumption of the autobiographical "I" also has implications for form. In its more conventional structure, autobiographical narrative focused upon "public or professional achievements" and traced stages of growth either "horizontally," by "expanding the horizons of self and boundaries of experience through accretion, but always carrying forward through new growth that globe of an irreducible, unified core," or "vertically," by exploring inwardly in order to locate "the irreducible core" (Smith 18). A woman would have discovered an immediate challenge to being represented in terms of public achievement, since she herself would have frequently been consigned to the private sphere. She might also have found herself negotiating with a prescribed literary structure and wrangling with the very form that had predetermined that, first, a central position in the narrative would be denied her and, second, that a woman's cultural assignment was located beyond the scope or logic of autobiography. A woman writer might also devise internal rhetorical strategies with which to evade or subvert allotted subjectivities, that is, a woman writer finds ways to manipulate the "I" such that her own experientially based history would be privileged beyond a prescribed history of essentialism (Smith 22).

Carr was one of those women for whom her autobiography provided a discursive arena in which she could both articulate a seemingly universal self and also employ narrative strategies that ran counter to normative, teleological autobiographical trajectories. As such, *Growing Pains*, which focuses on her public life as a painter and was published posthumously in 1946 through the concerted efforts of Dilworth, contains complex and paradoxical impulses. She clearly strives for disembodiment in the attempt to stage the universal subject, the "I" that embarks upon a public journey that is individual and yet representative of a developing nation, which is unique and yet expresses communal values. She writes a narrative that moves horizontally, seemingly in emulation of more conventional autobiographical structures: that is, in a chronological fashion, she traces "stages of growth" to explore how her experience is expanded, how she grows and matures as an artist.

Yet, even in gaining access to public discourse through the performance of the normative subject and in securing a sense of privilege associated with a sense of male agency, Carr still "crisscrosses" the genre and seemingly evades complete surrender to the normative "I." She does so by performing within the narrative her rebellion against those institutions of authority that would have authorized her silence, in particular, the restrictive patriarchal family unit, as represented by her father, and religious institutions. Thus, *Growing Pains* seems to contain those normative masculinist values by virtue of its form and of its adoption of the normative "I," and yet resists these same values in its content. At the same time, the series of male figures she presented within her narrative as having sanctioned her literary practices and to whom she defers, and the dissolution of self as occasioned by her pursuit of national transcendence, seem to suggest that Carr proceeded to relinquish the very autonomy and self-agency she so vigorously pursued. Against this, I argue that she strategically performed such deferral and represented herself as having had approval conferred upon her by key male figures, with whom she closely allied herself. These male figures were often crucially associated with major cultural institutions – and anticipated her relationship with Dilworth. Her decision to leave her literary materials and then her autobiographical manuscript in his hands might thus also be read as part of this well-mapped strategy.

That strategy also shows itself in the narrative development of her autobiography. By its linear trajectory, *Growing Pains* is conservative in structure. Susanna Egan observes that the "conventional Romantic autobiography assumes the growth and blossoming of the artist," but argues that the entirety of Carr's "writings offer not growth but the 'patterns of reprise'" (170).[7] If assessed, however, as an individual text, *Growing Pains* does indeed follow a "horizontal" model, that is, the trajectory or the "growing pains" of the artist who develops and comes to maturity in terms of skill and accomplishment, and who comes to be recognized for her achievements. In Part 1 of the book, she begins with her "Baptism," the title of the first chapter, and traces her first experiences, early growth, and art training in San Francisco to show how, as in "Colour-Sense," her artistic impulses needed "to be tormented out of the girl" (62). In Part 2, she records her journey from Canada to London, where she continues to pursue her art studies; where she assesses as aesthetic subject matter the inadequacy, albeit pastoral beauty, of British landscape and comes to a finer appreciation of the magnificence of Canadian landscape; and where, in conversation with British citizens, she comes to appreciate her national identity in relation to British modes of understanding. So she observes:

> These people called us Colonials, forgot we were British. English colonists had gone out to America with a certain amount of flourish years and years ago. They had faded into the New World. Later, undesirable not-wanteds had been shipped out to Canada. It was hoped that America would fade them out too – all the west side of the earth was vaguely "America" to England. This courteous old gentleman recognized Canada as herself – as a real, separate place. (131)

In exploring the challenges inherent in being a female artist in the period, Carr simultaneously explores those related to being a "Colonial," the non-British Others, the "undesirable not-wanteds" that were designated, like women, to the margins of experience (see also 237–8). Her purportedly "irreducible, unified core," already suspect given her gender, is thus challenged by the likes of Mrs Radcliffe, a British woman who asserts that "London will soon polish Canada off you, smooth you, as your English parents were smooth" (138). By her continued resistance to such impulses to "polish" her into good English breeding, Carr's "irreducible core" apparently remains untouched and she thus feels comfortable declaring that she remains in essence "Canadian."

In this section, she also examines her failing health and her admission to the East Anglia Sanatorium, to which she was given entrance under medical authority because of the sheer physical strain of living out of Canada. Those apparently "irrational desires" she feeds in order to study abroad and to pursue her career as an artist take a toll upon her body, as they would have, more largely speaking, when to be an artist was a much greater struggle for a woman.[8] These "irrational" desires erupt at this moment in the narrative, as she physically endures a virtual nervous collapse (see Blanchard 90). Carr thus quarrels with her sister, who seemingly did not believe in Carr's work and who "wanted to take [her] home immediately": "The doctor would not let me travel. She called him a fool, said he knew nothing" (247). The doctor's authority apparently prevails over her sister's judgment: Carr does not return to Canada until she has recovered.

In the third and final part of her autobiography, she explores that return, "not with 'know-it-all' fanfare, not a successful student prepared to carry on art in the New World, just a broken-in-health girl that had taken rather a hard whipping, and was disgruntled with the world" (272). These are in part the "growing pains" to which Carr alludes in the title – but from which she recovers in the third part. So she convalesces, restored by the "healing, restful" spaces and forests of Canada. Although by the end of the second part she may not have succeeded publicly or professionally in ways that would be typical to autobiographies that show "horizontal growth," by the third part she has achieved moderate success. She shows herself as one who has grown and matured as both writer and painter. Significantly, by this part, she records her return to France for further training; her introductions to Harris and Dilworth, who contributed to the furthering of her artistic and literary career; and her public celebration, even endorsement, as a Canadian author and artist.

Even as she follows a more conventional literary form, however, she defies in her content those social and political structures that bear down upon her, that would prescribe certain modes of conduct and expression. By opening *Growing Pains* with "Baptism," she demonstrates from the outset how she must resist, first, religious forces as represented by the Presbyterian parson, Dr Reid, who "tips" her "flat like a baby" in order to baptize her when she is four, and, second, patriarchal forces as represented by her father. Upon writing her and her brother's name in the Bible's covers, for example, her father "banged" them closed in an attempt to "[shut] us all in" for the rest of their lives (3–4). Her father's "unbendable iron will" (5) that directed her childhood home "with mechanical precision" (6) contrasts with her mother's gentle and kindly disposition; so she significantly sets up the second chapter, titled "Mother," in direct opposition to the first. Although she is still following the "horizontal model" by beginning chronologically with her childhood experiences, in this second chapter she characterizes her mother as generating a sufficiently nurturing force that extends well into Carr's adulthood. By contrast, her father is seen as providing a "tyrannical reality [that] shriveled up and was submerged under our own development" (5). She will later see her national inclinations, her longing for Canada, her "quiver of homesickness" (37) for her country whenever she is abroad, in similar terms: Canadian nationalism and modesty will be seen as a counterbalance, for example, to "beastly London" (109) and to the air of superiority that the British hold over her and her clearly inferior Canadian ways of being.

Even so, if Carr is in part successful in her employment of a form that ordinarily privileges a male – if not an imperial – subject, she seemingly relinquishes the very autonomy she effectively attains in "crisscrossing" the genre in terms of content because of another underlying impulse that appears to run counter to that success. That impulse is related to her increasing dependence on Dilworth: to his advice and instruction she seemed consistently to yield. He thus intervened and selected stories for *Klee Wyck*, as one example, but also negotiated the publication process for *Growing Pains*, *Pause*, and *Heart of the Peacock*, from their beginnings to the page proofs. Published posthumously, these three books reveal his vital role in getting her work into print. However, her reliance upon him in the forging and shaping of her autobiography demonstrated the manner in which she found legitimacy through a male subject, even as she resisted patriarchal control. She gained status as an individual artist because her own artistic practice was accorded national identification and value; in this process, Carr carefully negotiated the terms through Dilworth.

Male Interventions and Sanctions

Dilworth was certainly not the first male figure to endorse Carr's autobiographical writings, nor was he the first from whom she sought support. Indeed, her consistent tendency to seek male approval of her work also suggest a desire to position herself legitimately as citizen and artist. Of the early male figures, the painter Lawren Harris was most prominent. When she announced her intention to write a story, he supported this initiative as well: "Why don't you plan and do an entire book ... There would be nothing like it and it would be a real contribution. It could be illustrated by your paintings." To these assertions, he added that the book would be "worth doing, very well worth doing. Contributions to the life of men are made in no other way."[9] The origins of the writing of her biography – a cornerstone book in terms of staging her centrality as an artist with national aims – thus may in part reside with Harris. The gender-specific terms he draws upon here are important: if men contributed to public life and men wrote books about their accomplishments, he still valued Carr's contributions. Indeed, he later came to endorse theosophy, which disregarded gender and viewed it as immaterial to one's soul (see Blavatsky 1978–9). That "men" were generally regarded in the period, however, as the category to whose lives one must contribute, to whom one must appeal, before whom one must justify one's work, and by whom one would be legitimated might suggest why she limited her cooperative dealings with women. In a letter dated 24 June 1933 Harris articulated the other problems he perceived women would confront in attempting the autobiographical form:

> I still maintain that I am not entirely wrong about an autobiography, though strange as it may seem to you, a soul in a woman's body finds it very much more difficult than one in a man's body – perhaps that is far from being strange to you, though.
>
> Somehow a man gets a kick, a release out of writing his autobiography for any old person to read – it's a positive assertion of himself – but the lady is negative as regards herself, her person.[10]

His assessment of the effect of autobiography confirmed circulating ideas about women's embodiment and justified why women would not be able to experience the "positive assertion," the "kick" of identity, as a man would. Elsewhere in the same letter, he argued that friendships were strongest between men and women – two halves of a soul coming together in complete understanding: "One 1/2 in a lady's outfit, the other in a man's that can stand it and thrive and bloom and understand the grace of God." Carr may have inferred that, first, she would never be able to write an autobiography in a way that was anything but unusual for a woman: as Smith would argue, her "absorbing embodiment" would have been perceived as a contradiction of the discourses of subjectivity, of the disembodied male gaze, and of the teleological drift of unified selfhood. She may have also concluded, therefore, that she required another "half" to come together to create complete understanding.

In spite of his conclusions about women and autobiography, Harris remained persuasive about her position and currency as artist. He therefore strove to include her in a movement that legitimated her efforts and that rendered her art in terms that were larger in scope than she had previously been able to access.[11] In one letter, he noted that member of the Group of Seven Arthur Lismer, who had been out west, "left a creative stir" and "had great things to say about your present work": "he could see it emerging into its own fruition."[12] The accolades were a means by which Carr was sanctioned and embraced by their national project. If she was implicitly inducted into an aesthetic agenda that was national in scope, however, it was also clearly masculinist, and obliged her to be strategic in her interactions.[13]

That masculinist agenda also explains why she represented a series of male figures in *Growing Pains* as expressing approval for her writing.

The first of these was a medical professional. The reason for her turn to writing practices, she claimed, sprang from ill health. So, by her account, her medical doctor, Dr Baillie, forbade her to paint because of the strain on her physical well-being, although he determined that writing was permissible if it did not tax her further:

> "Doctor, may I write?"
>
> "Write? Write what?"
>
> "Describe places I've seen on my sketching trips, woods, Indians and things – nice Canadian things of the West, things that will heal, not rile my heart."
>
> "You can try, but don't get excited, don't overtire." (1946, 359)

In a passage that follows almost directly upon the heels of this one, Carr explains that she wrote against "book rules," of which she knew very little, and made up two of her own: "Get to the point as directly as you can; never use a big word if a little one will do" (360). The contradictions inherent in these two scenarios, her simultaneous acquiescence and rebellion, are clear: on the one hand, she represents an authority figure like her medical professional to demonstrate that the male and public world has approved of her artistic or literary production, but on the other hand, she wishes to "rebel" against those rules that appear to govern *how* she ought to write or express herself. She clearly desired, at the very least, to assert her own rules of literary style.

In the same chapter, "Alternative," Carr claimed that another male figure, Eric Brown, the director of the National Gallery between 1912 and 1939, invited her to write her autobiography some years prior to her having met Dilworth. She apparently dismissed the idea to do so at first because, as she suggested, she didn't "know how to write" (360). She eventually conceded, however, because she "wanted to please him" (360):

> While I was in the hospital, Eric Brown wrote me … "Will you collaborate with a biographer? We want the 'struggle story' of your work out West written" ….
>
> I said, "Nobody could write my hodge-podge life but me. Biographers can only write up big, important people who have done great deeds to which the public can attach dates. I could not be bothered with collaborators, nor would they be bothered with the drab little nothings that have made up my life. However, *to please you*, Mr. Brown, I will have a try." (360–1; italics mine)

That she subsequently mentions this anecdote in her autobiography is relevant: Brown is one of a series of well-positioned male figures that she presents as conferring approval and sanctioning her literary and artistic endeavours. She represents herself as striving to write simply because such figures invited her to do so. As importantly, she refused to work with "collaborators," such as Dorothy Livesay, who offered to help write her autobiography: Carr was determined to write her own story on her own terms (Livesay 146). She poses, however, as a submissive subject in *Growing Pains* in order to validate her representation in the public sphere and to secure the approval required to move through it with greater ease. She would therefore later argue that the reason she was inspired to write an autobiography at all was because "Brown wanted me to, but he died before I got a chance to send it for his crit" (1990, 307). This seeming displacement of responsibility for taking up the pen thus becomes a key strategy that Carr reiterated when she met Harris and then Dilworth.[14]

As the archive shows, Harris, like Brown, apparently spurred her on to write her own autobiography around 1933: "It might take a few years ... Would it interest you?" (qtd. in Walker 394). He is one of the key men whom she allowed to read her biography, as she admitted in a letter to Humphrey Toms: "my publisher, Editor, & Lawren Harris [are] the only three I have allowed to read my biog: say she beats Klee Wyck Small & the rest" (Walker 403). Interestingly, it is Harris to whom *Growing Pains* is dedicated because of this very encouragement of her artistic and writing practices. It is he, she proclaimed, who had "harp[ed] on 'the Biog' idea. ... probably he put the idea into my noddle originally, when I decided to write it" (2006, 131). So she suggested in a letter dated 15 February 1942, that

> Lawren tried to persuade me to write a Biog:[,] practically the thing I *am* doing[.] I remember jeering & saying "Who'd want to read it?" & "What had *I* to write about?" and dismissing it from my thoughts[.] Maybe it did not register *then*[,] maybe it sowed the idea[.] I don't know[.] I *thought* it was *really* because Eric Brown asked me to[,] said [if] I wouldn't[,] someone else would. I was amazed to see in these old letters it was just the type of thing he suggested. (2006, 111)

Carr's attitude as expressed earlier towards Brown and then here towards Harris also suggests her performed self-deprecation when considering whether or not her life bore any kind of importance to the national imaginary – "big, important people" who have accomplished "big, important things" have biographies written about them. She anticipates the "jeering" she might receive by holding herself up to mockery, only to demonstrate that it is both Brown and Harris who see the effort as legitimate. The moment allows her to perform a necessary modesty, given her gender, to prevent her from being regarded as violating the public sphere without proper invitation. She thus finally turned to writing her own autobiography, an indication that she too saw her life's artistic endeavours as vital to a national context.

When Dilworth first entered Carr's life in 1941, Harris began to collaborate with him in managing her affairs until his role significantly diminished. They operated what became the Emily Carr Trust Collection, in which an archive of her paintings that expressed her achievements was developed. They chose canvases for exhibits together, organized their shipment, and decided where her work was to be exhibited. In one letter dated 29 June 1942 Carr wrote to Harris to allow him to send her show to Seattle for a summer exhibit (of British Columbia artists) because "I have complete confidence in my Trustors." But well before this point, on 14 April 1942, Harris had written to her about his contact with Martin Baldwin, of the Toronto Art Gallery, and with the Montreal Gallery for its own exhibition of the Emily Carr collection. He reassured Carr that, having had "no reply from them to any letter written more than one month ago, ... I'll fire again." In these letters as others, he showed that he was consistent and reliable. In the same letter, he deployed a terminology that was charged with his appreciation for her work:

> They are creations every one of them = and the creations the like of which Canada won't see again. They are a heritage of the Can people, particularly of the West coast and believe me if Ira and I did not feel that down into our boots we would not have entered into the Trust – we would not have been and remained determined that the Emily Carr collection find a home worthy of its great contribution to the real Canadian culture – the peoples.[15]

He registered his belief in her contribution to Canadian culture, his sense of both the importance of *her* work and the importance of *his* role in its staging and development. These were the very terms Dilworth was to espouse when evaluating her work; these were also the terms Carr had initially used about the Indigenous iconography she featured in her canvases when she attempted to donate them to the province.

The Growing Pains before *Growing Pains*

Unusually, however, Carr did not immediately turn to Dilworth or to another male figure for support of her literary career. A cursory examination of the publication of *Klee Wyck* and her early editors shows how Carr learned by precedent to write according to the literary expectations in place, which were later applied to *Growing Pains*, and why Dilworth increasingly played a key role in this process. Indeed, Carr did not even meet Dilworth until 1939. Her initial attempts at writing non-fictional sketches and her autobiography, which were tentative, culminated in her first non-fictional work, *Klee Wyck*, four years before her death in 1941.[16] There were, unusually, three female editors who intervened in the three years before she met Dilworth: Dr Ruth Humphrey, Flora Burns, and Margaret Clay, referred to as "faithful women friends" in *Growing Pains* (361). Yet she eventually expressed deep impatience for them and found them ultimately wanting.

In Carr's early search for "understanding sympathetic ears & eyes," she encountered Humphrey, an English professor at Victoria College between 1936 and 1945 (Carr 2006, 134). They met in May 1936, when Humphrey offered to critique Carr's stories in return for a sketch (Blanchard 259). She also encouraged her to write a series of "little short Indian incident fragments" (262) that might be developed from her sketching trips to various First Nations villages: these sketches were the beginnings of what was later to be published as *Klee Wyck*. Humphrey became less available to Carr by about 1940, however, because she was travelling abroad. They corresponded regularly and Carr continued to send her manuscripts, yet she increasingly became impatient with the delays involved in receiving Humphrey's responses: "I have not sent more [stories] because moving round as you are now it's a bit hopeless" (Humphrey 117). Although she overlooked these lapses when Humphrey at long last would write substantive letters that "atoned for premier shoddiness of letter writing," Carr began to turn to others for assistance with her work (Humphrey 123).

She thus came to rely upon Clay and Burns. Director of the Vancouver Public Library, Clay advocated on Carr's behalf to get her stories published. Clay was also instrumental in having Carr's painting *Vanquished* sent to Amsterdam for an exhibition arranged by the International

Federation of Business and Professional Women (see Walker, 60n1). Specifically, when Carr sent twenty-five stories to Lorne Pierce, editor of the Ryerson Press, in February 1938, Clay wrote a lengthy letter of support in which she suggested that those such as Humphrey and Dr George Sedgewick, a professor of English at the University of British Columbia, had already shown interest in Carr's work.[17] The stories she sent, however, were an eclectic mix that were not considered suitable for publication in book form: nineteen, which were to be used later in the final version of *Klee Wyck,* pertained to her painting trips to First Nations communities, and six were about her childhood. It may be this unfortunate first attempt to collect her stories that caused Carr to characterize Clay as an ineffectual mediator and editor; as a result, Carr infrequently consulted her. Upon reading "Chins Up," an early version of material for *Pause,* for example, she was frustrated by the fact that Clay had to "*see* the words" rather than have it read to her: "Said she liked it, but you know things don't plop in that sort of still water[.] they gurgle round & round slowly till they reach bottom" (Humphrey 126). Carr felt more indebted to Burns, because she, like Humphrey, was appointed a "listening lady" who had been "very patient in listening to my script" (Carr 1946, 461).[18] Carr would read out her work to both Burns and Clay in order to hear how her stories sounded and edit them accordingly. Of the two, she particularly valued Burns's "clear brain & memory: [she] can read a thing *once* and get at it right away & hang on" (Humphrey 117) and regarded her as on equal footing with Humphrey. As she declared in one of her letters to Burns, "I owe to you & Ruth": "I *know* heaps of [faults] in every way yet how could I help it? Good writers take years to make."[19] Carr thus continued to send Burns samples of her writing until 1941, after which time she began to solicit the editorial assistance of Dilworth, the inception of which was mediated through both Humphrey and Burns.[20]

Specifically, Carr came to believe that without Dilworth's assistance, *Klee Wyck* "might never have come into being except as a still-born."[21] Carr's belief had some basis in fact: it was only until Dilworth intervened, selecting stories that he provided to W.H. Clarke, publisher and manager of the Canadian branch of Oxford University Press, and setting the terms of the stages of publication, from beginning to page proofs, that her first book was accepted for publication. Concerning the title, for example, he wrote to Clarke on 5 May 1941 that "Miss Carr has had quite an inspiration ... She suggests that we call the volume 'Stories in Cedar.'"[22] He then wrote to Carr about three weeks later to say that he had conveyed to Clarke how much "we both like the title 'Sketches in Cedar.' I think we should definitely decide on that." ("Sketches in Cedar," the original title of her manuscript, was eventually changed to "Klee Wyck.") He evidently had some understanding of their strategic relationship in producing one of Carr's books: when *Klee Wyck* was finally published, he wrote about the "thrill" of having "*our* book in my hands."[23] That Carr did not take offence at his suggestion implies that she accepted the growing intimacy between the two, and his role in the production of her books.

There are two reasons that explain his success with her, both of these related to the principle of kinship. The first involves their growing intimacy, also evidenced in the informal names they adopted for each other, the means by which they characterized her books, and the rings they exchanged as tokens of affection.[24] Over the course of their deepening friendship, they shifted from more formal appellations to informal ones: he referred to her as "Small," the child-self represented in the second volume of her stories, and she to him as her "Guardian." The terms of kinship were enacted as he became the caregiver and was invited to protect not only her child-self but also her books, which she characterized as her own offspring. In one letter, dated 18 August 1943, she noted that Small, whom she often conflated with *The Book of Small*, sought "sanctuary" in Dilworth's breast pocket "when E. is depressed in long wakeful hours" (Carr 2006, 223). In another remarkable narrative she appended to a letter dated 7 November 1942, she recorded how Small felt the "joy-feel of his deep true friendship" on the day Dilworth legally became the executor of her estate: that experience supplanted "the feel of a fathering love I lost when I was a little girl" (Carr 2006, 317). The terms of kinship are extended here, from Carr to her books; in assuming the role of parent not only to her child-self but also to her manuscripts, he could be trusted to usher her books into being and represent them in the symbolic.

The second reason for Dilworth's success with Carr is that he was better able than her early female editors to represent her in the public sphere. He identified what publishers at this time desired in terms of the autobiographical form: evenness and consistency in terms of the representative "I" and the subject matter over which it presided, and a more coherent narrative line. By contrast, her early manuscript of *Klee Wyck*, edited by these "faithful women friends," was rejected on three different occasions. The explanations offered by publishers focused on Carr's attempt to represent facets of her personal life and work simultaneously.[25] Non-fiction editor J. King Gordon of Farrar & Rhinehart, for example, rejected the manuscript because he could only see the merits of the stories as individual units: "I have read them and find them delightful, and some of them masterpieces of their kind."[26] However, they did not conform in their arrangement and content to his sense of what would constitute a unified autobiographical entity (see Carr 2006, 9–11); he saw the stories as "more suitable for magazine than for book publication."[27] The various personae she adopted within *one* manuscript undermined prevailing notions of the coherent, autonomous, and masculinist self that governed the non-fictional form. Carr's inability to find an interested publisher for *Klee Wyck* thus seems to demonstrate how her range of experiences, which informed the multiple roles she concurrently adopted, could not be contained within a more conventional autobiographical form (even if not a proper autobiography). The limits to the form and to subjectivity imposed by the publishing industry in mid-century Canada would not allow for a book in which an "incoherent" self, that is, the representation of multiple selves, would be rendered. Dilworth clearly understood the demands of the publishing industry in this period.

More broadly, Carr regarded Dilworth as the pivotal male agent who could articulate her concerns in the public arena. Indeed, by August 1941, as a letter from Carr to Humphrey suggests, Dilworth had entirely replaced both Burns and Humphrey as editors:

> I love working with him ... He has made a lot of new copies, & there will be heaps to go over ... Ira had a new copy of "Bobtails" made – he gave me splendid crits on her. So now I will have a copy, & you can read it. (Humphrey 139)

From this point on Carr never again asked Humphrey to critique her work. The dynamic between Carr and Dilworth – her appeal to his editorial eye, his readiness to assist – set in motion the growing intimacy between the two that was fundamental to the trajectory of her literary career. So she wrote to him in December 1941, "I do value having *you* to talk my work over with for I know you understand." In another letter to Humphrey, she articulated how she valued the fact that he "is so good, so understanding & comfortable as a backer." She appreciated that he provided criticism that was "stiff and merciless," yet "*very* complimentary and encouraging" and detailed: "Each section had its separate comments" (Humphrey 144).

The shift from her listening ladies to Dilworth occurred over the span of approximately three years. If Humphrey was no longer invited to provide editorial criticism, Burns quickly deferred to Dilworth's authority. After the publication of *Klee Wyck*, for example, Burns sent him a letter, dated 18 November 1941, in which she thanked him for his "untiring efforts" and "enthusiasm" in relation to the book, and "for what you have done in bringing to publication in such perfect form a great contribution ... to Canadian literature." How she conceives of his place within the national literary scene is of relevance here – for it was to become one of the reasons Carr would become so closely allied with him. Dilworth's response to Burns, however, indicates that he recognized he was one in a succession of editors and that, correctly, he alone could not accept praise for his contributions to Carr's work. He appreciated "how much [she] and Miss Humphrey did for Emily in the early days of her struggle with literary form."[28] That struggle found resolution after his attention to standard literary and publishing practices regarding the autobiographical form allowed him to steer Carr's manuscripts to publication.

Carr deliberately sent her manuscripts directly to Dilworth for a number of reasons: his geographical proximity made it feasible to visit her both to critique her writing in person and to nourish the friendship she sought; he was able to offer an intimacy that eventually distinguished him from all others; and his positions as, first, professor at the University of British Columbia and then, from 1938, BC regional director for CBC Radio meant he was educated, qualified, and well connected to those who would thereafter read her stories over the air and, ultimately, see them to publication. It is perhaps with the experience, diplomacy, and knowledge that comes with such positions that he usually suggested only minor changes to her writing. Often, he allowed such criticism to be enfolded within what he saw as the merits of her writing, "the impression of simplicity and lack of effort." Almost invariably, such criticism was counterbalanced by his desire that his remarks not be taken too seriously, a posture that meant Carr ultimately retained authority over her texts – even as she respected his editorial decisions. On 17 August 1941, for example, he suggested that "perhaps [the story is] better as it stands and I am just suffering from one of my frequent blind spots" (Carr 2006, 42). Whether this kind of comment was an indication of genuine or performed modesty, or of his respect for her final authority – or both – he was patently successful because she almost invariably expressed appreciation for his insights.

More generally, Carr was delighted by his involvement in every aspect of her career and in furthering her interests. These interests often focused on the public side of her career, a side she herself eschewed. Their intimacy allowed him to represent her at lectures he gave of her stories at the Vancouver Art Gallery and at the University of British Columbia, and readings he conducted over the radio for the CBC. For the latter, the stories were initially read by Sedgewick (in January and February of 1940) and then later entirely by Dilworth himself. After the broadcasts, he wrote Carr supportive letters: "We had a great many very interesting comments on them. A great many more, I should say, than we have had on any other talks or readings."[29] On 16 April 1943 he also read from her work for Oxford University Press at the University of Toronto Women's Club. He described the latter as a "room very well filled with an extremely interesting, alert-looking audience" (Carr 2006, 203). Dilworth was savvy in terms of recounting to Carr how she was featured as the author in such moments and he as secondary. In this particular instance, he noted that "had it not been for the warm spot over my heart where Small kept watch ... I think I might have got cold feet and run out on the good ladies" (Carr 2006, 203).

He was also enormously useful in arranging introductions to persons who might further Carr's literary career and those from the larger artistic circle of which he formed a part: Nellie McClung, Robertson Davies, and Duncan Campbell Scott are examples of distinguished Canadians to whom Carr was introduced, directly or indirectly, through Dilworth. Some of these connections were brief and tenuous. There seems to have been only one direct meeting with McClung, to whom he referred in a letter to Carr. A subsequent letter from McClung addressed to Carr survives, in which she asserted that "I hear of you often through our mutual friend, Mr. Dilworth."[30] Dilworth also forwarded "a charming long letter from Robertson Davies," who had written a positive review of *Klee Wyck* in *Saturday Night* and whom Dilworth at a later time met for lunch.[31] Yet it is Scott who appeared to have held greatest sway, as Dilworth's letters suggest. In a letter dated 11 July 1941 he observed that Scott "thought [the title selected for your first book] was the best of those I told him of ... I am not sure whether or not I told you that Duncan liked it. I know his judgment will mean something to you." Carr was indeed an admirer of Scott and would have likely felt connected to a larger national cultural scene by such mediations of correspondence and discussions. These interactions did in fact position Carr within a wider Canadian cultural scene and included her with other such cultural producers of the period.

On numerous other occasions, he mediated her interactions with figures that were of importance to the development of her public persona, including Clarke, her first publisher. Believing he could "speak for [her]," he responded directly to these persons about matters related to her work.[32] However presumptuous his gestures may appear, Carr gave him full licence to do so and suggested that her "feelings should [not] be consulted *too* much" about such matters.[33] Indeed, as he did so, she continued to compose *Growing Pains* and to confer with him about a number of matters, including whether or not she ought to delineate the development of her literary career: "The last phase will be most difficult & is the worst remembered, partly because it is *too new*[,] partly because my brain is old. Is it necessary to include my writing? Is the Biog *me* entire or just the story of my *painting*?" Ultimately, she asserted, he ought to "choose which you want"[34] because, as she suggested in a letter dated 12 October 1943, the "Biog" was no longer hers: "it[']s *yours* & before I alter it[, it] *must* be with *your* consent."

The question she asks is revealing: should her autobiography be the story of "me," that is, her private self, rather than of her public career as an artist? It may suggest her uncertainty about what is essential to an autobiography; but it may also suggest that she recognizes Dilworth as her primary audience and connection to a public to which she would otherwise not have had access. It further demonstrates her learned understanding that an autobiography might be concerned only with a singular, coherent, and public life – and therefore a masculinist one – rather than a private one. She had learned this lesson when attempting to publish *Klee Wyck*. Finally, and most significantly, it reveals the degree to which she believed a biography might be exchanged for "me," might operate metonymically, a stand-in for Carr's own person. Under Dilworth's disembodied gaze and by the terms of kinship set, therefore, Carr *and* her manuscript would be sanctioned as legitimate subjects in the public sphere. The conferral of the "Biog" and the manner in which she defers to his authority – "choose which you want" – is also enormously revealing, inasmuch as it suggests that literary decisions ultimately were in Dilworth's hands, and that he would therefore be responsible for her public representation of her "self" (especially given her own metonymic understanding of books). For similar reasons, when Lawren Harris read the "Biog" and suggested "some additions," Carr "refused to make [them] without Ira's consent, as the M.S. belongs to him."[35]

This gesture of relinquishing the "Biog," and even the comments she makes above, may seem to suggest that Carr gave Dilworth unilateral control over her manuscripts; however, the gesture is more complicated. It was a sign of their growing intimacy and mutual understanding, of her complete trust in his ability to articulate her concerns, and of her desire to be represented, but mediated more properly by a male subject in the public sphere. A revealing letter to contemporary artist Myfanwy Pavelic indicates that she felt that, for example, Dilworth's corrections were made only when utterly necessary and, more significantly, he did not overstep the bounds of his role: "My Editor will not change or allow to be changed one word. He goes over punctuation & points out sometimes if he thinks I have not made a meaning clear. But he *never* re-writes or re-words me[.]" Again the emphasis on her *self*, the "me" that he might have reworded, rather than her book, indicates that she felt editorial interference might have censored or altered *her person*. In other words, Dilworth was a protector of Carr's interests rather than simply her editor – their intimacy allowed for Carr to express herself without impediment or interference, to move beyond the embodiment to which she as a woman had been consigned.[36]

Still, Carr was initially obliged to test him and his fidelity: the intimacy and trust that became central to the dynamic of the relationship unfolded over time. Since she claimed that her previous publishing attempts were "disastrous" and that her own stories were "not up to much" given the indifference they had elsewhere inspired, she was uncertain about how Dilworth might respond. In *Growing Pains*, she expresses her anxiety as follows: both "the stories and I awaited our Editor" (364). The capitalization of "Editor" underscores the place of authority she was to confer upon him, but only *after* she recognized that he appreciated her work and would fundamentally respect her wishes. The appellation also gestures towards how she would later personify her books, a key to understanding her literary work as an extension of her sense of embodiment and the need for his disembodied gaze to complete the "half" she had sought. Thus, she feels his "kindness" profoundly in having "lifted a tremendous load from me, just as if he had kicked all the commas, full stops, quotes and capitals right to another planet" (364). The "load" he lifts is presumably related to her uncertainties about the worthiness of her writing – but also to her finding someone who might respect the "rules" of grammar without altering her vision or understanding of her work.

However dismissive she may have been about her "little life," she enjoyed the public attention her literary and visual work received. She represented Dilworth's approval as if it were a form of national endorsement, perhaps strengthened by his prominent position as the regional director of British Columbia for CBC Radio. This perception seems most evident in one memory she recounts in her autobiography, "Seventieth Birthday and a Kiss for Canada," when a party is held in her honour to celebrate the success of her book *Klee Wyck*. In *Growing Pains* she describes the moment thus:

> Then everybody began to chatter at once. Praise, praise, praise for *Klee Wyck*. I ducked my face into a box of beautiful chrysanthemums and red carnations that the Canadian Press had sent me.
>
> I did not see or hear Eye cross the room, but suddenly I was aware of a great kindness there before me and the kindness stooped and kissed my cheek!
>
> It was the proudest moment of *Klee Wyck*'s success when, before them all, Eye stooped and gave me that kiss for Canada, prouder far than when *Klee Wyck* won the Governor-General's medal for best non-fiction for Canada. (373)

Her description of Dilworth's bestowal of the kiss as on behalf of Canada suggests the position he occupied within her imaginative framework.[37] He embodies "kindness," the root of which, according to the OED, suggests "kinship" and the "natural affection" arising from such proximity. She was being "seen" by the Canadian public, through Dilworth's mediating gaze. His kiss was an endorsement of her work, her position within the Canadian national imaginary, which was corroborated by the national distinction of the Governor General's Award. Yet, the intimacy and distinctiveness of their relationship was privileged beyond the recognition associated with a national award.

Her name for him in this account, "Eye," was one she adopted in their correspondence. That she would often begin letters with "my dear Eye" reveals the mechanics of the relationship: this appellation suggests the close, attentive reader whom she characterized as part of *her own body*. It is perhaps a metaphorical description of her inability to see her own work clearly, as it is also a means of displacing her own sense of embodiment and allowing his "disembodied" perspective to represent her in the public sphere. It may thus be interpreted as a sign of the repressed desire to be the "Self," the male subject who occupies the symbolic, who can therefore confer approval, and who has the kind of decision-making authority Carr had been striving for much of her life. In support of this view, Dilworth's role extended well beyond operating as her "Eye" – he also operated as her "voice." He mediated, for example, her interaction with Graham McInnes of the National Film Board.[38] For this film production, in which Carr categorically refused to appear and for which she refused to speak, she agreed Dilworth might do so on her behalf. He also evidently derived some pleasure from these collaborative efforts and regarded them as national in proportion. As he suggested on 26 October 1941, "It has helped me to realize a bit of myself and has given me a small share in a great piece of work for Canada ... I have never before been so thrilled about a piece of work in which I had a part" (2006, 51–2).

Carr strategically uses this blurring of identities – the manner in which her "Eye" helps to represent her "I" – and her intimate disclosures to Dilworth to gain a sense of agency. This process becomes most clear in the writing of *Growing Pains*. Although she had subtitled it "An Autobiography," she takes steps to see that *he* oversees its shape, even asking him to write the foreword. She only did so, however, after she felt sure he would do as she required. Thereafter, she gave the book entirely over to him:[39] "Thank you for being glad about the Biog. being yours – What shall you call her? I called her first edition 'Growing Pains.' Ruth did not like it but could suggest no better[.] Maybe you will think of [a title]."[40] This invitation to reconsider the title may have also served as a test, since it was shortly after Humphrey's disapproval of naming the work "Growing Pains" that Carr sought out another editor. As Carr continued to write sequences for the book, she conferred with Dilworth about a number of matters, each time reiterating that the book was his. So she wrote on 12 October 1943, "it[']s *yours* & before I alter it[, it] *must* be with *your* consent" (2006, 241). It became clear that the autobiography was only his because he consistently returned to Carr to ask for her consent first and to exercise her wishes.

Her strategic forfeiting of authority to him in order to allow him to manage her manuscripts and then her records is significant: his decisions were vital in locating publishers, securing her first book publication, and launching her career as a writer. She ultimately achieved the independence she had vigorously sought since the beginnings of her career as an artist. That she decided to write her autobiography reflects, at some level, her growing belief that her role as artist had acquired both public and national importance, and that such a role was integral to the national imaginings of this period. Dilworth's role also implicitly demonstrated how her work might fail to be published in this period without "proper" editorial interventions and without the terms of kinship that would have otherwise precluded Carr's person. As their friendship deepened and as she characterized him more frequently in terms that called upon principles of familial affiliation, she increasingly depended on Dilworth to facilitate her entry into the public sphere and to allow her to participate in a larger, transcendent idea of national citizenship. His efforts may seem to reinscribe her as a subject submissive to masculinist control and national governance and to incur the loss of the agency for which she so vigorously struggled, but these efforts also paradoxically allowed for her to acquire ontological weight, to be rendered a legible subject in a national imaginary that would have otherwise excluded her. For Carr, these kinds of negotiations demonstrate the means by which she tried to render herself a legible subject in the national imaginary.

If, as I suggest in chapter 1, Johnson found a way of addressing her audience directly through her embodied performances, Carr was no less successful by speaking and working through Dilworth. Whereas Johnson used intimacy to reconstruct the eroticized body as a body of violence, to engage her audiences sympathetically while subverting the male, colonizing gaze, Carr's use of intimacy supported the terms of kinship by which her manuscripts were eventually preserved and published. Her intimate relationship with Dilworth allowed her to represent her concerns publicly but without endangering these concerns or her status as author. If Antigone reminds us that political participation for women may involve "the violent forgetting of primary kin relations," Carr showcases how such a process might be complicated and even bypassed: Dilworth could promote her books publicly and mediate her political participation, but without threatening the polis or symbolic masculine authority. It is therefore unsurprising that she would relinquish first her autobiography and eventually all her literary papers to his care, and that he would faithfully represent what she desired in the public sphere. The reasons Sheila Watson, the subject of the next chapter, would have for leaving her papers with her close friend, Fred Flahiff, are considerably different, but her story nonetheless has a critical feature in common with that of Carr: they both worked cooperatively with male figures to locate a sense of self-agency, to establish their archives, and to extend the boundaries of their status as authors in mid-twentieth-century Canada.

3 "It's What You [Don't] Say": Sheila Watson, the Imminent Narrative, and the Archive of Displacement

In the last few years of her life, Sheila Watson (1909–1998) became preoccupied with housing the papers of her husband, Wilfred (1911–1998),[1] in an archive at the University of Alberta before turning to her own papers. We might say, as with Emily Carr, that the principle of kinship informed her efforts, and that these efforts would be initially applied to the materials for someone else's archive rather than her own. However, her motivations were rather different from those of Carr, and she was more concerned about the proper housing of her records. In his capacity as biographer, Fred Flahiff noted that, once she had set up her husband's archive, she was provided "with a precedent and a space for shoring up her own papers" (324). Yet it was of utmost concern to her that her papers not suffer house arrest, by having them stored with those of Wilfred at the University of Alberta. Flahiff notes that "she felt no hostility towards the institution or the city, only reluctance to be archivally proximate to [him]" (325–6). Ultimately, she eschewed formal institutions as a final destination for her records, instead without advance warning, sending her papers and books in a series of boxes to Flahiff in Toronto. It was he who would eventually locate the institution, St Michael's College, where her fonds would be established. When he unpacked the boxes, he found "a series of notebooks – twenty-seven in all – which contained, aside from notes she made of her reading, journal entries spanning more than forty years" (326). With her permission, he transcribed these because of the importance he attributed to them, with the view that they ought to be published after her husband's death, undoubtedly an act of discretion because of some of the personal details contained therein. He conveyed his thoughts to her by telephone, which he notes in his biography of Watson as having inspired "silence at the other end of the telephone line, and then: 'I want my story told'" (326).

The resonant assertion may have referred directly to her journals, but may also encompass her archive, that is, the Sheila Watson fonds at St Michael's College where her papers at last came to be preserved; it is certainly integral to her desire for self-representation, as it also bears relevance to the means by which researchers and literary critics approach her archive and her journals. If we assume the journals – like other materials in her archive – are important to the dissemination of her personal narrative, we might conclude that they are intimately involved in mapping her private life. Yet an examination of the entirety of Watson's journals, especially those from her time in Paris, reveals that the entries are inconsistently engaged with what has already been identified as private and central to "her story": her relationship with her husband, which Flahiff characterized as a "long, sometimes tortured and always tortuous, relationship" (x; see also Scobie 2010, 107–8). Instead, one pattern that emerges is a curious form of "withholding" her personal story, what Gerald Prince might call the "unnarratable" or "nonnarrratable." He defines the latter as that which

> *according to a given narrative*, cannot be narrated or is not worth narrating either because it transgresses a law (social, authorial, generic, formal) or because it defies the powers of a particular narrator (or those of any narrator) or because it falls below the so-called threshold of narratability (it is not sufficiently unusual or problematic). (297; italics in original)

Even though what "is impossible in one context may be *de rigueur* in another one," this impossibility of telling is not the case here (Prince 297): Watson does not refrain from disclosing elements of her narrative because her story transgresses a law, defies her powers of articulation, or falls below the threshold of narratability. Nor is the material she omits a function of the "unnarrated" or "nonnarrated" – those "frontal and lateral ellipses" that impede narrative rhythm, characterization, and so forth (298). Prince's final category, the "disnarrated," which encompasses "unrealized possibility" or "purely imagined worlds," is also uneasily applied to this situation (209–300). To Prince's evocative categories, therefore, another must be added.

Watson constructs what I define in this chapter as an "imminent narrative," one that is related to how one approaches and characterizes her archival records, and specifically her journals: a story that is almost disclosed but not quite, a technique by which she draws attention to herself and to her story. In her case, that which is on-the-cusp-of-being-narrated becomes a kind of strategy: it is "what she doesn't say," to misquote purposely from one of the more familiar anecdotes Watson relates about her father.[2] From this anecdote, Watson derived the conclusion that "people can only interpret what you *say* to them"; however, to this observation one might add that what is *not* said is equally significant. Her averted gaze, the withholding of elements of the narrative, means she does not directly anatomize her marital relationship, with considered effect. What she does not quite disclose heightens the journals' emotional content and the nature of the private story to which she only briefly and occasionally alludes. Her decision to leave both her archives and her journals in the hands of another, then, might be read as a complementary strategy to that of imminence: one of displacement.

Imminence and displacement register power by virtue of the demand for collaboration, and thus are associated with the third understanding of unarrested archives, as I characterize them in the introduction: that is, archives that both mobilize and are mobilizing in terms of, respectively, their eventual formation and subsequent effects. The establishment of Watson's archive and the telling of her story are contingent upon others for their formation, continue the process of imminence, and ensure that several others would be engaged in narrating her life well after she was no longer able to tell her own story. Indeed, the setting up of her fonds at St Michael's College and the telling of the story she expressly wanted told were intentionally contingent upon others for their formation and extend the process of imminence. The researcher and scholar become key in this paradigm: the mobilization of ideas, of research that will be cultivated from working in the Watson archives, eventually becomes key to the archive of displacement. Although most archives might be approached as such, we will see that Watson's literary strategy paralleled what she was attempting to do with her archival records.

It may also be argued that, although she is engaged in performing an autobiographical "I" in her journals – or rather minimally performing it – she does so in such a way that seems to underscore her sense of alienation. Indeed, one journal entry offers an insightful remark related to her desire to be "freed for a moment from the burden of feeling the need to excuse myself for being what I am – indeed for existing at all" (qtd. in Flahiff 114). It may seem that she would lose the very empowerment associated with telling her story because she does not fully disclose it. Yet, as she refrains from ruminating extensively about marital strife, she renders the occasional remark about revisions to *The Double*

Hook and far more detailed observations about scenes in Paris. Regarding the latter, a second pattern thus emerges by virtue of the pose she adopts, one that might be characterized in terms that Stephen Scobie employs in *The Measure of Paris*: the privileged stance of the avant-garde *flâneur*, the anonymous, wandering, and yet *male* spectator who does not interact with others and whose urban peregrinations and empowering visionary gaze focus on the streets of Paris. Even if she is not quite characterized as such, at least it is certain that her seeming disengagement from her marital situation is counterbalanced by entries in her journal about explorations of the city. In so doing, her journals seems to shift from representing her private self and her interior life to focusing on an external and public sphere – if we assume her private, emotional life is the story she wanted represented after all.

At first glance, however, her declaration about her desire to have her story told suggests the opposite: the autobiographical element to both her archives and her journals and the empowerment that would result from having her story "told" or divulged. Indeed, her declaration initially seems freighted with more traditional autobiographical assumptions related to the singularity and coherence of story, the unified self, truthfulness of the autobiographical narrative, and an "I" that is autonomous. Traditional autobiographical forms emphasize the public role assumed by a man, whose achievements singled him out as representative of what a nation might realize. It almost does not need to be said that a woman would not have been regarded as a representative figure, in view of assumptions about her sole social responsibility in relation to reproduction and her inherently irrational nature. Her access to the public sphere and her claims to articulate an autobiographical voice and identity had been denied, at least up to the modern period.[3] The rise of modernism, with its attendant breaks from previous literary currents and epistemological assumptions, allowed for an expansion of who might be represented as it also complicated notions of traditional autobiographical representation and communication, including those forms that were deemed worthy of consideration (Smith and Watson 123). The writer taking up an autobiographical form in or after the modern period would have thus been more consciously involved in creating a cultural artefact than a factual profile of one's life: that is, a writer would have understood that, by definition, any autobiographical form would inevitably fail to recreate one's life.[4]

Watson's journals, and more largely her archive, remind us that she was producing cultural artefacts, not a factual profile. Even if her declaration is contextualized by the particulars of her life, especially those associated with her challenging marriage, it also needs to be considered in relation to autobiographical theory and the literary developments of modernism: she wrote, after all, a substantial part of her journals between 1955 and 1956 while in Paris, the city where modernism reached its apogee and, as Alex Goody identifies in *Modernist Articulations*, in which "memoirs, autobiographies, newspaper articles and academic treatises inscribe a particular version of modernism that highlights the expatriate, urban experience" (118). As the notes from her reading patterns confirm at this time, she was in fact selecting books judiciously, including texts by modern authors Simone de Beauvoir, Samuel Beckett, Simone Weil, and T.S. Eliot, from whom she frequently quoted. These reading patterns offer a cultural assemblage out of which she worked, offer instances of modern literary techniques and philosophies to which she had been exposed, and suggest the temper and climate of her journals. These patterns immediately heighten in her Paris journals, among other possibilities, the pervasive sense of alienation and detachment – perhaps a version of that "expatriate, urban experience" to which Goody alludes – as they also complicate conceptions of the story she wanted told.

At second glance, her insistence that her story be told reminds us of the importance, even urgency, she ascribed to establishing her archives and to the publication of her journals; however, it simultaneously raises a question about *what kind* of story she wanted told, how she wanted it told, and by whom. When I first read, for example, the excerpts from her journals that Flahiff had selected for publication in his biography and then later all her hand-written journal entries as I sat in the archive at St Michael's College, I was haunted by the succinct, fleeting entries that captured her husband's seeming emotional indifference, even the cruelty with which he received telephone calls and telegrams from his mistress in his wife's presence, and the stoicism with which she endured these series of betrayals. Watson was able to tell her own story and do it well. The passive construction of her assertion, however, invites someone else to partake in telling her story, and thus has implications for self-agency. A cursory assessment of her assertion seems to mark the autonomy of the subject, one who assertively expresses her desires; but there is a vital contradiction embodied or expressed in the passive construction, a seeming side-stepping of responsibility for the assertion of selfhood. It implies the need for an involved reader or witness, one who will hear and then tell her story on her behalf. That story is one she herself ultimately writes, but it requires a responsible mediator who will both take up the cause of telling it, especially when she is no longer able to do so, and see to the publication of her journals and the setting up of her archive – after her and her husband's deaths. These gestures explain why her archival records might be seen as both arrested (eventually contained within an institutional repository) and unarrested (released by Watson and then later by Flahiff for the sake of integrating others in the process of telling her story): they speak to the necessity for creative collaboration, but a form of collaboration that is also deferred.[5]

Watson thus invokes a twofold strategy in relation to her archives and her journals: imminence and displacement. Allowing someone else to publish her journals reproduces in gesture the act of leaving the materials for her archive in Flahiff's hands. The story will at length be told – at a later date and by someone else. The passive voice confirms that another person is implicated in the process – of setting up her archive, of telling her story. We might conclude that a certain measure of agency is lost in such a gesture, or that at least she reveals an unwillingness to act on her own behalf; however, we may instead read the gesture as consistent with evidence from her earlier professional life, which evolved distinctly and independently from that of her husband. An examination of how she negotiated her first published book, *The Double Hook*, to its ultimate publication also shows otherwise: even though she then also had "champions" of her work, she negotiated ably and autonomously. Deferral and displacement were not necessary strategies. This form of the unarrested archive entails leaving her archive and her journals in the hands of someone else and generating contingencies: it is incumbent upon future researchers who approach and peruse her archives to position her story and her significance within the Canadian literary and historical record. In other words, collaboration is key not only to seeing her papers housed or her journals published, but also to telling her story. Her assertion is thus also ultimately a contradiction of the singularity imputed to "her story," for, since others tell that story, various narrative strains are inevitably engendered and even multiply.

Within this chapter, therefore, there are three stories I track, beginning with Watson's public literary career, to demonstrate how she established an independent literary career. Her professional life shows to what extent she was skilled at dealing with her own affairs, and at dealing with men with whom she negotiated ably and who supported her; it also provides the context for and raises questions about why she would leave her archival materials, including her unpublished journals, in the hands of another. The latter part of the chapter examines first the formation of her archive and then the imminent narrative contained within her journals, which would have been affected by currents of modernism. These two sections, in particular, demonstrate the alternative means by which she asserted a sense of agency that involved working through an intimate connection (i.e., displacement) to cultivate a form of self-representation that was purposely deferred (i.e., imminent) and that demonstrated how she valued collaboration.

Reading in the Archive: Sheila Watson's Literary Career

Sheila Watson was both an academic and creative writer, like her husband; as such, they were to a limited extent involved in each other's work. Wilfred Watson was primarily a poet and dramatist, and she a novelist and writer of short fiction; both eventually found tenured posts at the University of Alberta in the Department of English. He earned his PhD in 1951 from the University of Toronto, where she later earned hers, and was hired initially to teach at the University of British Columbia for two years before moving to the University of Alberta in Calgary. Two years later he was transferred to the Edmonton campus to take up a post as a professor, a position he would occupy until his retirement in 1977. He was a prolific writer, whose first volume of poetry, *Friday's Child*, was accepted by T.S. Eliot for publication with Faber and Faber in 1955 and was awarded the Governor General's Award. Although his next collection, *The Sorrowful Canadians and Other Poems*, did not appear until 1972, in the intervening years he turned his attention to writing plays. His first major play, *Cockcrow and the Gulls*, was performed at the University of Alberta's Studio Theatre in March 1962, and was followed by *Trial of Corporal Adam* (1963), *Wail for Two Pedestals* (1964), *Let's murder Clytemnestra according to the principles of Marshall McLuhan* (1969), and *O Holy Ghost, DIP YOUR FINGER IN THE BLOOD OF CANADA and write, I LOVE YOU* (1967), among others. In addition to introducing a form of experimental poetry, number-grid verse, he also co-authored *From Cliché to Archetype* with Marshall McLuhan in 1970. As critic Diane Bessai noted about him in 1978, he "steadily conducted a one-man revolution in Canadian letters from the 1950s to the present" (382).

Sheila Watson may have been much less prolific, but she was considered an equally or more formidable presence on the Canadian literary and academic scene.[6] Regarding the latter, she had to be. Writing her own doctoral thesis on Wyndham Lewis, at the University of Toronto under the supervision of McLuhan, and even teaching a course with him, she clearly envisioned herself as eventually working in a university environment. Yet that environment was not always supportive, as is evident in an exchange she had in this period with A.S.P. Woodhouse. He called Watson into his office on campus, seemingly to "discuss her future" with her, but observed in an apparently characteristic "long withdrawing roar": "Mrs. Watson, in the aaacademic worrrld a woman must beee as gooood as tennn mennn" (as qtd. in Flahiff 188). Sheila famously responded thus: "What men?" (188). Flahiff would later record this incident in his biography as an instance of what it might have been like for a woman to move through the ranks of the academic world in mid-fifties English Canada. Indeed, although Woodhouse was trying to help her, the incident also evokes the patriarchal nature of academic circles in which she would be obliged to move and, simultaneously, her unwavering resolve when confronted by such attitudes.

Notwithstanding barriers, the historical and archival record shows that Watson made enormous strides as both a writer and an academic. She was widely esteemed for her writing endeavours, literary criticism, pedagogical approaches, and techniques in the classroom. In 1962, even before she completed her doctoral work on Lewis (in 1965), she assumed the position of assistant professor at the University of Alberta in Edmonton, where her husband was already teaching. There, in January 1971, she edited and published the first issue of the literary magazine *The White Pelican*, which she founded with her husband and a number of other writers, including Dorothy Livesay, Douglas Barbour, Norman Yates, and Steven Scobie.[7] She published two novels, *The Double Hook* (1959) and *Deep Hollow Creek* (1992), the latter nominated for a Governor General's Award. She also finely crafted a number of stories that were published in prestigious journals, some of which were eventually collected in *Four Stories* (1979), *Five Stories* (1984), and *A Father's Kingdom* (published posthumously in 2004), and in 1984 was awarded the Lorne Pierce Medal for her literary achievements. All of the negotiations for these publications, aside from those published posthumously, she managed adeptly and with full awareness of her need to be involved at all stages of the publication process.[8] In one letter to her husband, for example, she wrote to suggest how her experience with her first book had taught her to consider carefully the decisions that had gone into crafting her novel: "I know from the publishing of *The Double Hook* that one has to have one's mind made up, otherwise one is stampeded against considered judgment, especially when there is a gap between the time of composition and the time of execution. I use the word with its full force."[9] Watson's punning on "execution" wittily exemplifies her sense of what might have happened to her work without proper negotiation and authorial care – and, when necessary, intervention.[10]

Perhaps the best examples of proper negotiation and authorial care – to which both the holdings in her fonds and her journals attest – are her interactions with the publisher Jack McClelland and Frederick M. Salter, key figures who saw *The Double Hook* to publication. Salter was the chair of the Department of English at the University of Alberta and a specialist in medieval drama, specifically the York Cycle of plays; as Flahiff notes, he also taught Shakespearean drama and, most pertinently, creative writing in the Department of English (81). Negotiating with these male figures did not pose a problem for Watson. Even if the fact of her being a woman, "more fundamental say than the fact of a one legged man," was inescapable, Watson did not think of herself "specifically as a woman": "There's not much difference between being a man or a woman" (qtd. in Flahiff 188). It may be that this attitude enabled her to negotiate effectively with Salter and McClelland in the academic or publishing world – and they were principally respectful of her. She thus often found support from male figures throughout her writing and academic career, including McLuhan. The latter was far from being blind to gender, as an incident she records in her journal suggests; in one instance, he "laughed at the femininity of V[irginia] W[oolf]'s 'My back is against the wall'" (qtd. in Flahiff 188).

Even without such immediate support, Watson began working on *Deep Hollow Creek* in the 1930s and *The Double Hook* much later, although their publication dates would suggest a different timeline. She commenced *Deep Hollow Creek* well before she met and married Wilfred in 1941. The novel grew out of her experience of teaching in Dog Creek in the Cariboo county of British Columbia over a period of two years. It "provided her with her first experience of interracial rurality, and the raw materials for her fiction" (Bowering 2002, 1197). That first novel, however, did not find immediate publication. Archival evidence shows that in 1948 she sent the manuscript and a part of a new novel, the latter presumably the origins of *The Double Hook*, to McClelland & Stewart. Sybil Hutchinson, editor at McClelland & Stewart, wrote that she appreciated the merits of *The Double Hook* and was trying to send it to presses in England and the United States – standard practice in this period (cf. MacSkimming 122) – and particularly to Falcon & Grey

Walls Press. The latter responded that they would be interested "in not too long manuscripts of non-fiction, Canadian setting," a sensibility to which Hutchinson evidently thought Watson's novel might appeal (qtd. in St. Onge 22).[11] She also suggested sending it to Robert Weaver for the CBC Talks series and then recommended some changes to expand it and simplify its style: "that could be done without sacrificing good writing." But Weaver decided against using it because he found it "a little insubstantial" (qtd. in Flahiff 77).

Watson was not to be so easily deterred. She submitted the manuscript of *The Double Hook* to publishers both in Canada and abroad; if it initially met with resistance, as it did, that reception was occasioned in large measure by its experimental, modern form, which was bewildering for its readers.[12] The novel was eventually accepted by Jack McClelland, despite ambivalent readers' reports. McClelland had called upon Earle Birney to evaluate the manuscript. The latter responded that while he viewed it as "a remarkable piece of writing" and "a stylistic *tour de force*," he also found it "monotonous, self-conscious, artificial, and lacking in real fictional interest" (qtd. in MacSkimming 130). He admired Watson's "remarkable gifts as a writer" but disparaged what he regarded as her lack of "fictional clarity." McClelland clearly agreed with the observations concerning the novel's exceptional nature because he decided to publish it. So he wrote to Watson on 8 August 1958:

> We think very highly of your book. It is an outstanding piece of writing and there has never been any doubt in our mind as to whether or not it deserved publication. It's the sort of thing that makes a publisher feel it must be published. Unfortunately, it has been a general consensus of opinion that it is not a sound commercial publishing risk.[13]

To offset the risk, the company considered publishing it as part of the New Canadian Library paperback series, which "concerned itself only with Canadian 'classics'" and what they considered "a 'quality' paperback line" designed to sell at a fraction of the cost of hardback covers.[14] Initiated in 1958 by Malcolm Ross, the series was designed to target both the educational market and the general trade, in order to facilitate "greater teaching and research in the field of Canadian literature" (Friskney 153). At its inception, it seemed to be less concerned with creating a canon, since "[n]umerous titles had no claim to canonical status" that were published with NCL (Friskney 154). Clearly, however, McClelland envisioned Watson's novel as occupying a canonical status, such that it would indeed be considered a "classic." The advantages of this form of publication, he suggested, were wider readership and broader critical attention, while the book would still be affordable for students. This approach is striking when one considers his simultaneous unsuccessful efforts to establish a partnership with an American publishing company, a convention by this point for Canadian publishing companies because it meant sharing costs (Friskney and Gerson 134).[15] Since the Canada Council had not yet established its infrastructure to support developing publishing companies or writers, this partnership was imperative for financial reasons.

Yet American publishers were especially reluctant to take on the novel. McClelland thus already knew that the market for Watson's novel would also be vastly limited because, as a letter dated 21 September 1959 indicates, his own publishing company had already made "a considerable effort to interest an American publisher in *The Double Hook* – as indeed did Mrs. Watson before we came on the scene": "we submitted the book to Knopf, Harcourt, Atlantic-Little Brown, Doubleday, New Directions and Grove." The reasons American publishers gave for their hesitation and then rejection of the novel, according to McClelland, were not related to the quality of the book: "Most American publishers have reacted enthusiastically as far as the merit of the book is concerned." Instead they seemed to suggest that it was "too good for U.S. publication."[16] But another common response offered a different kind of logic: the book's lack of commercial viability no doubt related to the fact that, at the time, "neither Canadian literary fiction nor poetry had much international appeal" (Friskney and Gerson 134). As a result, publishers in Canada were wary about engaging material submitted by Canadian authors and did so only at great risk to themselves (Friskney and Gerson 134). Most Canadian writers, naturally, turned to publishing companies abroad because the domestic industry was so limited (Karr 59). McClelland, however, was clearly willing to take a risk. He was sufficiently confident of the book's merit that he was prepared to publish Watson's novel in a new and inexpensive paperback format alone – a risk and anomaly in English-language publishing, although regarded as standard practice in European countries.

In May 1959, *The Double Hook* was published in hardback and paperback. McClelland worked with Salter, who had already written a foreword to the novel for Watson.[17] McClelland used some material from that foreword for a publicity endorsement,[18] and included instead "A Note from the Publisher" in which he addressed the distinction of a novel appearing as a paper-covered edition from the outset and then made reference to Salter's essay. Publishing in paperback (alongside the hardback) was significant, for McClelland was pairing an experimental novel with an experimental publishing move; and McClelland's reference to Salter was specifically significant for Watson, for Salter had been a strong advocate from the novel's early stages, even if she felt that he did not understand certain facets (Flahiff 141). As a letter from McClelland to Salter indicates, the latter's early support and observations about the book "had tremendous influence in making me feel that we must find a way to publish it": "When I read the manuscript myself I had the benefit of having first read your foreword and being prepared so well, I both enjoyed and was tremendously impressed by the book."[19]

Salter's endorsement was important in other ways. On the one hand, it demonstrates the kind of support Watson and her work generated; on the other hand, it lends support to Carole Gerson's claim that the "allographic" or "externally authored introduction ... issued from authority figures who were usually male" (2010, 48). Gerson adds that, in many instances, such prefaces revealed "the magnitude of the masculine authority that was brought to bear on women's writing" (56). These authority figures would "intercede between the author and her public, confidently proclaiming her significance, often in a landmark first volume or final publication such as an author's collected works or a posthumous memorial edition" (48). Salter might be conceived as one such authority figure, asserting such masculine authority to declare Watson's significance and to intercede on behalf of her work. That McClelland replaced him in this role may suggest that such male authority was indeed instrumental in the approbation of Watson's work.

Salter was, moreover, an early editor for her work, one whom Watson appreciated. In fact, his involvement suggests that he acted as a literary agent without its more formal aspects. As the next chapter on Jane Rule will show, this kind of relationship is relevant in that even the most independent authors seek the services of an agent. Agents serve specific functions, one of which is to act as an early audience or witness to a text, and another to draw up contracts and advise on financial concerns. Salter, however, did not submit Watson's manuscript to McClelland & Stewart; it was sent by Kay Mathers, who had worked at Clarke Irwin, who became a friend of Watson,[20] and whom Flahiff characterizes as acting as her agent (196). Nor did Salter attend to the financial aspects of the book, a more crucial function of an agent, as Mary Ann Gillies notes (7). However, much of Salter's other work on her behalf bears similarities to what an agent would do. He remained in touch with McClelland after the novel's submission and wrote to Watson to assure her of his unwavering resolve to see the book to publication: "He says like Cleopatra he is 'marble constant' in his opinion about it."[21]

He was a supportive colleague, to be sure; however, he also did much to guide the novel to publication. He effectively did all else associated with the role of agent, including distinguishing between high literary and commercial forms of writing. As an academic, he would have understood the "formulistic" kinds of fiction that might more easily have found publication (Karr 59), but he valued Watson's innovation. In so doing, he espoused a modernist agenda that valued an elitist, experimental literary form over a conventional or popular novel. The book she had created, he noted in the foreword he drafted for it, reached beyond local, regional concerns:

> She finds him in a pocket of the Rockies, but the exact geographical location matters little; the scene is, as it were, accidental ... Mrs. Watson does not dwell on racial distinctions, nor does she attempt a "regional" novel, though she might have done. She is concerned with the reponse [*sic*] to life of *homo sapiens*, and her conclusions, drawn from an untutored group, may be equally valid in the most sophisticated society.[22]

Salter was trying to make a case for a novel whose implications extended beyond Canadian borders, which had the kind of appeal for a small, more literary and international market. Therefore, he would not have persuaded Watson to seek financial remuneration, but rather publication in "respectable venues"; he would have eschewed operating as a "professional bargainer" (Fetherling 668). Instead, he served the function that, as we will see, Jane Rule demanded of her own agents: first, he acted as Watson's primary audience, by making corrections and suggesting changes to the manuscript to render it a more coherent whole; second, he encouraged her to submit her work to the kinds of markets that would have been appropriate; third, he proclaimed and protected the literary and moral vision that her work espoused; and fourth, he endeavoured to create a wider and more appreciative audience for it. So, Watson noted in a letter that he had suggested to her that he would "crusade in the East when he goes to meetings of the learned societies in May."[23] In another letter, dated 10 September 1954, he noted that after reading *The Double Hook* he was "prepared to defend it against all detractors."[24]

In terms of his first responsibility – that of audience to her manuscript – he was an appropriate candidate. He was a sensitive reader and prepared to provide early editorial feedback for her novel. The alterations to the novel, Flahiff argues, are "traceable both to Salter's editorial suggestions and to his formulation of what it was he saw in *The Double Hook*" (81). He was detail oriented, as Flahiff shows, correcting those errors that might have escaped a less attentive eye and even going "to the trouble of mapping the countryside" to be sure that her references never slipped – as they did not (qtd. in Flahiff 82). He even challenged her title, because he believed "there are no double hooks," a fact she later disproved by buying one on the bank of the Seine in Paris (1974–5, 182). At a public reading in Edmonton, Watson acknowledged his role in the book's structure:

> He used to lecture me every once in a while and say, "The way you write a novel, the way you put a novel together is the way you put together a pigpen – you do it with craft and skill, and in an orderly fashion." He read the manuscript and he combed it through trying to find that the roads didn't go in the right direction or the people had on the wrong clothes or the clock was telling the wrong time of day. (qtd. in Flahiff 82)

Above all else, he was an appreciative audience, who was perceptive about her design and intent: "Of the quality, artistry, moving power of your book there isn't, and cannot be, the slightest question. It is an amazing performance" (qtd. in Flahiff 82). In this sense, he offered her consistent support and, whenever necessary, critical feedback.

Salter's involvement extended beyond editing the text and making suggestions about where to place her short stories. He believed that "'a campaign' had to be mounted" to convince a publisher to take on the book because "in the ordinary way, no publisher will take it" (qtd. in Flahiff 83). In other words, like a literary agent, he evaluated what venues were most appropriate for the work and made a case for its publication. To that end, he began by approaching the editor of *The Atlantic Monthly*, to whom he also sent a copy of his "foreword," a "defense" of the novel, that is, an explanation of what Watson had accomplished. He wrote to Watson to let her know why he did so: "It would, of course, be best done by yourself – provided you did not get off into the cloudy abstract and unintelligible symbolic. Such an explanation would not only show the publisher and editor what sort of goods he was dealing with, but it would give readers a necessary leg-up for the ride" (qtd. in

Flahiff 83). But he perceived that, if Watson had written a most extraordinary novel, she was not necessarily up to the task of writing a lucid prefatory note to explain her accomplishment: "What amazes me is that you should do such a perfect work and not be able to explain it" (qtd. in Flahiff 83). If she disagreed with this assessment, she did not say so: she allowed him to write his foreword.

In his letter to *The Atlantic*, dated 17 December 1954, Salter suggested the serialization of *The Double Hook* and, for that purpose, sent only his foreword, not the novel itself: "If you are dismayed by the difficulties which are described in the Foreword, we shall both save time by keeping the novel home" (qtd. in Flahiff 83). Salter was being shrewd in targeting *The Atlantic*, for, as Flahiff notes, it was associated with the Little, Brown publishing company, and publication with one might well mean publication with the other. *The Atlantic* sent for the novel. Since the magazine was hosting a competition at that time, Salter asked that the judges consider Watson's novel, which came to be one of the seven hundred entries submitted.[25] Watson anticipated a rejection, for she was already considering New Directions as the next publishing company. She waited, however, as "since Mr. Salter took so much trouble with it, I can't do anything until it comes back."[26] Watson was correct. By early May 1955, the director and editor of Atlantic Monthly Press, Dudley Cloud, replied that the novel would not be accepted, nor had the jury reached consensus about its merit. Instead, the jury was "divided quite sharply" and so, he wrote, they would not be able to "make a success of the book" (qtd. in Flahiff 83). Fortunately, McClelland would.

Watson's professional relationships with both Salter and McClelland anticipated something she herself would appreciate when it came to the design for the cover of *The Double Hook*: reading and creative work both require active participation and, to some extent, collaboration. As Salter noted in his foreword, she would find "her audience among those whose reading muscles are capable of exercise and development." *The Double Hook*, he added, would "inspire enthusiasm; and it will inspire a demand for more experience in shared creation." So it was with the book cover, designed by Frank Newfeld. Newfeld had been hired by McClelland & Stewart to design books for their paperback series. He was to "become the first notable postwar book designer in Toronto, and [McClelland & Stewart] would openly declare the primacy of innovative book design" (Bowering 2002, 199). For the cover, he photographed one of two double hooks that Watson had bought in Paris and enlarged the image, so that "all the imperfections – the beautiful imperfections of hand work began to show." She appreciated his design and considered it a "sensitive and creative response to the text" (1984, 167). Elsewhere, she noted that "it seemed like a co-creation. It was the first thing that happened after the writing of the book, that is, it had caused someone else to make something else which I thought was in itself very lovely" ("What I'm Going to Do" 182). As Flahiff observes, she "had been told something about her book by its cover, and she came to respect, even to revere, Newfeld's co-creative comment" (199).[27] Watson recognized collaboration and inspiration as facts of the publication process, even with the release of her first book.

If materials arrested *within* her fonds at the St Michael's College archive showcase how she valued collaboration, this fact becomes especially clear in terms of *how* she allowed the fonds to be established through Flahiff's mediations – and explains her inclusion in this study. Collaboration and even co-creation in her publishing life and in relation to her archive shed light on and provide the context for the cooperation she later sought in ensuring that her journals would be published and her story would be told. In part, the decisions to relinquish her papers and leave them with Flahiff, and especially to avoid housing her papers with those of her husband, exemplify the tensions and intricacies of being a women writer and the means by which her literary commitments were both impeded and facilitated. She demonstrated clear independence in her writing career and negotiations related to her literary and academic work, which is underscored by the means by which she preserved her literary, personal, and archival voice – in this instance, as a separate entity from that of her husband and through the interventions of a friend. Her autonomy in her publishing efforts reveals that she did not need someone else to set up her archive. The act of displacing her archive, then, became a key strategy of her self-expression.

Archival (Dis)placements

In the journals that Watson included as part of her archive, she reflected in one of those rare, intimate, and insightful moments upon her marriage to Wilfred Watson, and particularly the vows they had exchanged on 29 December 1941:

> I remember thinking on the steps of the Courthouse in Vancouver – without more than natural grace – This is for always – whatever I have thought since, this thought has never been in question.

> There is no comparison with other contracts, which are in their nature material and temporal ... There is marriage and there is a marriage contract – the contract is material and temporal ...
>
> The law does not make marriage – It protects or rather tries to protect often bunglingly and inadequately in a temporal world something, which is not temporal, although rooted in beginning as human life – and, I suppose, even the soul is – though one does not think of soul as temporal. (qtd. in Flahiff 54)

Watson was musing about their marriage at a time when the situation was most turbulent and when divorce seemed certain. She believed that, though divorce might have been sanctioned by the law and the marriage contract alterable because temporal, yet there were higher, more spiritual claims to which she at least felt answerable. "Till death do us part" was a commitment that she was bound and determined to honour. Watson therefore kept her vow to her husband: they only ever parted ways temporarily, in geographical terms, at times for the sake of financial and work-related exigencies. He worked on the completion of his undergraduate degree at the University of British Columbia, for example, while she worked in Mission City, in the Fraser Valley. He later served in the Royal Canadian Navy, and thereafter the two lived together in Toronto.

Yet I think it arguable that Watson was shrewd enough to find a loophole in the marital contract for both her temporal and spiritual commitments. The conditions by which her archive was eventually formed, notably separately from that of her husband and through Flahiff's mediations, suggests that she had indeed found a legitimate means of parting ways and representing herself as a distinct author on her own terms. Her own story, independent of that of her husband, would eventually find its expression in and beyond the very archives that presumably contained it. Another version of her story that might be told by others, therefore, concerns the negotiations involved in setting up her archive. Whatever agency she exercised in her negotiations with the publishing industry and the academic world, Watson had reasons for her diligence in this capacity: her husband was also an academic and writer, and she was therefore careful to carve out and make claims for an independent professional life, entirely separate from his, while being certain to give primacy to his own efforts. This diligence suggests interesting possibilities: that she thought it possible that her independence would be undermined; that there was the danger of being subsumed by each other's careers; and, concomitantly, that she believed in respecting the integrity of their respective writing professions. Tracing her literary productivity and her work in a male-dominated academic environment reflects some measure of the efforts she made to establish an independent literary life. Indeed, as already shown, she sometimes saw her working relationships with men as forms of collaboration. But contextualizing her achievements within a marriage that was somewhat more intensely oriented towards the success of her husband's career lays emphasis on her desire to set her life and her writings apart. This tendency shows itself most prominently in the gesture of leaving her archive, the materials for which she selects beforehand, and her unpublished journals, which she begins with the crisis of her marriage, in the hands of Flahiff.

If Watson laboured to have a literary life separate from that of her husband, perhaps the most evocative articulation of this desire shows itself in her decision to have her papers preserved in a different institution from the one to which his papers were consigned. Although she had taken care of her husband's papers, he did not assist her with hers. Her solicitous conduct – that is, ensuring that her husband's papers were in order before her own – may suggest the primacy she attributed to his accomplishments. However important and however much she herself valued it, her work was at times approached as less important than his – if not in value, then in terms of the care she took with his writing. Perhaps this care was part of her perception that her husband was also threatened by her own accomplishment. She thus wrote to Flahiff on 15 September 1993 that a "critical moment" in their relationship was "the publication of *Deep Hollow Creek* before his volume of stories *The Baie Comeau Angel* by NeWest and what he believed to be the lack of recognition of that publication."[28] Watson must have appreciated the dynamic of the relationship well before that moment, or understood its early rhythms many years prior to the publication of her second novel. As if in either warning or ironic self-commentary, she noted in a journal entry dated 7 September 1955 that their landlady in Paris, Madame Gouzien, said, "as if telling me a truth, 'The life of an artist's wife is not easy – especially if she has children. If she has none then it is her duty to be compliant in all things if she can'" (Flahiff 2005, 94). The Watsons had no children, and she could scarcely be characterized as "compliant." There is sufficient evidence, however, that her commitment to her husband's writing was great, though it did not surpass her commitment to her own work. In other words, the roles of artist's wife and artist were not always compatible.

The "shoring up" of her papers thereafter was to be of great concern to Watson, who had "developed a morbidly comic sense of her own isolation in this enterprise, and a growing sense of urgency" (324). Flahiff notes that she spoke with "grim humour of piling everything – herself included – on a barge, setting it alight, and being borne into the Straits [*sic*] of Georgia and oblivion" (308). He notes too that, although she did not "ask [him] to undertake th[e] task" of setting up the materials for her archive, she needed him to "to ensure that it be performed" (ix). Of utmost concern to her was simply that her papers not be kept under house arrest at the University of Alberta, where those of her husband are to be found. When she spoke to Flahiff about her concerns about deposition, he suggested the National Library in Ottawa, a curator from which had already approached her about her papers. In one letter, Flahiff thus noted that

> Toronto would love to have [your papers] – even St. Michael's, although I'm not sure you want to be cheek-by-jowl with Chesterton and Newman. The National Archives still seems to me to be the best – and logical – place. With Marshall's papers there, there would be much to interest anyone working on either of you … And it is a *national* place – and I have a sense of it as a *national pressure point*. (italics mine)[29]

Watson was clearly not compelled, either by her papers' proximity to her former doctoral supervisor's or by the national proportions and inflections by which her work would be characterized if her papers were to be housed in the Library and National Archives, for, apparently, she did not respond to his suggestion (Flahiff 325). To the idea of her papers being held in St Michael's College, she was far more receptive, "less dismissive." Flahiff justified it as an appropriate institution for her papers thus: "An aunt, her father's sister, had, after all, been a nurse here in the twenties when the College and the College School had shared the same space. And she had worked with Marshall McLuhan [here], with whom she taught a course … And she had other friends here as well; Father Charles Leland, for one, who said Mass for her every intention" (Flahiff 2009, 1). These reasons may have served the purpose, for St Michael's College is indeed where her papers came to find a home, but only after Flahiff had temporarily housed her papers in his own place of residence.

Intimate connections and associations, the very means by which Watson initiates the process of establishing her archive, became important in relation to the archival institution where her papers would find a permanent place, rather than claims of national or international recognition. It would be these kind of connections upon which she would rely in setting up her archive. Such an aspiration to set her story "within zones of familiarity and comfort" would inform her decision about whom to approach in establishing an archive, where to house (and not to house) her papers, and why she would set up an archive at all (Berlant 281). Flahiff notes that her reasons for keeping her papers concerned an "obligation to herself and to those who valued what she had done. But she also realized an obligation to those who, by nature or by happenstance, had come to be a part of the fabric of her life" (Flahiff 2009, 1). In other words, her gesture towards preservation was based on recognition not only of the importance of *her life* to others, but also of the constellation formed by others who inhabited the same sphere. Yet the reasons for her insistence on leaving her papers in an institution separate from that of her husband may well be related to what Paul Tiessen calls "the search for voice": he argues that she "seem[ed] to have felt it imperative that the primary voice embodied in her archive – although it contained much by way of the respective voices of Wilfred and Marshall, just as theirs contained much of hers – should in various ways remain distinct from the primary voices in theirs"; but she may have also "appreciated that, among the three archives, hers, constructed last, would contain something of a last word" (263). A voice that was distinct and that would be preserved as such, and a home for her papers that would be contextually appropriate and meaningful, perhaps for others more than herself – these reasons seem to have been of utmost concern.

Certainly, the deposition of her papers was to be no small consideration, not the least of the reasons being the material she included in the deposition. Much to Flahiff's dismay, some of this material Watson had destroyed, including the journals she wrote while she lived in Dog Creek. There is no way of knowing what unarrested materials were lost, except for that which is suggested by the journals that have survived. Even so, as critic Julia Creet observes, there is a kind of "violence inherent in the process of archivization itself":

> Once private ephemera of private lives, letters become public documents held under institutional restraints, the institutionalization of domesticity locking lives in boxes. A necessary trade-off, we might say, in order to allow researchers to mine these long-dead souls (sometimes not-so-long-dead; sometimes not dead at all) for their historical relevance and revelations.

> No longer just the traces of a life lived, archived papers become public documents and their writers become public figures by virtue of their textual traces rather than their worldly accomplishments. (313)

Creet evocatively suggests here the convergence of public and private spheres in an archive. Watson surely understood the implications, not only for the meaning of where her papers would be stored but also for those papers she chose to retain and others she chose to destroy. These cultivated gaps in archives, that is, the wilful omission and even destruction of documents, suggest that researchers are encouraged to approach archives in particular ways. She did not decide, after all, to pile all her papers on a barge and set them alight – only some of them. Watson was, therefore, also choosing to shape the story she wanted narrated by others, and indeed to influence which "others" would be involved in the narrating and archiving process.

The primary person implicated was undoubtedly Flahiff, and one can only speculate about why he was chosen. There are several possibilities here, not the least being that she regarded him as an honourable candidate to serve as guardian of her work. But it was also he who had insisted upon the publication of *Deep Hollow Creek*, which had languished in manuscript form for decades. McClelland & Stewart's appeals to see another manuscript did not persuade her.[30] McClelland himself wrote five years after the publication of *The Double Hook* to suggest that whether or not they made money from her first book was immaterial: "it has ... been our privilege to publish it." He added that "we do ask for more. We want another book from you."[31] Whereas McClelland did not seem to know about the extant manuscript, Flahiff did. By his account, when she began to speak of destroying her papers, he insisted she leave the typescript of *Deep Hollow Creek* behind:

> "Whatever you do, don't destroy it," I said.
>
> She stood at the door as I was leaving.
>
> "You bastard," I remember her saying as she handed me the typescript. "You've got what you wanted." (Flahiff 308)

That desire was not only his; as he playfully intimated in a letter dated 30 October 1990 in response to a Duthies bookstore employee expressing regret that Watson had not published more, he was "glad that I had got what I (and not only I) wanted." It had been thirty years since McClelland & Stewart saw her first novel to publication, but that had not diminished their desire for another novel: they asked to see it immediately.[32] A letter to Watson from Ellen Seligman later acknowledged the manuscript and her contact with Flahiff, "who has no doubt told you that we will be making an offer for it."[33] Flahiff was recognized by Douglas Gibson, McClelland's successor, as playing "a vital role in bringing the new book into existence," and so he sent to him a copy of her new book, "hot-off-the-press ... with my compliments and my gratitude."[34] Flahiff had thus already shown himself to be an interested party, someone who shared her aspirations within a zone of familiarity and comfort.

If the weight of accountability was part of her hesitation in publishing, it was surely also a factor in deciding about where to leave or papers – or with whom.[35] In some sense, by giving her papers over to Flahiff, she was being more or less freed of the responsibility of publishing any more of her work, especially her journals. Of course, Watson did not *say* much by way of establishing her archive either; she freed herself from the responsibility of setting up her archive by allowing Flahiff to take it up on her behalf.[36] He wrote about his general apprehension over the duties he had taken on: "I sometimes think that you are putting your life in my hands – and I hope they are the right hands."[37] Watson clearly thought so. He wrote or telephoned to ask her questions, at which time they also discussed the idea of his writing her biography. He ruminated on his status as the person who had been the recipient – of her friendship and her papers: "I wander between friendship and scholarship."[38] He confessed that he would "at best be an uneasy biographer," and so tested out his initial ideas about its structure with her:

> I think of a biography whose form is monistic and whose sense of detail and accuracy is impeccable. I think of writing backwards – from what I know – with your Paris journal as the bridge between the Sheila I know and the Sheila I know of. I shouldn't be writing to you about these things, I suppose, but with whom else can I consider them?[39]

His latter remark indicates that boundaries of impersonality and impartiality may be considered hallmarks of scholarship and archival theory; their friendship, however, made these perceived boundaries less clear.[40] Perhaps, however, Watson had understood that intimacy was a factor in setting up an archive – and researching in one. Such attachments, which "make people public" and produce "transpersonal identities and subjectivities," would effectively be a driving force behind the formation of her archive (Berlant 283). But her archive would not generate stable or consistent forms of her story and, in this sense, would be far from "arrested"; instead, it would continue to inspire various collaborations, generate scholarly fervour and interest, produce scholarly work, and "make her public." Flahiff would be one of these collaborators.

Watson's decision to leave her papers with Flahiff might thus be understood as a strategy. The shared interest in setting up her archive allowed for the displacement of responsibility for its production and the imminent expression of her story; both of these techniques were to be reiterated within her journals. Ultimately, the collaboration that she both directly and indirectly sought would extend beyond leaving her archives and journals in Flahiff's hands to the very reading and telling of the story, and even stories, she wanted told. It seems fitting, then, to move on to the journals in which Flahiff recognized something of importance, of which he selected some for publication, and to which he refers as the "soul" of her archive (Flahiff 2009, 1).

Reading in and beyond the Archive: The Paris Journals

As Flahiff organized the materials Watson had sent in preparation for the archive, he came across her Paris journals. He was astonished by the extraordinary quality of her writing, which heightened his sense of the tremendous loss of her Dog Creek journals: "The journals you have kept – especially in Paris – are among your most important and most startling writing."[41] He proposed that these too be published: "What I have read of your journal entries suggests in time some kind of edition."[42] He was not forfeiting the idea of "a biography of unraveling" but, he told her, "the voice of the journals is my first concern. They must someday be published."[43] Watson again clearly thought along similar lines, not only because she preserved these rather than her Dog Creek journals, but also because it was this remark that inspired the notable rejoinder "I want my story told." The Paris entries cover the years 1955 to 1956, years when Watson claimed she was not writing: Salter remarks upon the fact that Watson had sent him a letter in which she observed that "In Paris I stopped writing altogether."[44] She likely meant she had stopped writing any fiction, for the regular entries she made in her journals in Paris would suggest otherwise.

Flahiff selected only some of the journals for publication, which in effect generates one of the narratives she likely anticipated would be told about her. I wanted to read through all of them, however, to compare the two accounts, so I made my way to St Michael's College to read the journals in their entirety, or as much as she provided for the record. The journals offer a sophisticated example of the kind of reading – and reader – required, particularly related to strategies of imminence and displacement. These are important techniques in that they hinge upon the collaboration of the reader: the story to be pieced together in the journals will be told later, by a perceptive reader who can draw inferences from what Watson wrote. She had elsewhere argued for the importance of readerly attention and acuity, the proper development of a literary consciousness: "The understanding of the reader depends on his ability to bridge gaps, to grasp implications, to understand references, to relate his experience, which is often acquired only through previous reading, to the subject which the writer is discussing" (qtd. in Flahiff 59). The literary consciousness and educated imagination she expected of the reader meant that a proper act of collaboration would follow – she would see an editor, such as Flahiff, for example, as involved in such an act of co-creation. Clearly, she performed as such a reader as well. In a 7 October 1955 entry, for example, Watson commented on how she "read" one particular theatrical figure:

> Barrault himself is curiously fascinating. He centres in on himself. His art is the art of concentration. When he declaims the spell is broken until the gesture re-establishes his central remoteness again. *He compels attention by looking at himself as a man in the street can draw attention to a cat on a fence simply by staring at it.* (qtd. in Flahiff 105; italics mine)

Watson was referring to the French actor and director Jean-Louis Barrault, whose work with both avant-garde and classic plays was integral to French theatre after the Second World War. This entry is the first of three that Flahiff publishes in which Baurrault is mentioned.[45] However, he was no small source of fascination for Watson, since several entries in which he is mentioned or featured appear thereafter, none of which appeared in Flahiff's biography: on 12 and 15 October 1955, another two in December, then again in January 1956, and repeatedly thereafter, on 1 and 15 February, 24 March, and 13 April, all focusing on his "impassioned miming" or his technique and talent: she remarked, as another example, on 20 December 1955 that "he was the weight at the centre" of the performance she had seen. These passages strike me as significant, which indicates that I am preoccupied with a narrative that was not of equal interest to Flahiff and that we are perhaps engaged in constructing different accounts of Watson's life.

The way in which Watson characterized Barrault's performance – "he was the weight at the centre" – offers a useful approach to understanding the significant writing practices that Watson adopts in her journals and that, in gesture, parallel the conferral of her archive upon Flahiff. Like Baurrault, she directs her scrutiny elsewhere, to guide her readers' attention to Paris street scenes. In so doing, she renders her narrative imminent, deferred until the reader returns the gaze to the very person directing his or her attention in the first place. Like Barrault, Watson also "centred in" upon herself yet compelled attention by vacillating between glossing over her private life in a detached manner and focusing on scenes in Paris, by which she also generated that "central remoteness." She does so, not by declaiming or analysing the particularities of her relationship with Wilfred, but rather by alluding to them, then guiding attention away from the situation in which she found herself towards urban scenes.

That redirected gaze has been interpreted by Stephen Scobie as essential to characterizing her "flânerie": "the detailed knowledge of the Paris streets; the quality of being an observer of, but not a participant in, the life of those streets; a deep-seated sense of being alone but not lonely; and the capacity to transform this experience into art, to move from walking to writing, from being a flâneur to being an écrivain" (2010, 109). As critic Mary Gluck notes, the *flâneur*'s "anonymity to the point of invisibility" was "the distinguishing marker of the *flâneur*" (73): "his ability to perceive the world was accompanied by the inability of the world to perceive him" (73). The *flâneur* is virtually anonymous, his status confirmed by a gaze turned outwards. Watson is, however, writing a journal, an autobiographical form for which a narrator's gaze would habitually be turned inward; typically, the narrator locates agency in the telling of his own story, as it is shaped within and contributes to a public sphere. These two patterns initially would seem to operate at cross-purposes. The performance of the "I" in her journals, however, such as it is, is engaged with suspending or not fully disclosing the autobiographical narrative – creating an "imminent narrative" – and then shifting her gaze towards urban scenes of Paris for strategic effect.

Watson's journals certainly do have some passages that directly address her fraught relationship with her husband, and these serve as deft touches in providing a strong emotional undercurrent to her time spent in Paris. So she writes on 4 September 1955, "Somehow tonight I can't sleep – W's misery cuts across my heart" (Flahiff 2005, 94). In another entry, dated 10 January 1956, she observes, "All day today W. was looking at me as the dorade [a type of fish] did – as if my existence was some frightful crime against humanity ... Whatever came or did not come in the post this morning has loosed W's anger against me" (136).

But other passages are largely oblique or indirect in their references to her marriage, when these passages treat the subject at all. For example, on 1 October 1955 she writes, "There are things I would write, but can't. Could one write a history of love systematically destroyed –" (103). The evocative dash at the end suggests irresolution, the need and yet powerlessness or inability to address what is evidently a marital crisis. Even when she does comment on her own suffering, her remarks are rendered obliquely or with this sense of withholding, as for example in the entry dated 18 September 1955: "Sitting here with my arms on the old wooden table I am terribly afraid – not of what will happen but of myself – ." The entry ends, poised for further telling, but dangling on the precipice of yet another dash. Then there are those passages that do not recount her dreams but only reference them, as, for example, one dated 28 April 1956: "For two nights before yesterday I dreamed my dreams – the ones I have not written down" (153), and another dated 7 November 1955: "It is three thirty. I woke in the middle of a terrible dream crying with the tears running back into my eyes like knives" (120). What precisely Watson dreams is never disclosed. One final example, an entry on 28 July, showcases the means by which she removed herself from the narrative:

> At five-thirty was awakened again by the telephone. It was daylight and the birds were talking in the court. W. answered the telephone. I heard Mme G. get up and go to the bathroom, and then W clicking the receiver too. At breakfast time a man came with a wire.
>
> Tonight it is raining.

The "I" is almost absent (except to observe what she heard) and conveys a remoteness from – and yet real pain about – the moment being narrated. Watson's almost fleeting autobiographical "I" thus might be characterized as alternating between embodiment and alienation. The alienation might, of course, be related to the difficult relationship with her husband, as another journal entry on 25 October 1955 suggests: "Love purely is to consent to the distance. It means worshipping the distance between oneself and what one loves."[46] One could also read such distance as what one holds away from oneself – a detached view of things for the purposes of observation and, indeed, preservation.

That detachment in some ways is more typical of the *flâneur*, at least in the sense of disengagement from much of what it is she observes and sometimes the oblique means by which she did so. This narrative approach, of course, was informed by currents of modernism: in the Paris of the time modernism had reached its zenith. As both the literary form and techniques adopted in *The Double Hook* and her journals would attest, she was intensely aware of these modern theoretical and literary currents and artists (such as Maurice Utrillo, Pablo Picasso, Barrault), of the circulating theories of representation – of one's life, one's story – and even of the impasses in communication. The journals would, to some extent, confirm these techniques and also the modernist understanding of the difficulties of communication. In one instance, for example, she observes that a man, who has directed her attention to a building, tells her "that the building was the Hotel de Severs and was thirteenth century"; to this she adds, "I am not sure that I understood what he said" (109).

Many of the journal entries are seemingly not about Watson herself, but rather scenes upon which she gazes or people she observes in the city. The fact that she does not offer extensive personal ruminations, as one might expect in a journal, confirms, as Scobie suggests, that she acts like a *flâneuse*. Take, for instance, the narrative of Mme la concierge, her husband, and "la petite Claude," who is ushered off to the country for the sake of her health, or the death of André Dumain, the butcher's son (133); or general street scenes, such as that of "rue Coquilliere," which she describes as "crowded with people buying and eating oysters – baskets of oysters and baskets of empty shells" (131); or as she wanders the streets of Paris, the comments about Le Louvre, the Galerie Carpentier, the Place Vendome, Montmartre, Notre Dame des Victoires, the fish stalls, the linen counter, or the button shop; or scenes between complete strangers, that of "a young man with a scarf about his throat and a plump elderly man in a tightly buttoned coat kissing goodbye in front of the Bureau des Postes – the right cheek, then the left" (119–20). As she observes upon seeing "a tray of large heavy-legged crabs which looked as if they had lived long in the sea," with a kind of indirect self-commentary that is characteristic of her writing: "Peripatetic speculators too" (113).[47]

Watson does allude to the role of the *flâneur*, in one instance on 21 October, when she visits the outer office of Foreign Affairs. There, she meets a "curious little man" who claims that "He knew what an 'écrivain' was – not someone attached to a school – not someone studying under a master – but a man who lived in the city, who went here and there, peered into this corner and that – walked about looking, looking" (113). But, of course, we must remember the example she sets up with

Barrault. In directing our attention to the "odd man" and his definition of the *écrivain*, she compels the reader to turn his or her gaze back to the *écrivaine* who is narrating the anecdote and whose assumption of the role of *flâneuse* allows her the privilege of "looking and looking": indeed, Watson seems to suggest with some sense of irony that she has adopted a role habitually ascribed to men. Scobie notes that she assumes the role because she "left [their] apartment on rue Vignon and walked around Paris, leaving Wilfred at home to write" (109), that he occupied their domestic space, their flat in Paris, and that she was thus "driven by the dynamics of her domestic situation" (108). Even if her husband were not there, it is clear that Watson did not feel at home in their flat; she records on 14 January, "When I am too tired to go out, as I was today, the walls bend in. It is a dreadful thing to outstay one's welcome." It is worth remembering that her forays into the city were not just those of the artist, but also those of the exile – not from a country, but from her domestic life, from her husband. In being shunted to the margins of her married life, displaced from the domestic sphere, as she was, she is also permitted a vehicle for the rearticulation of her experience – one that allowed her to express alienation by roaming through the streets of Paris, during which time she visited the galleries, churches, and concerts to which she refers in her journals. We now know that her husband took her to Paris rather than his "young friend" because the latter declined the invitation, and as Flahiff observed, Watson "mediated between [her husband] and the world" (89). The Paris journals were written *because* of her very experience of marginalization, by being relegated not to the domestic sphere but to the streets of Paris, ordinarily the purview of the male subject.

The journals thus in effect represent a series of reversals or cultural contradictions: the domestic space, to which she would have been consigned as a woman, is apparently claimed by Wilfred, with her occupying the urban centre; and she rather than he takes on the role of *flâneur*. She might be seen, as critic Michael W. Jennings remarks about the *flâneur* in general, as "as much at home among house facades as a citizen is within his four walls … Buildings' walls are the desk against which he presses his notebooks [and] newsstands are his libraries" (19). But the reversals do not stop here, for, as Walter Benjamin observes, with the decline of the arcades displacement had become characteristic of the *flâneur*, invariably a male subject who, like the autobiographer, required the presence of a woman as "a marker of absolute alterity [that] guarantees [his] subjectivity" (qtd. in Goody 120); Benjamin also defines the "*flâneur* as a masculine social figure" that then serves as "a metaphor for the modern artist" (qtd. in Goody 124).[48] A woman would ordinarily serve as means for the securing of the *flâneur*'s subjectivity, but if Scobie is correct that Watson assumes the role of *flâneuse*, then it is her husband who serves as a marker of alterity. She thus adopts a series of roles that are habitually ascribed to men: autobiographer, *flâneur*, modernist artist.

Paradoxically, however, she remains invisible as observer in her text and may be seen to assume a "non-status" that, while being read as a male prerogative for male writers, is interpreted otherwise for women writers. Elizabeth Podnieks, for example, observes about journals and diaries that such invisibility is typical not only of women's experiences but also of the genre. Citing Shari Benstock's essay "Expatriate Sapphic Modernism," she suggests that modernist women who wrote "were exiled within male-centred literary movements, and women who wrote diaries were exiled even further in terms of genre" (72). Exile was already a feature of modernist writing, but it was thus more pronounced for women who, in choosing to pursue the life of artist or scholar, were involved in "flight[s] from femininity": that is, "freedom of mind and spirit meant above all freedom from family pressure to conform to conventional feminine norms" (Friedman, qtd. in Podnieks 74). Yet modern writers, male and female, were concerned with "escapes" that were "not only geographical but also psychological" (73). This self-imposed exile was complicated for women by the fact that they could never "completely exile themselves *from* a patriarchy because they [were] always being exiled *by* the patriarchy" (75). In this sense, male writers could *choose* exile, but women writers could not entirely do so, since they experienced exile as a function of their gender. They could only choose exile by virtue of their disinclination to accommodate themselves to a patriarchy (that had already marginalized them) and by their choice of literary form. Watson would have been aware of the cultural climate instantiated in such attitudes. T.S. Eliot, for example, noted only a few years prior to her journey to Paris that "I struggle to keep the writing as much as possible in Male hands, as I distrust the Feminine in literature" (qtd. in Podnieks 77). Yet she was not exiled from a male-centred literary movement, as is evident by the support and backing she received in relation to the publication of her quintessentially modern first novel *The Double Hook*, and by its later critical reception.[49] She actively read the modernists; as she suggests in interview, she had read Eliot, Ezra Pound, James Joyce, and D.H. Lawrence before she "ever went to the Cariboo," and certainly before she wrote *The Double Hook* or her journals (untitled interview 360). Instead, it seems reasonable to suggest that Watson was strategic in the forms and approaches she adopted. As Shirley Neuman notes, women's modernist practices demonstrate that they could both choose what empowered them and reject what disempowered them (213).

Instead, it may be argued that her journals contain another technique, of the kind that Glenn Willmott observes in her storytelling: "Darting in and out of minds, moods, mouths, and eyes like a fish refusing to be caught, Sheila Watson frees herself from storytelling. Or rather, the storytelling we have come to expect is soaked up into something else, into what seems an unfolding, unfurling riddle" (2004, 87). So it might be said of her journals and, for that matter, of her archives: she frees herself from telling her own story, which becomes absorbed into "something else." In so doing, even in employing the journal form with its private dimensions, she simultaneously reinforces the isolation she experienced, geographically in Paris and by the circumstances of her marriage, as she also invites the reader to partake in her story's telling.

It may at first seem an oddity that in assuming the privileges associated with the roles of observer, modernist artist, and autobiographer, Watson would not take greater liberties in her journals, one of the more private of (gendered) genres, instead of refraining from telling the story. Her very illegibility, even anonymity, and her sense of alienation as expressed in the journals *is* the experience of women, the *flâneur*, and the modernist artist. The narrative that is imminent heightens her sense of alienation, and allows her to express such alienation without declaiming. Even so, Watson does tell a story, by virtue of what she does not say, by indirection, poised for fuller telling – by someone else. So the peculiar manifestation of her literary records and her journals reflects her story, which the techniques of deferral and displacement capture: those records and journals may be arrested within a centralized repository, but they are also unarrested as researchers interact with and generate various narrative lines from the materials therein. In his remoteness, Barrault does not disappear; so in her seeming detachment from her personal life and her focus on Paris and its street scenes, neither does Watson. As readers, we may look in the direction in which Watson directs our gaze, but eventually we will turn back to look at the woman who was directing our attention and who is curiously fascinating, in order to participate in telling at least one version of the story she wanted told. Jane Rule, the subject of the next chapter, would also direct the gaze of her researchers and readers, albeit through entirely different means: through a distinct form of the arrested archive. Like Watson, she would preserve an impressive volume of her papers and carefully consider where to leave them, in the understanding that both her papers and the archival institution she chose would influence the shape of those narratives that would proliferate well beyond her lifetime.

4 Jane Rule and the Archive of Activism: Negotiating Imaginative – and Literal – Space for a Nation

Jane Rule (1931–2007) – novelist, short story writer, activist, and contributor to the gay liberation periodical *The Body Politic* (1971–87) – was as fastidious about her writing life as she was about preserving the documentation surrounding that life. Over fifty boxes of papers and other materials – manuscripts, letters, newspaper reviews, photographs, and so forth – were preserved in the first of several accessions made at the University of British Columbia almost ten years before she died.[1] Indeed, she was so meticulous in recording her career as an author that she retained even letters that castigated her and her work, in a folder titled "Hate Mail."[2] The sheer volume of the materials in the Jane Rule fonds bears witness to how, as T.L. Cowan puts it, "keeping our shit" is supremely important to feminist endeavours and commitments, to revealing the struggles women writers endured, and to expanding the "law of what can be said" about women (79). These materials, moreover, demonstrate that house arrest is a crucial initial stage in the process of setting up an archive that, in Rule's case, showcases both the networks of support she generated during her lifetime and the careful means by which she negotiated her career with agents and other professional figures in order to protect her commitments to the queer and feminist communities.[3]

The Arrested Archive: The Case of the Canadian Gay Liberation Movement Archives

Rule's diligence in preserving her materials finds its logic in the example set by the Canadian Gay Liberation Movement Archives (GLM) Archives. The need for and yet the complexities of "arresting" documents for posterity become evident when Rule's personal practice is contextualized not only in terms of the GLM Archives, but also in two legal entanglements that preceded the preservation of her own papers and were connected to her career as author. Both of these entanglements call upon the negative valences of the meaning of "arrested," associated with criminality. The first involved the archives of *The Body Politic*, owned by Pink Triangle Press, and the leading Canadian queer news magazine; it would become "the mouthpiece for the Canadian gay liberation movement." Shortly after its inception in 1971, the magazine created the GLM Archives, a private establishment located in downtown Toronto (Barriault 99), which would in 1975 be renamed the Canadian Gay Archives and in 1993 the Canadian Lesbian and Gay Archives. These archives were developed as a means of extending the magazine's advocacy for queer rights and, to that end, made use of the *The Body Politic*'s advertisement space to call for materials, to "communicate with a readership that might include potential donors" of archival material (100). In 1977, the metropolitan and provincial police raided their offices and seized archival and other materials in response to an "investigative article on hebephilia, titled 'Men Loving Boys Loving Men'" (100). These materials, which included editorial material, personal correspondence, books, and subscription lists, were not returned until 1985, eight years after the raid.[4]

A regular contributor to *The Body Politic*, Rule was involved in several controversies that arose as a result of the magazine's ideologies, including the seizure of its papers. In her own archive, for example, she preserved documents that pertained to her regular column for *The Body Politic*, provocatively titled, "So's Your Grandmother," in which articles such as "Closet Burning" and "Why I Write for the Body Politic" appeared and which sometimes elicited polarized responses from its readership. *The Body Politic* incident offered Rule a crucial model for how to prepare her archive, what repository to choose for the preservation of her papers, and why she would consider leaving such materials for posterity. She had clearly learned what to preserve based on the example set by the GLM Archives: thus she also retained articles that appeared in *The Globe and Mail* and elsewhere, and brochures circulated by the Toronto Gay Community Council in relation to both the "arresting" of documents from the GLM Archives and the several appeals that the prosecutor, Roy McMurtry, made each time the Pink Triangle Press was found not guilty by the courts. Indeed, on 10 August 1982, in her capacity as contributor to *The Body Politic*, Rule wrote directly to

McMurtry to castigate him for his inability to "listen to the verdicts of your own courts":

> Your attempt to uphold the morality of your community by suppressing serious discussion of ranges of sexuality in *The Body Politic* has by now become an example all over Canada of immoral abuse of government power. You cannot, in the long run, destroy the paper. Its support comes from all over the English speaking world because it is the most respected and responsible paper of its kind, serving a community which has faced centuries of abuse and has never been entirely silenced and never will be.[5]

Rule here appeals to freedom of speech – the "serious discussion" that is being repressed by the "morality of [McMurtry's] community" – and later in the letter further grounds her argument by denying charges of indecency and asserting the respectability of the magazine. These documents within her archive show her awareness of not only the problems the queer community generally confronted, but also the problems specifically related to depositing papers in a private establishment.

Rule's decision to establish an archive that was both extensive in its holdings and placed at a university rather than in a private archive was assuredly influenced by the precedent of the GLM Archives, which had not sought the protective auspices of a formal, government institution. Still, when Laurenda Daniells, a University of British Columbia librarian and archivist, approached Rule about depositing her papers within its precincts, Rule was initially reluctant. Daniells knew Rule personally through their mutual connections in the Department of English at the University of British Columbia and believed her papers would be of value. In 1987, therefore, Daniells visited her and her partner, Helen Sonthoff, to "show Jane how [her papers] would be organised should she decide to deposit them with us."[6] At the outset, Rule expressed uninterest; moreover, the funding Daniells had hoped to secure to purchase Rule's papers "was not forthcoming." Yet well after the GLM incident, Rule decided to pursue housing her papers at UBC.[7] Perhaps she considered the protection she would be offered by the principle of academic freedom, so intrinsic to university life. The government raid of the GLM Archives would have impressed upon her the importance of safeguarding papers as a form of activism and as a means of ensuring access to those papers in order to increase visibility and social awareness of queer and feminist histories. In other words, she understood the potential for extending her commitment to advocacy for the queer community through the contents of her fonds. The materials therein could further mobilize ideas she so vocally espoused during her lifetime; as these materials bear witness to her efforts to create legal and imaginative space for the queer and feminist communities, the archive itself further protects and authorizes those efforts and that space.[8]

The second legal entanglement, to which I draw greater attention in the latter part of this chapter, concerned the Little Sisters Book and Art Emporium, which imported queer literature from the United States. Rule was directly affected when in December 1986 a shipment of their books was detained by Canada Customs on grounds of obscenity. In 2000, in a landmark Supreme Court case titled *The Little Sisters Book and Art Emporium vs. Canada*, the bookstore owners, Jim Deva and Bruce Smythe, pursued their right to sell materials that represented the queer community and to import such materials for this purpose. For this trial, Rule was called upon as a key spokesperson. In both of these legal entanglements, the act of arresting – papers or books – becomes literal, a material reality, and demonstrates that even after Rule made considerable efforts to protect her contributions to the rights of the queer and feminist communities, these efforts could be waylaid or impeded.

The legal dimensions of both these examples suggest how archives – both institutions and the fonds held within them – and literary production are closely regulated by the state and vigilantly guarded. Arrested archives are thus not simply related to an author's decision to protect his or her papers within a state-sanctioned repository, but rather, as the following chapter on M. NourbeSe Philip will also show, these matters become nuanced when we consider who safeguards the materials, what purpose informs their safe-keeping, and what eventually becomes endorsed as legitimate fonds or archives. In effect, the node that differentiates these forms of "arresting" materials is related to access and, quite literally, to the "law of what can be said": whereas one gesture is intended to thwart the circulation of particular discourses, the other is intended to promulgate them. Rule likely "arrested" her papers and deposited them with the University of British Columbia to extend her activism, to secure and allow for greater public contact with her papers, the contents of which were not congruent with heteronormative values. Conversely, the arresting of papers and books by the state was meant to impede the mobilization of particular ideas: that is, state officials intervened and "arrested" both the papers from the GLM Archives and the books en route to the Little Sisters bookstore to hinder their wider circulation and to protect the national imaginary they perceived as threatened by the contents of those materials. These entanglements highlight why Rule was careful with her professional development as a writer and then later with the development of her archive.

These entanglements also invite researchers to consider what Rule so desired to protect, aside from the obvious manifestation of the effort involved in building her literary career. The legal incident with the GLM Archives provides an important precursor by which to consider how Rule needed to shield her papers against the incursions of the state, but also suggests that her papers might have been as threatening as those housed in the GLM Archives. Indeed, in spite of her diligence, towards the end of her career Rule was obliged to grapple with a legal system that wished to circumscribe the circulation of her books. It is not surprising, therefore, that she would have taken great pains with how she managed both her professional literary life – how she engaged with publisher, editors, and agents – and, ultimately, her archival records. The careful attention she paid to her writing life and to protecting the moral issues that she championed was applied to her decision to arrest her own archival materials within a formal, academic institution. I have thus approached her fonds at the University of British Columbia as offering a space that not only legitimates her papers and her career, but also extends the activism she pursued in her lifetime: these papers bear witness to her vigorous attempts to achieve self-agency as an author, to protect her moral commitments to the queer and feminist communities through her professional engagements, and to expand the space for their public representation. Rule's painstaking safeguarding of her materials thus offers an example of how a writer might create imaginative, even literal space for women and queer writers, as well as revealing the challenges in fashioning her career and establishing crucial groundwork for those writers who follow.

Homesteading a Territory

As her archive shows, Rule was unambiguous about what she believed her role as writer entailed and about the challenges of the profession. She commented in 1986 that she was "homesteading a territory. Where I am may turn into a ghost town, or it may turn into a city."[9] She clearly devoted her life to homesteading that territory, that is, to making space in what was a heteronormative and often intolerant environment, to which the documents in her archives testify. Even years later, when she withdrew from public life as a professional writer,[10] she wrote to

Margaret Hollingsworth about the "horrible vulnerability" of sending out work to an "indifferent" or judgmental audience. She concluded, however, that the "world's judgment is not really the point; the making is."[11] Drawing upon the vast wealth her archive affords, this chapter demonstrates how Rule strove to make an impact on socio-cultural conventions through her writing and worked hard to move beyond the limits imposed on this by the publishing industry; her papers showcase this process and the spaces to which she lay claim, even literally within a centralized repository. She could thus make such a declaration to Hollingsworth because, by that point, she had considerable experience in negotiating with national and international publishers, agents, literary figures, and governmental institutions and with the challenges she faced in her activist pursuits.

Her interactions with those involved in the publishing industry, especially her agents, have been meticulously preserved in her correspondence. Indeed, it is precisely the richness of her archive that allows for this chapter's close and extended study of her interactions with others in the publishing industry. Those interactions, and particularly her editorial battles, underscore how she consistently struggled to safeguard her freedom of expression and her literary integrity over the span of her career, and to expand the space for the articulation of queer concerns. Those interactions show what was at stake in the struggle: the archive Rule preserved bears witness to a lesbian woman's struggles to achieve literary independence in mid-century Canada, and to articulate and protect the moral interests of the communities she valued. Clarence Karr notes in *Authors and Audiences* that legends of such struggles have "a special appeal for Canadians, who take delight in seeing themselves as David confronting Goliath" (58). The materials in Rule's fonds show that she relentlessly laboured not only to publish her work but also to resist censorship in daily practice. Her negotiations with various publishing figures and institutions, such as Robert Weaver of CBC Radio, Carol J. Meyer of Harcourt Brace Jovanovich, and *Chatelaine* magazine, and with her literary agents over matters related to socio-cultural censorship, suggest what they conceived their roles to be in the publication process. These negotiations also showcase Rule's part in redefining expectations and protocols that determined the value of her work, the degree to which her work was edited, and the venues in which her work appeared. In other words, she understood that how she told her stories was as important as where they were published, even as she tried to write for an audience that had its distinct needs and desires. Disagreements with two of her agents, Willis Kingsley Wing and Kurt Hellmer, would become especially significant in obliging them to render their business terms more clearly and in making plain what Rule demanded of her literary agents, and would showcase why her relationships with two other agencies, Hope Leresche & Steele and the Borchardt agency, would run more smoothly. These disagreements and successes also reveal the process by which she sought professionalization as an author and explain why she assiduously preserved such an abundance of materials for her archive: both were fundamental to revealing how she achieved literary integrity, her contributions to enlarging the space for the articulation of queer commitments, and the larger moral vision she espoused.

Rule's negotiations with the publishing industry must be understood in the context of both where she worked and the period in which she published, especially from 1956, when she moved to Canada from the United States, until 1990, when she announced her retirement from writing. As Janet B. Friskney and Carole Gerson note in their assessment of twentieth-century conditions for publishing in Canada, the country did not have a sufficient readership to sustain its writers financially. Writers were therefore compelled to resign "themselves to writing part-time" or to seek "to advance their work in the major English- and French-language markets of the United States and Europe" (131): "They not only had to negotiate different ideas of the social and cultural role of the writer generally, and of the Canadian specifically, but also had to navigate the expectations of foreign as well as domestic publishers" (132). Rule would have experienced less difficulty in working with publishers abroad, since her first attempts at publishing were made while she was living in the United States. She would have neither approached other publishers as foreign nor regarded their expectations as unfamiliar. Compared to her writing colleagues in Canada, she would have had a greater degree of awareness of publishing practices abroad.

Still, like other authors, she would have been obliged to negotiate with and distinguish between literary and popular markets, the latter being dominated by magazines. Mass-circulation magazines, which accepted both popular and literary forms of writing, were more lucrative than book publication; however, they also depended upon "advertising income, which was calculated on the basis of circulation" (132). Editors, who were reliant on "advertising revenue of brand-name products" to absorb their costs, could not "afford to misinterpret their readers' interests" and risk circulation numbers (Karr 59; Friskney and Gerson 132). Karr shows that magazine fiction was thus disparaged by academics for being "formulistic and unworthy of the status of great literature": it was accused "of being episodic, unsophisticated in plot and structure, often written to order, and eschewing the intellectual, the controversial, and the political while catering to a bland market of mass readers" (59). After moving to Canada, Rule would have discovered that the domestic magazine trade, which "came into being at the start of the Second World War," was increasingly rendered more complex by the influx of imported magazines, mostly from the United States; these imported magazines paid writers considerably more than Canadian publications (M.D. Smith 261).[12] Even so, writers in Canada were expected to respond to the call for a high literary standard in both domestic and foreign magazines.[13] Many writers thus turned to publishing venues outside the country, especially the United States where the literary market was considerably larger. Even if the expectations remained the same, the remuneration was more attractive.[14]

The novel in Canada had an entirely different set of expectations and problems, which Rule for the most part adroitly sidestepped by employing agents who usually found publishers outside of Canada first. Indeed, by mid-twentieth century, most writers in Canada submitted manuscripts to publishing companies abroad because of the limitations of the domestic publishing industry (Friskney and Gerson 134). Book publishers sometimes expected writers to adapt their work to "public taste" and thus were not so far removed in their practices from magazines (59). Writers were also more likely to be published by the likes of McClelland & Stewart if a British or American publisher first agreed to "share costs" (134). The situation in Canada began to change by the 1960s, at least in terms of support for the publication of work by domestic authors; at that time, "new infrastructure support, such as Canada Council programs" enabled writers to "create a fresh wave of literary excitement" (138). The effect showed itself in the emergence and thriving of smaller presses. By 1970 there were thirty-two small presses printing fifty or more English-language, Canadian-authored books; by 1980, the number of presses had leaped to eighty-nine (MacSkimming 247).

That "wave of literary excitement" was well past due for queer literature, which was trying to find its own way in the 1950s.[15] Peter Dickinson's *Here Is Queer: Nationalisms, Sexualities, and the Literatures of Canada* is mindful of how national literatures have their own "closets" and how received national orthodoxies assume a heteronormative literary canon: "the identificatory *lack* upon which Canadian literary nationalism has historically been constructed ... is in large part facilitated by, if not wholly dependent upon, a critical refusal to come to grips with textual *superabundance* of a destabilizing and counter-normative sexuality" (4). As Donald W. McLeod notes in "Publishing against the Grain," by the 1950s in Canada "explicitly gay male (and some lesbian) material" still had not yet made a full literary appearance; instead, it surfaced in "regular gossip or tidbit columns," which provided the foundation for "the beginnings of Canada's gay and lesbian press" (326). Jim Egan, "Canada's pioneer gay activist," also wrote articles in the 1950s that seriously explored issues related to homosexuality for the venue *Justice Weekly*. By the 1970s, *Long Time Coming* emerged from Montreal and, of course, *The Body Politic* from Toronto. McLeod observes that the latter's appearance confirmed the "strength and visibility" of the gay and lesbian community in Canada (326).

In the United States, the flourishing of paperbacks in the 1950s allowed for "an underground literature of lesbianism" (Showalter 419). Women writers' freedom to choose their subject matter, however, remained limited. As Elaine Showalter notes about American fiction, "if the kitchen was the only room of her own for the American Eve ... it was a prison, and women writers were due for a break" (421). Her assessment of American fiction might provide some parallels for what was happening in Canada. As John Morgan Gray of Macmillan Canada, for example, noted about the domestic industry in 1950s, the "big decisions, editorial and commercial, [were] made in New York and London and in the interest of his author a Canadian editor dare not forget it" (qtd. in Friskney and Gerson 135). By the 1960s, the various liberation movements in both countries related to race, sex, and gender began to affect the production of literature as a whole (Showalter 422). Poetry remained the most "effective medium for social, political, and cultural transformation," with the novel "generally slower than poetry to react to historical change" (423). Longer fiction was just beginning to register the "inchoate frustrations of women in the years leading up to the second wave of feminism" (424).[16]

In both her magazine fiction and her novels, Rule explored such "inchoate frustrations" – and met with the same in terms of publishing her work. She had initially tried to publish without literary agents but then turned to them almost immediately for assistance, although the practice was unusual for writers working in Canada in the period. As Douglas Gibson notes:

> When I started out [in March 1968], there was one literary agent at The Canadian Speakers' and Writers' Service in Canada, and some Canadian authors had New-York based agents but most people we dealt with didn't have agents. And then, through the 1970s, and more specifically through the 1980s, a number of literary agencies sprang up. (Evain 80)[17]

Well before the 1970s, Rule was one of the few authors in Canada to have a New York–based agent. Indeed, in 1954, just before she moved to Canada from the United States, she made her first unsuccessful attempt to secure one. As the archival record shows, Russell & Volkening, a New York–based agency, refused to represent Rule because "we cannot ... work well with material in which we don't have a very considerable confidence."[18]

Her first long-term business relationship with an agent emerged shortly thereafter and set the conditions for virtually all subsequent publishing-related interactions. She began to work with Willis Kingsley Wing, who sent out her stories to both popular and literary magazines. Wing was associated with A.P. Watt and Son of London, Britain's top agency (Karr 77).[19] His professional relationship with Rule commenced around early 1957, when Rule began to pursue the professionalization of her career more actively; that relationship dwindled by August 1962. Under his purview, she published her short stories in several magazines, including *Redbook* and *Chatelaine*, which were oriented towards working women and mothers. He was followed in October of that same year by Hope Leresche, of Hope Leresche & Steele,[20] and Kurt Hellmer, who represented Max Frisch and Friedrich Dürrenmatt, among others.[21] These two agents attended to the publication of her first novel, in a manuscript titled "Permanent Resident" (published as *Desert of the Heart* [1964]). In May 1966 Hellmer was replaced by Rule's last and most successful American agent, Georges Borchardt, whom Leresche recommended. Borchardt's agency, co-founded with his wife Anne, was established in New York in 1967 and dealt with French writers like Roland Barthes and Pierre Bourdieu.[22] Her success with this final agency is indicated by the fact that thereafter some (although not all) of Rule's manuscripts found publication with greater ease than did *Desert of the Heart* – although such ease might also be explained by her more prominent reputation as a writer and changes in the socio-politics of the national literary market.[23]

At the same time as Rule increasingly and cooperatively worked with agents, she also worked independently of them.[24] She often dealt directly with publishers or publication venues. Three telling incidents, which occurred decades apart, might be seen to characterize the range of her editorial and publishing relationships. The first of these was with Robert Weaver, the renowned CBC Radio broadcaster, literary editor, and anthologist. Her association with Weaver commenced virtually at the same time as she began working with Wing, who eventually mediated some of the negotiations with Weaver over payment for her stories.[25] Rule had sent Weaver a tape recording of one of her stories, "A Walk by Himself,"[26] which initiated an awkward exchange related to his mistaking her for a man. His error was engendered by the pitch of her voice in the recording and exacerbated by the manner in which she signed her letters at the time, as "Jinx Rule."

In the same letter in which he addressed her as "Mr Rule," he answered a question that for Rule was almost consistently at the forefront of her concerns – that related to censorship. In answer to her inquiry, he wrote on 28 March 1957 to say that CBC Radio had "very few taboos." In fact, he noted that they had broadcast "a number of stories which magazines would not consider because of their themes":

> However, a few years ago, there was a good deal of protest from listeners about the use of certain four-letter words in CBC drama and short story readings and we agreed at that time to cut out this kind of language instead of running the risk of possible censorship of the themes themselves. In other words, I think we would have to cut a few of the expressions you have used in your short story.

In response, after correcting his mistaken impression about her gender, Rule said how pleased she was by CBC's handling of the matter of censorship, even though her story was not broadcast on the CBC program *Anthology*: "Yours seems to me a very sane policy … If you can manage large audiences, offering them good stuff with only occasional cutting of four letter words, you're doing a wonderful job."[27] It was largely an amicable relationship because they shared similar views about such restrictions and about editing. That relationship remained unchanged even after Weaver rejected her next three stories, "The Chosen Two," "My Father's House," and "Her Own Funeral." The archival record shows that it was approximately two years later, on 19 January 1959, that Weaver accepted one of her stories, "On the Way."[28]

The second of these exchanges was a revealing one with *Chatelaine*, which took place in the late 1960s. As Valerie J. Korinek argues, the magazine's focus had become more intensely focused upon feminist and political issues during the 1950s and had thus shifted from its earlier espousal of apparently more traditional feminine roles. Yet despite claims of greater political liberation, which was credited to the editorial interventions of Doris Anderson, its conservative legacy was to continue to show itself.[29] *Chatelaine* hosted a contest in 1968, the rules of which foreclosed any opportunity for Rule to submit a short story. In a letter dated 15 September of that year, Rule wrote to the "Mrs. Chatelaine Contest" to explain that, although she had "read the directions" for entering the contest, she had deliberately and flagrantly defied their entry form, which asked for the name, occupation, and income of the submitter's "mate." She noted that the questionnaire had disqualified her because "I'm not single. I'm not married."[30] Rule's partner was Helen Sonthoff.

To their request for such information, she made the rejoinder: "This magazine does a much better job with articles and with stories than lots of its kind. It could put some imaginative effort into questionaires [*sic*] as well." She added that she was voicing her protest by "disrespectfully submitting my entry."[31] After supplying the requisite information for the contest, Rule proceeded to object "disrespectfully" by offering an additional five pages of information, including the following: her occupation and annual income; her favourite company menu (many of which, as she claimed, were pilfered from the *Ten Minute Gourmet Cookbook*); and her "Special Projects." The latter, she explained, involved working against such questionnaires:

> Late at night I sometimes answer form questions, to test my own sense of identity against the identity I'm supposed to have, to test my own life against the life I'm supposed to lead. It's more of a hobby than a research project, but it keeps me in touch with how hard I have to work in order to write clear, hopeful little love songs to Mrs. Chatelaine because she's the one who sends the checks for the kids and I like to participate in the larger community.

As Rule wrote in her covering letter, "You don't have to imagine me. I've done it for you." Her "Conclusions" also explored the implications of the contest's stipulations. Contestants, it would seem, were obliged to model themselves upon prevalent notions of marriage, heterosexuality, and family life: the contest was not, as it proclaimed, "open to all home makers in Canada," but only to those "with husbands and 'real' children." In so doing, *Chatelaine* predetermined who might publish with them well before considering the literary merit of the work. On this occasion, it was primarily the *Chatelaine* contest form to which she was reacting, although it was clear at a later date that her literary material was not always consonant with their publishing agenda either. A letter from Winthrop Watson, a representative for Georges Borchardt, indicates that even a decade later her material was being refused on conservative grounds. Barbara West at *Chatelaine* had written to him to say, "we have a very conservative readership that would not readily accept a story with a theme of this kind. Many of our readers would not understand it, and those [who] did would probably be offended."[32] If Rule had offended Chatelaine during these exchanges, she was not prevented from publishing several other stories with them over the span of close to fifteen years,[33] nor from being asked to judge one of their fiction contests in March 1978.[34]

The last of the exchanges in which she acted independently of her agents occurred a decade later, in the 1970s. Employed at Harcourt Brace Jovanovich as an editor, Carol J. Meyer was an ardent admirer of Rule. She declared as much in a letter dated 21 December 1979: "Your books have been an absolute staple in my life."[35] If Rule was publishing more easily with *Chatelaine*, however, she still on occasion found it difficult to find publishers for her longer manuscripts, notwithstanding the editors who championed her work, such as Meyer and, later, Kate Medina of Doubleday and Hy Cohen of McCall's.[36] Showalter's sense of the conservative cultural politics that affected the publication of novels rather than magazine fiction shows itself here. Harcourt Brace had agreed to publish *Contract with the World*, which appeared in 1980, after the manuscript had already been turned down by Macmillan, Collins, and Doubleday.[37] The reader for this book was Carol J. Meyer, who considered the novel "a wonderful book, a stunning book": "you *write* so well, and you know so much," she gushed, "that I am chastened by it."[38] In 1979, Rule also submitted the manuscript for *Outlander* (1981) to Meyer, who believed that it was a "book I am not going to be able to take on." In part, her refusal to do so was related to the genre of the book – "collections [of stories and essays] don't sell." She also observed that

> I don't think HBJ is quite ready for it. They are advanced enough to publish a novel with homosexual themes, but I think this might be a bit much ...

> *Outlander* is certainly *not erotica,* but so much of the book has to do with lesbian sexuality that I doubt that the more "straight" publishers (and here I am using the word to mean conventional) will know what to do with it.

Although Harcourt Brace Jovanovich, founded in 1919, worked to become more politically open, Meyer admitted that it remained quite politically conservative and that it would require a champion of Rule's work *within* the organization to push forward the book's publication (Tebbel 1981, 179). She was initially unprepared to take on that role: "I don't think I have the courage to make so direct a political statement, and I don't think the other people on the staff would be comfortable enough with the material to do a good job of publishing the book without an editor who is willing to be ferocious and insistent."[39] Only a matter of weeks later, on 22 April 1980, Meyer inexplicably changed her mind. She declared that, with respect to the "risks involved in sponsoring this book, I have no problem with that now ... I had problems with the collection, because I felt guilty and insecure, but I definitely do not feel that way about this one." Nonetheless, in spite of her enthusiasm, the Borchardt agency sent *Outlander* to Daughters, which rejected it, and then, in June 1980, to Naiad Press, which subsequently published it.[40]

Encountering the resistance of a conservative publishing culture, Rule needed the support of her agents. Indeed, she regarded them as champions and protectors of her work when other publishing figures or institutions would not act as such. Generally, agents are seen as important to "various facets of publishing – from publishing contracts to advertising campaigns for books to public relations for authors" (Gillies 7). As Gillies notes, the emergent figure of the agent responded to authors' financial considerations and needs. George Fetherling characterizes agents as "professional bargainers": "they allow the relationship between author and publisher to remain positive and creative, unvexed by the crassness of commerce" (668). Rule was irked, however, by the prioritizing of financial considerations over what she perceived as unnecessary or detrimental editing of her work. She came to assign at least four responsibilities to the literary agent: first, act as audience of, witness to, and critic of the literary text; second, understand the various kinds of markets to which a writer may appeal and then locate the most appropriate publishing venue for the work at hand; third, negotiate the economic terms for the work; and forth, but perhaps most crucially, protect the moral imperatives of the literary text by guarding the latter from textual editing, expurgation, or any other form of censorship. It was this latter point that was to be most contentious.

Willis Kingsley Wing

Rule began to work with her first agent, Willis Kingsley Wing, around early 1957. Her relationship with Wing was initially characterized by the fundamentals of agent-writer relationships: the working out of economic details related to appropriate markets and venues for the publication of her short stories. It was also distinguished by the frank and open remarks that Wing made about the literary merit and quality of the work she submitted for the purposes of finding suitable publishers. He managed negotiations for publication in magazines that included *Atlantic Monthly, The New Yorker, Mademoiselle,* and *Playboy*; book publishers that included Faber & Faber, Doubleday, Random House, and McGraw-Hill; and radio programs that included *Anthology,* the CBC program directed by Weaver. Wing also anticipated the challenges Rule would encounter, as a letter dated 16 December 1957 suggests: the "kind of short fiction that interests you as you discovered in your relations with editors before showing your work to us is hard to market. Even with the most successful story the market is desperately narrow." He thus suggested she shift her attention to longer fiction – in particular, the novel.[41]

With respect to literary quality, he commented freely in several letters, as in one dated 11 April 1957.[42] Therein he noted that one story, "My Father's House," was "uneven," "wordy," and "lack[ing in] direction," and that the dialogue of the characters was at times "irritating and pretentious." He suggested that another story, "The Coward," conveyed "dark emotional depths" without "explain[ing] them clearly": "Unless the story is meaningful and is clear in its meanings the reader is going to feel cheated." In making such remarks, however, Wing also made another intriguing observation related to the two markets *between* which Rule seemed to have landed. He considered these same stories "too literary for the popular markets and not quite authoritative enough for the other markets such as the *New Yorker, Atlantic, Mademoiselle* and so on. It seems to me your principal need is to work out motivation and the end results of your interesting characterization." The novel, it seemed, was the direction in which he was gently encouraging Rule to move.[43]

His insistence that Rule appeal to one market or the other, however, raised alarms, for he found himself placating her in his subsequent letter, dated 30 April 1957: "I'm not urging plot and motivation on you for the sake of adherence to existing forms or patterns. We have trouble in this business with semantics." Even at this early juncture, his remarks reveal that Rule refused to adhere to "existing forms and patterns" and wanted to develop new ones. He thus eventually shifted from offering criticism to appeasing her or showing support for her work. By way of encouragement, he noted that "I think you are in the process now of finding out exactly what you can do best and if the target isn't hit every time, you can reassure yourself that this is not an uncommon experience."[44] When he was not available to give such direct support for or attention to her work, his colleagues strove "to do the best for [their] authors in the British market without detailed instructions from [him]."[45]

He was especially careful to assert his authority in financial matters. On 8 April 1957 he came to understand that she had been working with Weaver to have "A Walk by Himself" read over the radio. He advised her that, even if she retained publication rights, "major magazines would not want to publish after a radio program had used the story." In all such instances, Wing remarked that he ought to be referred to "for contract negotiations."[46] In other words, however Rule may have conceived of his role, Wing emphasized that he had the final say over her financial contract. In another letter, dated 8 July 1957, he reminded her that even if she submitted stories independently to magazines in the Canadian market, the agency was still entitled to commissions from her publications:

> As to the Canadian market and the question of submitting your stories there yourself, you might like to know that the editors of *Chatelaine* and *Maclean's* are clients of this office and that we have quite wide contacts in Canada, but, of course, if you prefer marketing your manuscripts there we have no especial objection on the understanding that it does not affect our commission position.

It is clear that at this point Rule was still learning the protocols related to financial agreements and markets when publishing through an agency. Later, within the course of their developing business association, she came to define such protocols by elevating her concerns about censorship above the financial rewards that might involve compromising her moral commitments and the integrity of her work.

Tensions showed themselves on 25 November 1958, when Wing wrote that "we could do a lot better if you could enjoy the give and take of a personal conversation." There is even an element of defensiveness in his letter: "we've invested quite a bit of time and money in your affairs and I should like to continue but don't feel any obligation." A month later, he sent a conciliatory letter, in which he suggested that he was indeed trying to remain attentive, to do his "utmost" as her agent, although he hoped she would understand that, given a choice between doing his utmost in the market and spending time writing letters of assurance, he might prefer the former. Indeed, he added, the time the agency had "devoted to [her work]" was a register of their confidence in her work: any lack of success she had thus far had, he observed, was a "marketing problem for which neither you nor I are responsible." He was to reassure her again later by suggesting that the market itself had changed, had "become more selective," but this shift was no reflection of her real value.[47] He was evidently trying to differentiate between his representation of her work and the ideological constraints of the existing market.

Clearly, Rule was appeased by his remarks because her ire was not roused again until about two years later when the editor of *Housewife* magazine,[48] Alan Wykes, was granted permission by a London-based representative of the Wing agency to condense her story, "Your Father and I."[49] Wing quoted a letter from his London associates sent on 16 January 1961 wherein he stated that, as it was "Wykes who [was] doing the work, [he saw] no cause for objection." Apparently, Wykes had an established reputation with the magazine and within the industry. Wing himself therefore believed "this to be sufficient assurance."[50] He asserted, "all our dealings through our agent in London with British magazines have, on the whole, been satisfactory up to now. British editors have always had the right to anglicize stories of North American origin up to a reasonable point." Claims of convention were to become his strategy for displacing responsibility.

Rule, however, would point out that the editing went beyond convention. In a letter dated 9 September 1961 she angrily observed that those apparently "satisfactory" dealings extended well beyond anglicizing her story to making excisions of "over a thousand words. In a six thousand word short story such cutting can hardly be considered minor." She proceeded to list the changes made, which were the result of "poor judgment and poor taste." He changed, for example, the setting of the story from Reno to Exeter, altered idiomatic expressions, and made egregious stylistic changes. The modification in the setting, she observed, "posed such difficult problems, Mr. Wykes solved most of them by simply dropping out the central section of the story, the trip across the country which develops the tensions between the husband and wife and reveals something important of the daughter's trouble." Rule also observed that he altered the speaking passages of the main character, Richard, who no longer simply said "something" but "murmured" or said "gently."[51]

Rule then insisted that, since the damage to her published story was irrevocable, she receive greater assurances that "no contract of mine is made for me that allows any alteration of my work without my specific permission." She scarcely waited for his response before she wrote a follow-up letter (of the same date),[52] in which she addressed Wing's belief that she had "jumped to the conclusion that it was [his] contract arrangements that made this handling of the story possible." As she noted, the "contract was vague enough to allow Mr. Wykes to make the radical changes he did" presumably because, as Rule noted ironically, "Mr. Wykes has a good reputation as a responsible editor":

> It seems to me that you take a pretty fantastic risk in setting up a contract that gives an editor these liberties without permission of an author. I don't see how it could protect an author from gross misrepresentation. Or do you think this handling of a story not a gross representation?
>
> … I cannot feel easy about other contract arrangements unless you can assure me that … *no* alteration, no matter how small, will be made without my permission.

Wing explained that magazine proofs were typically not given the same attention as those for novels. He thus quoted the editor of the magazine who had written to say that "cutting and sub-editing by British editors of women's magazines ... is a fact of literary life which the authors writing for these magazines have to accept."[53] Yet he tried to assure her that "we will be especially insistent to see that such a problem doesn't arise again." Rule did not feel persuaded by his seemingly vague reassurance. In a letter to Leresche, she noted that he was unable to satisfy her desire to "have final say in all editing, no matter how insignificant."[54] When he also advised her that, in her discussions with publishers independent of Wing, she "listen to what they have to say, and like the timid wife, 'refer them to your agent,' making no commitments," it is likely that she realized he could not ever represent her concerns properly.[55]

Rule's response to this letter does not survive, although her ardent commitments to feminism and queer sexuality would have surely recoiled before a sexist and heteronormative remark about playing the role of "timid wife." That she lost confidence in his abilities may have manifested itself in at least one letter she directed thereafter to a publishing company rather than through the agency itself. In November 1961, rather than asking Wing for an explanation, she inquired directly to the Macmillan Company of Canada about its early "reservations" regarding "Permanent Resident," which her agent had mentioned but not elaborated upon. Kildare Dobbs, then employed at Macmillan and warmly praised by Wing as "a man of background and character,"[56] on 14 November 1961 responded to her letter thus:

> For your own information, the reservations of which Willis Wing spoke are these: (a) We're not sure that you've got away with reversing the Narcissus story. (b) We don't always know how to take the Lesbian theme and can't see quite what you're trying to say about it. Is it offered as a solution for any women? Or just for these women? Or is it an ironic comment on the sterility of romantic love? The relationship as you show it is fairly superficial and "immature." I realise that this is supposed to be characteristic of homosexual attachments but it isn't placed as such.[57]

Some of the prevailing attitudes in the publishing industry show themselves here – that romantic love was exclusive to the hetornormative domain and that "homosexual attachments" were immature and therefore unworthy of serious consideration in high literary forms. However dissatisfied she may have been with Wing, she must have been equally if not more chagrined by this response, especially given Dobbs's latter, unflattering remark about the nature of queer relationships. No response by Rule survives.

Wing thereafter noted that her "faith" in their work was "very easily shaken": "I treasure my reputation greatly but if you and I can't agree on it, I haven't the slightest desire to continue with your work."[58] Over the next year, Rule indeed would no longer treasure his reputation as much as Wing did: this editorial fiasco was a sticking point with her until their working relationship petered out by 16 August 1962. Apparently, Rule visited his office and spoke with one of his assistants about the problems she identified in their working relationship.[59] The associate relayed this information to Wing, whose surviving response confirms that Rule felt his agency neither adequately represented her nor protected her interests: "In view of your doubts about the Watt office in the British field and ourselves in North America," he coldly remarked, "I think there is no value whatever in continuing," as the flourishing of an "agency relationship" required "mutual trust, good faith, and an agreement to work happily together."[60] Since Rule had lost faith in Wing's ability to market and protect her work properly, she decided to give another agency the opportunity to fare better.

Hope Leresche and Kurt Hellmer

By early October 1962, Rule began working with a new agency, Hope Leresche & Steele, formerly the Sayle Literary Agency.[61] The relationship was almost instantly successful, especially if one considers that by October 1962 Leresche had secured Secker & Warburg as the publisher for Rule's first novel, *Desert of the Heart* (1964; in manuscript titled "Permanent Resident"). Initially, Leresche warned Rule that the novel would be difficult to place, "for even in this day and age the Lesbian element may prejudice it in some quarters."[62] Yet only a month later, she announced the novel's successful placement with Secker & Warburg, the first publisher she had approached: she observed that "[it] would be about the best imprint for it and ... it is a house with whom I felt you would be happy." To this remark, she added that she thought "the author-publisher, author-agent relationship is important." This kind of remark would have pleased Rule, and did. She responded: "I will always assume that, if you approve a contract, you have done all that is necessary to protect your interests and mine."[63]

The evidence shows that Leresche was indeed skilled at making such relationships run smoothly, in spite of heteronormative attitudes. When David Farrar of Secker & Warburg suggested that, although he did not object to "the Lesbian element" of her novel, he did not wish it to be the "theme in every book," Leresche told Rule that she had replied thus: her client had aptly explained the "meaning of the book and he was as pleased as I had been by your intelligent reasoning."[64] Leresche also successfully negotiated the rights for Rule's book with the Canadian wing of Macmillan.[65] By this point, Rule understood the markets for which she was writing and recognized that "the Lesbian relationship makes the book a problem on the market." She clearly identified a clash between her moral and artistic aims and the markets with which she must work; she understood that it was a problem "from the point of view of sales" when her "chief purpose" was to explore "a particular society's moral response to sterility." Rule realized, that is, that the novel was "too well written for the trash market where this kind of subject matter is apparently becoming popular."[66]

Less successful was Leresche's American counterpart, Kurt Hellmer. Although Leresche had suggested Hellmer, she was displeased when Rule somewhat naively initiated the professional relationship on terms agreeable to her and Hellmer without consulting Leresche in the negotiation process. Rule had agreed to Hellmer being responsible for both American and Canadian markets; yet, as Leresche pointed out, it was "customary publishing practice that if a book [was] sold first in England, then the Canadian market goes to the English publisher; if on the other hand a first sale [was] made in the States, then [the] American publisher [got] the Canadian market in his contract."[67] Rule had assented to the provision because she believed Hellmer's location meant she would be able to secure "quick answers to questions on local business," but she came to agree with Leresche and, after some discussion, Hellmer operated on Leresche's behalf in the American market alone.[68] In the first few months, Hellmer and Rule had a seemingly happy working relationship.[69] Like Wing, he and his assistant, Sally Nicklas, offered critical insights into her work. Both were enthusiastic about her novel, "Permanent Resident." In discussing its publication, Hellmer made remarks that reflect the publishing conditions of the period: Macmillan "might be interested in a book, but it is doubtful they would go to the expense of producing it themselves. Canada is just too small a territory to make publishing pay."[70] Macmillan did agree to publish the novel, but only after Secker & Warburg had first committed to it. Some of these interactions showcase how satisfactorily he operated as the protector that Rule desired for her work.

She was apprehensive about the delayed publication of the American version of *Desert of the Heart* given some of her previous experiences with *Housewife*. She admitted that she must "sound more like a patient nervous about an operation than a writer about to have a book published."[71] Some of these heightened anxieties and preoccupations revolved around minutiae: "the use of commas in separating adjectives."[72] But she understandably also wanted reassurance that no editing would be done to *Desert of the Heart* without her prior knowledge and approval. Hellmer wrote on 18 November 1962 to suggest that she need not worry, "since you will receive the copy-edited manuscript before it is [sent] to the printers, thus assuring you that no changes [will be] made with which you might not agree." Even so, she was worried because Aaron Asher of World Publishing Company, which had agreed to publish *Desert of the Heart* in the United States, was refusing to alter a contract in a way that accommodated Rule's concerns. So again she wrote to Hellmer on 21 November 1962: "I would like you to do what you can to persuade him to accept my second suggestion, either the repeating of the sentence already written into the contract or a sentence like 'All copy editing is subject to the final approval of the author' to be placed at the end of the copy editing clause." Happily, he could write by November 26 that her first suggested change – the omission of two words related to unauthorized editing – stood "the way you have changed it."

Even Leresche impressed Rule in operating as a protector of the literary text. Indeed, the editing of her first novel was virtually nonexistent. There were concerns over changing to accommodate British spelling and vocabulary. About these changes, Rule argued that it was "important to keep American terminology for an obviously American setting. The context for all these terms makes their meaning clear." In a subsequent letter, she added that a "book so obviously American in setting should stay in American idiom except where meaning is seriously threatened."[73] Other concern revolved around libel laws because some of her fictional characters and place names corresponded to real persons and place names in Las Vegas. Secker & Warburg therefore requested that she submit her novel to their lawyers to be certain that it could not be accused of libel in Britain and invited her to submit her manuscript for legal review in Canada.[74] A letter from F.A. Upjohn of the Macmillan Company of Canada on 20 December 1962, indicates that he was alerted to the possibility of libel by Rule herself. She had based her story on an actual place called Harold's Club, at which she had worked, and it was the recognizability of this venue that lay at the heart of the company's concerns. He thus forwarded her letter and manuscript to the company's lawyers for their perusal. A response from Wright and McTaggart, Barristers and Solicitors, to Macmillan, dated 4 January 1963, indicates that changing a few names was sufficient to allay any anxieties in relation to libel.[75] According to Peter Wright, the lawyer who penned the letter, the question of libel apparently posed a greater threat because of the sexual orientation of Rule's protagonists. He observed that, in the event of a lawsuit, a court "would be unsympathetic to the underlying theme of the book and that therefore some of the presumptions that would be made in ordinary cases might not apply here." Fortunately, little was required to accommodate legal concerns. As one example, Rule simply changed the name from Harold's Club to Frank's Club, and the issue was largely settled.[76]

Aside from these matters, there were three concerns raised by the printer. The first dealt with the use of obscenities, about which Rule ironically noted that she believed "all this had been settled at the trial of *Lady Chatterley*." The second dealt with the "physical descriptions of love making," to which Rule made the rejoinder: "all of them are so abstract that there isn't any point in modifying them unless the very acknowledgement of the nature of the relationship is to be ignored."[77] The remaining critique was an inquiry from the print setter. As Rule recalls:

> One of the characters, Evelyn, says "my husband and I" quite self consciously, and then says "feeling like the Queen of England in her Christmas message." The printer had underlined this, and had written in the margin: "Is this offensive to the Queen?" I wrote underneath, "No." And that is the only critical exchange I had about that book.[78]

Even if Rule felt the concerns about libel laws were "not the ordinary exercises of an author preparing a book for publication" because "in the early 1960s, novels were not being published about erotic relationships between women," she stood her ground.[79] Leresche supported Rule's decisions: "You may have struck rather a prudish printer who chose to voice a personal opinion ... Don't let this worry you and here again you are perfectly free to stick to your own words and phraseology."[80] Rule's sense of the market was far from incorrect, as the letter from the lawyer indicates and as Showalter has more widely shown. Still, the conservatism that persisted in the period did not substantively alter the subject or quality of at least this particular novel. "Permanent Resident" found publication.

After the initial period of success with Hellmer, problems emerged. The first real conflict with him surfaced approximately one year into their professional relationship, on 15 August 1963. She received the September issue of *Redbook*, a literary magazine that redefined itself in 1951 to appeal to post–Second World War women and mothers (Tebbel and Zuckerman 1991). Her story "No More Bargains," which appeared in that issue, suffered from significant grammatical changes and egregious omissions for which she had not given approval.[81] In profound agitation, she wrote to Hellmer to castigate him for allowing such modifications without giving her warning:

> A copy of the September issue of REDBOOK arrived this morning, forwarded from your office. As I read through the story NO MORE BARGAINS, I discovered that it had not only been cut but also revised since I last saw it, and it is ... a butcher's job. The cutting in the first scene, for instance, makes the whole scene meaningless, a waste of space. As for the revisions, there are some real corkers, sentences turned into blatant nonsense, straight statement turned into appalling cliché. Additions like "For suddenly she knew" belong to a category of errors that I should think even true confession magazines would be ashamed to admit. There is no point in my making a list of the numerous changes in which the editor achieves such brilliant grammatical clarity as having the juice and coffee stand up instead of the man drinking them.[82]

In part, Rule's indignation was rooted in her sense that, as an instructor at the University of British Columbia, she had a standard related to good writing to uphold: "I teach at a university. I teach English. I teach writing ... explaining to my colleagues and students that I didn't make [these errors], that they were made for me, doesn't help. Any responsible writer does not allow himself to be so used." Although these reasons gave more than sufficient grounds against further unapproved revisions or omissions, a number of other issues surfaced as she and Hellmer exchanged fiery words over the incident.

The dispute escalated because Hellmer insisted on showing fidelity to the existing markets rather than to Rule. So, on 16 October 1963 in a searing letter to Hope Leresche, Rule wrote about her resentment of editorial interventions, especially about how Hellmer had failed to protect her from them: "He has done everything he could to avoid making a statement which would require him to arrange contracts that limited editorial rights. Apparently ... he feels he would be too limited by such restrictions because he keeps using vague phrases designed to placate me without binding him to any real agreement."[83] Her view was rooted in her deep conviction in the importance of literary integrity. The changes to "No More Bargains" were disconcerting because they affected the story's content, what Rule saw as embodying the "moral vision" of a work. These changes, moreover, were made to accommodate material interests – that is, to shorten the piece to make space for an advertisement for vacuum cleaners. As Rule went on to note, "One has to keep bad editing, and vacuum cleaners, in their place."[84] Perhaps to set herself apart from Hellmer's practices, Leresche wrote that "I would never have submitted a story of yours to the more popular women's magazines and when I sell, as I do regularly, to the better-class of magazine, I always insist on a proof for the author ... I see that not so much as a comma is disturbed."[85] She did show Rule support: "I am behind you absolutely in your insistance [*sic*] that you should see a proof of any story before it goes to print."[86] She acted as the kind of agent Rule desired, even demanded.

Rule became increasingly tenacious and rigorous in her dealings with Hellmer, insisting that he comply with her conception of his role as agent. She enlisted the aid of a lawyer to "make it impossible for my New York agent to sell any of my work without adequate protection from irresponsible editing."[87] After the *Redbook* incident, she vehemently insisted on allegiance to her interests: "if cutting and rewriting are done without my permission ... both you and I have legal recourse. Is it that you don't think you can get magazine editors to agree to these restrictions? If you can't, if such restrictions tie your hands in the markets you are primarily interested in, then you have a real problem, one you can't solve with me, and we should stop trying to do business." Here Rule identifies one of the key issues of their disagreement – his limited knowledge of or engagement with markets, which she supposed had exceeded her own.[88] In frustration, she wrote directly to the editor of *Redbook*, Barbara Blakemore, who eventually agreed to allow Rule to "have the final word" on her forthcoming work; announcing her triumph to Hellmer, she argued that "I must maintain final responsibility for my own work ... I want legal control in your hands and mine, not in theirs." Declaring that "you are useless to me as an agent unless you can give me protection against this butchering," she drew a line, one that he evidently crossed again, for on 29 May 1966 she replaced him with her last and most successful agent, Georges Borchardt. He was recommended by Leresche, who was certain, she noted in a subsequent letter, that Rule "would find him a valuable and stimulating support."[89]

Before Borchardt became her agent, however, Rule was to continue to be exasperated by a series of disputes over unapproved changes. Since Hellmer did not defend her work as she wished, she fought to protect that work directly. During a period of turbulent ownership, World Publishing Company had accepted "Permanent Resident," then transferred it to the New American Library – only to have it transferred back to World.[90] In February 1965 Benjamin La Farge,[91] associate editor at New American Library, to which World had by this point transferred the book, became caught up in one of these disputes over unapproved changes. He had been sufficiently careful prior to February; in one letter dated 25 January 1965 he explained that the title "Permanent Resident" could not be used for the American version of her book, since Secker & Warburg had changed her original title to "Desert of the Heart" for the sake of comprehensibility: "Although I can see why you might object to their title, I am afraid that we had no choice in the matter and we are under an injunction from the Federal Trade Commission not to change the title of a book which first appeared in England unless we clearly indicate the English title next to ours on our dust jacket." Rule agreed more readily in this instance than she had to the initial change of title, but was displeased with the editor New American Library hired to prepare her manuscript for publication in the United States. She thus felt obliged "to do a lot of recorrecting."[92] On 11 February 1965 LaFarge responded with what surely was for Rule too casual an approach to the matter of editing: "If our punctuation differs here and there from what you would prefer, it is at least consistent and does follow some rule or another." Her response does not survive, but only a few days later, on 18 February 1965, he responded to a letter in which she had evidently indicated her position on the subject, that she only committed to agreements or contracts that allowed her to have the final word. Thus he wrote:

> I was not aware that your contract with World gave you the right to approve the final changes made in manuscript, and I must therefore apologize for not having known this in time to let you exercise your right.[93]

LaFarge tried to placate Rule by adding that the "instances in which we have disagreed with your punctuation are not only few but comparatively minor and inconspicuous," that "our interpretation at least has the merit of making for a cleaner and more readable typography," and that "none of the changes we have made in punctuation has actually changed the meaning you intended." This dispute would have been prolonged had it not been for the fact, which LaFarge referred to in his letter, that the New American Library was no longer to be responsible for her book – shortly thereafter the rights reverted to the World Office in Cleveland.

As the senior vice-president of World, Roy D. Chennells, explained to Hellmer in a letter on 24 February 1965, the Times Mirror Company had purchased World Publishing, with the result that New American Library had become responsible for "publishing operations of hardbound fiction and so-called popular non-fiction"; Rule's novel fell under the former. When the arrangement did not "work out satisfactorily, ... the decision was reversed"; thus, her novel was transferred back to World. Throughout this process, Rule continued to struggle to assert her rights as an author. Her exasperation was thereafter directed towards World Publishing. She expressed her impatience without reservation on 20 February 1965: "you can imagine that none of this pleases me. I imagine there are marvelously understandable, institutional explanations for the disgracefully irresponsible handling of my manuscript to date. I am not really interested in them."[94] The publicity schedule had already been set to begin 17 May 1965, and, as Rule noted, such publicity would be useless if the novel's publication was delayed. Rule also wrote to Hellmer on 23 February 1965 to alert him to this dispute over the editorial liberties that also threatened the publishing schedule of the book, and of which he had not yet been apprised.

It was a situation that Rule was unable to negotiate, since her authorial and moral interests had been trumped by corporate ones. Her sole option would have been to withdraw her novel, which she did not do, much to Hellmer's relief: "I am glad you made 'no idle threats about pulling out,' because starting anew would be an uphill struggle without any certainty of success."[95] On 26 February 1965, Hellmer concluded in his assessment of the publishing shuffle that "we are the victims of circumstances beyond our control." The publication and corresponding publicity of her novel did proceed according to plan; by 4 May 1965 he could write that orders would continue to be filled by World. To this, he appended the apology, "from past experiences with them, I had no reason to doubt their efficiency. But you may rest assured that I will be most careful with your next book, or at least as careful as humanly possible." A letter Hellmer sent to Chennells a month before he wrote to Rule indicates he did make such an effort; he reminded Chennells that the agreement clearly stated that "the publisher agrees to make no changes in the text without the Author's agreement."[96] William J. Redding, the director of editing services, replied with assurances that no further changes would be made.[97]

Yet Rule's disappointments continued. World's publicity campaign seemed to be ineffective, not even securing a review in the Los Angeles *Times-Mirror*, the company that owned World itself. A brief review appeared in *The New York Times Book Review*;[98] otherwise reviews were sparse. The letters exchanged thereafter between Rule and Hellmer registered her continued annoyance. He attempted to defend himself:

> A publisher is interested in reviews even more than the author, because reviews mean sales – but there is no way to force a paper to review a book ... From my own experience, and from what publishers tell me, it very often happens that a book isn't reviewed at all, and certainly not in New York.

Attempts to mitigate the paucity of reviews would not have been aided by the fact that, in the same letter dated 11 February 1966, Hellmer was obliged to explain that the paperback rights had not yet been sold. They had not yet done so, he explained, because they did not want to "sell it to some third-class publishing specializing in 'lesbian novels.'" The remark was telling. It may have been an attempt to disguise his own ineptitude, but it also suggests their mutual understanding about her attempts to enlarge the space for queer writing: she wished to bring a subject matter related to sexual orientation and usually relegated to "third-class publishing" venues to a much broader audience. She thus refused to allow her novels, or their content, to be so compromised.

The timing of and increase in their disagreements had a bearing on his disclosure that he would be ending his association with Leresche and moving to another agency, London Authors.[99] Since Rule perceived her working relationship with Leresche as "easy and sane,"[100] the decision to remain with them was not difficult: the accumulated frustrations and disappointments she had experienced with Hellmer led her to decide it was time to move on. On 20 April 1966 she wrote to him to say that it was indeed "wisest for me to change agents": "I am sorry [your time and effort have] not been more profitable for both of us." He responded two days later, returning one outstanding short story, called "Joy,"[101] and wishing her the best. It was a seemingly peaceful resolution to a tumultuous professional relationship.

Rule's disappointments in the publishing industry would not end with the termination of this professional connection. Roughly six weeks later, on 7 June 1966, she was informed by World Publishing that sales were sufficiently slow that they found it "necessary to remainder stock on hand."[102] As *Desert of the Heart* was being remaindered by World, Secker & Warburg contacted her with similar news. Rule would receive further disquieting news about her second manuscript, "This Is Not for You": Secker & Warburg refused the novel "on the grounds that it would present the same problems in marketing" as had been posed by *Desert of the Heart*. As Rule observed in a letter to John Gray of Macmillan dated 14 July 1966, she could not assume "an attitude of sweet indifference," especially given her other communications with Macmillan on the same subject. Macmillan had published the Canadian first edition of *Desert of the Heart*,[103] and their press release indicates that they were confident in their backing of her work: "no novel of greater impact will be published in Canada this season."[104] Gray had been negotiating with Rule about her second manuscript; from the beginning, it did not go well. Although the correspondence was amicable, Gray did render his apologies at the outset for a seemingly insensitive and "casual suggestion of a major cut."[105] When he wrote to her again, on 14 September 1965, to enclose a reader's report for "This Is Not for You," he warned her that at moments she might "find [the report] hard to take." Indeed, the report did not mince words, suggesting that Rule had not quite overcome the "crippling technique" of second-person narration with which she had encumbered herself; that the protagonist, Kate, was a "thin-lipped martyr" and required revision; and that the "level often gets down to a pastiche of the worst women's magazine fiction," adding that "only now and then does the cool strength of *Desert of the Heart* writing show through." Rule addressed these points, not uncharacteristically, with some sense of irony:

> This particular reader has, nearly inadvertantly [*sic*], occasionally come upon my intention, dislikes it so that he (or she) has the charity to suppose I did not intend it and could correct it with some effort ... Kate is bitchy, self-pitying, a bit of a thin-lipped martyr, along with being a fairly strong, intelligent, sometimes likeable, occasionally truly pitiable character ... As for recasting "in a more flexible narrative style," again a difference of view is so profound that conversation about it is probably pointless. I don't deal with point of view as if it were simply a gadget for getting a story told ... The point of view is the book. Without it, there is no point for me in the tale to tell ... What it adds up to is that I am offering the book as an orange and being told, with some impatience, that it is a bad apple. And I am afraid, even if I were able to persuade such a person that what we have here is an orange, the final comment would be, "well, but I don't like oranges."[106]

Rule's letter was not written, as she herself noted, "in a fit of pique," for she expressed admiration rather than contempt for Gray. She understood, as she explained to Leresche, that he appreciated her "talent but not her book"[107] and added that she was cognizant of his "kindness, glad of the honesty of response." Indeed, his letter of 11 October 1966 suggests that "kindness" was characteristic of his interactions: he did let her book go, not with "relief" (as Rule had anticipated) but "regret": "I wouldn't agree that I don't like oranges ... All in all we have failed you I think, and I'm sorry." This exchange demonstrated that Rule extended her expectations of her agents to her publishers: she would not compromise her artistic integrity to accommodate their expectations.

But it was apparently neither Gray nor Macmillan whom Rule believed had failed her: Hellmer was the person with whom she expressed greatest impatience because he had inadequately defended her rights as an author. He retained his rights as her agent only in relation to *Desert of the Heart*, and thereafter suggested that she request the reversion of those rights, so that he would be able to "offer the book to paperback publishers" and she would not be obliged to share the profits with World. Rule did not agree, however, to offering the book to paperback publishers, and would not agree for another six years. Even when Hellmer suggested the incentive of a movie deal, in a letter dated 17 September 1968, which he claimed would lead to "a subsequent paperback deal," Rule did not agree until several years later, as his letter of 10 July 1972 indicates. Yet two years thereafter Hellmer remained unsuccessful in locating a paperback publisher[108] – the novel had been refused by Dell, Popular Library, Bantam, and Fawcett.[109] By 2 April 1975, however, Hellmer was able to write to her about an offer by Arno Press to do a "very small (200 copies) hardcover reprint edition for universities and colleges," which had already been permitted in England and Canada.[110] Rule agreed.

Hellmer continued to try to engage publishers in a paperback edition of *Desert of the Heart*, but received refusals from Pyramid, Avon, Warner Paperback Library, and Ballantine. In mid-May 1975, however, he unexpectedly passed away, leaving those who took over his agency, George Wieser and Patricia Falk Feeley, in great confusion. That these agents generally worked by different principles and that Hellmer had been remarkably tenacious about marketing her novel are facts evidenced by a passing remark that Feeley made to Rule in a letter dated 22 July 1975, the same one in which she announced Hellmer's death: "I should tell you that we don't work as Mr. Hellmer did – submitting to more than twenty publishers, sometimes, for upwards of three years. But we do work hard and, we think, effectively." Their promises would not persuade her: she looked elsewhere to find an agent who would properly assume the responsibilities of protecting her role as author and furthering her interests.

The Borchardt Agency

In search of an agent, Rule wrote to Georges Borchardt on the advice of Leresche, who wrote: "I had heard many good things of him and had some long sessions with him when he came to London last winter. I am very pleased indeed at his work so far."[111] He operated as a "sub-agent" of Leresche, to whom Rule was to give world rights over novels and to whom all novel-related contracts – even those made through Borchardt's office – would go first.[112] When she did negotiate her contract with Borchardt, she was careful to note that she needed advice from "someone who does know what would be wisest to do with this new book" but would only settle with an agent "who is not only interested in my work but [who] also accepts the limitations I want for contracts and places of publication":

> I want to be quite direct from the beginning about the problems I present to an agent so that you can feel free immediately to refuse to handle my work if the restrictions of sales are not in keeping with your own policies ... Though I am always glad of editorial advice and often find criticism helpful, I cannot accept any agreement [that] takes final responsibility of my work out of my hands ... Some agents I have talked to found this restriction unrealistic, and from the point of view of number of sales I am sure it is, but I am not willing to have my work published in any other way.[113]

She identified the possibly conflicting needs: "help me sort out a way to deal with the American market that is both responsible from my point of view and practical from yours." The tensions between moral and economic impulses required balance – but neither of these needs had been satisfied in her working relationship with Hellmer.[114] Borchardt accepted Rule on these terms, notwithstanding the "limitations" that suggested she was more interested in an agent who protected her rights and moral commitments than in one who secured the most lucrative contract: "Nothing of what you say frightens me in the least, particularly since I agree with your feelings about changes." Still, he added, "everything depends on how I feel about your work," and, to that end, he requested a copy of her new novel.[115]

Borchardt played the role of agent exactly as Rule desired. By 23 June 1966 he had taken swift action. He read *This Is Not for You* but, unlike the Macmillan reader, considered it "moving, original, and well-written." With this assessment Leresche largely concurred: she considered it "a beautifully written, strong, compelling book."[116] Borchardt outlined plans that coincided with those of Leresche and registered his confidence and support: "tell World that I now represent you, that you were unhappy with their handling of *Desert of the Heart* and would like to be released from their option." Borchardt determined a course of action that would leave the agency "free to negotiate with a publisher of our choosing." He took one other measure as well, in the event that World decided to retain its option to publish Rule's second novel: "if World decides to make an offer for *This Is Not For You*, we would then write into the contract as many guarantees as possible."[117] Rule must have appreciated the authority and rapidity with which Borchardt worked. By 11 July 1966 he asserted in unequivocal terms that he would never sell "a work of yours granting any editorial rights." He then provided her with further instructions about reverting the rights for *This Is Not for You* back to her, so that he could "get to work."

Borchardt demonstrated great capacity and acuity about both the material with which he was working and the markets to which he sent that material. At times, he rejected stories outright and returned them to her if he felt little confidence in them, or did not believe he could represent them, as he did with "A Good Kid in a Troubled World": "the story seems a little too mannered and doesn't read smoothly."[118] He also rejected "Grief" because it would have little appeal "either to the women's magazines or to the literary ones."[119] He consistently read her stories carefully before determining what was the best venue. Within a year, for example, he had sent her story "The Bosom of the Family" to *Cosmopolitan* even though, as he mused, "the more popular magazines [might] object to some of the undertones in it."[120] "House" he had sent to *Ladies' Home Journal*, because he believed it had "a good chance of selling to a women's magazine."[121] He had also sent her second novel to a number of publishers, including Farrar, Harper, Viking, Random House, Harcourt Brace, and Houghton Mifflin – a line-up of publishers that suggests he considered her novel to be literary rather than popular.

By 1967, Rosemary Macomber had become his assistant in negotiating on Rule's behalf with magazines and other venues. When "The List" was returned by *Redbook*, she wrote to Rule explaining what she had thus far learned in her interactions with the publishing industry: "The question of sales to these magazines depends somewhat on whether you can bring yourself to tailor them according to their rather rigid requirements." The rejection letter from *Redbook*'s fiction editor, Mrs Neal G. Stuart, expressed appreciation for the fact that Rule had conformed to some of these rigid – and decidedly commercial – requirements: she admired how "this story is hip deep in the vacuum cleaners, unironed laundry and domestic problems of our young readers," even as she "found the story's ambiguous resolution troubling."[122] To these remarks Macomber responded, not without some degree of irony, that the "only trouble ... from the popular market point of view is that the woman is thirty-eight":

> For *Redbook* (and in a lesser degree for the other women's magazines), if you're over 34 you're dead. They are all aiming at the young married market who are the big consumers of appliances, baby foods, cosmetics ... The exception to this is *Cosmopolitan*, which aims exclusively at the single girl on the make. But she's still apt to be dead if she's over 34. The women's magazine market has more rules than a convent, all of which can be broken if a sufficient big "name" is involved.[123]

Elsewhere, Macomber had questioned whether or not *Redbook* was in favour of women's liberation.[124] Despite her convictions, she asked Rule to consider changing the protagonist's age, if doing so did not "invalidate the idea of the story." In response, Rule behaved unpredictably: she agreed. *Redbook* still refused "The List," on the ground that revisions would be "a very speculative venture" and they were not certain about finding it desirable thereafter.[125] The story eventually found publication with *Chatelaine*[126] in April 1969, and, although the magazine did not send galleys because it was not part of their protocol, Macomber reported that that they had given a "solemn Canadian word-of-honour that they [would] change nothing in the story."[127] Perhaps reassured by Macomber's early conduct and by this promise, Rule did not protest.

Her seemingly greater pliancy with Macomber might signal the greater understanding between the two, or perhaps Rule had come to appreciate that negotiation and compromise were central to the publishing process. Macomber made clear that even if Rule made alterations to accommodate a magazine – in this instance, *Redbook* – other changes might later be requested:

> I just don't think they can give you a guarantee that nothing else will be cut or altered in the story before it goes to press. The most we can do is

> ask them not to make any cuts or changes without checking with you first. Will this do? I know it is hateful to see your work mangled, but one has to start somewhere with the selling of your stories, and I don't think we should erect barriers to acceptance.[128]

There was no outcry from Rule. Perhaps there was no need – thereafter, the publishers of many of her stories did not request rewriting or alterations, and apparently made few if any. "Moving On," for example, was published in *Redbook's* June issue, and "House" (published as "Not an Ordinary Wife") shortly thereafter;[129] "Her Name is Barbara"[130] and "A Chair for George"[131] were accepted by *Chatelaine*, "The Bosom of the Family" and "My Country Wrong" for anthologies by Oberon,[132] "Middle Children" for *The Other Persuasion* (Vintage 1977),[133] and "Anyone Will Do" by *Redbook*, albeit with some revisions that had been imposed by the magazine.[134] Macomber had to remind Rule that, in seeking serialization of *The Young in One Another's Arms*, a novel that had already been published by Doubleday (in both Canada and the United States) in 1977, they would inevitably have to consider "cutting and editing for complete-in-one issue." Anticipating the kind of protests Rule would make, she noted that it wasn't "really 'selling out' to allow this – it's just the exigencies of space limitations."[135] Even to the revisions for "Anyone Will Do" and those anticipated for *The Young in One Another's Arms*, Rule made surprisingly little rejoinder.[136]

Perhaps Rule appreciated the kinder, gentler tone Macomber adopted in her correspondence: she tended to be self-deprecating, suggesting often that she was "dreadfully literal-minded" or reiterating how much she appreciated Rule's work: "I did like the book and the way in which you showed the interpretation of these people."[137] In another letter, she suggested that, while she enjoyed Rule's non-fiction work in relation to *Lesbian Images*, she regarded her "essentially as an artist in fiction (and in a way in your life) rather than a writer for any cause narrower than a better understanding of human beings."[138] This response was gentler than that of Leresche, who initially tried to dissuade her by suggesting that "*tomes* have been written" about Radcliffe Hall and Gertrude Stein and that "the market would be very small indeed for a new book."[139] Macomber would make deft inquiries but not place demands upon Rule: she invited her to consider writing stories for particular venues, for example, as she did for a magazine called *Yankee*, on such themes as women's liberation, but she did not insist that Rule comply.[140] At a later date, Macomber reminded Rule that she needed to differentiate between agents and existing markets: while Macomber pushed and negotiated on Rule's behalf, there still remained "little that you or I or anyone else can do to improve the efficiency of publishers ... I don't think the distribution systems will ever achieve the level of something like General Foods."[141] Yet Rule was finding success and demonstrating that, through her agents, she was indeed expressing self-agency by making space for her literary work and moral concerns in markets that had at one time been closed to her.

Or perhaps Rule's confidence in Macomber grew for reasons other than those evident in the correspondence – that is, that Rule had become habituated to such negotiations and even learned to expect them, because there were still moments when certain publishing venues refused her work on the ground of its explicitly lesbian content. Yet it was also Macomber who more quickly and easily delivered news of Rule's successes: she became the bearer of good news. Macomber followed up Borchardt's initial attempts to place the novel *This Is Not for You;* she noted in a letter dated 2 April 1969 that it had been sent to Gambit and, in another letter dated 16 April 1969, that she had been approached by Hy Cohen, a former Delacorte employee since hired by the Book Division of McCall's, who had expressed interest in the novel. By 12 June 1969 Macomber would be able to write to Leresche with the news that McCall's was indeed interested in publishing Rule's second novel. The manuscript for *Against the Season* was also sent to Cohen and to *Redbook* at their respective requests. Although it found favour with the former, the latter requested "extensive cutting": "obviously the part[s] they would want to cut are the sections dealing with the lesbianism."[142] McCall's was considerably more accommodating: Cohen had had "some suggestions to make," but these were "entirely subject to your approval and willingness to comply." McCall's would otherwise be "happy to publish the book just the way it is if that is what you want."[143] And publish the novel they did: McCall's then attempted to make arrangements to have *Against the Season* distributed in Canada by McClelland & Stewart and Macmillan, but finally found success with Doubleday.[144] The British rights were subsequently picked up by the publishing firm Peter Davies and the paperback rights in Canada and the United States were purchased shortly thereafter by Manor Books, so that another edition of *Against the Season* was printed in 1975.[145] Within the same time span, *This Is Not for You* was reprinted by Popular Library.[146] Then in 1973 Talonbooks bought the rights to publish *Theme for Diverse Instruments* (1975) and shortly thereafter the rights to print a new edition of *Desert of the Heart*; Doubleday bought those to *The Young in One Another's Arms* (1977), as did Collins in 1978.[147] By 1982 CBC was serializing in dramatic form *The Young in One Another's Arms*, and by 1977 a movie bid had been made on *Desert of the Heart;* a film directed by Donna Deitch, titled *Desert Hearts*, would be released in 1985.[148]

In short, Rule's career was blossoming.[149]

In the agreements governing Rule's publications, Macomber may have been self-deprecating, deferring to Rule's literary talents, but she was otherwise certain about her role as agent: she was very firm about the payments that ought to be exacted for her author. She even reminded Rule that it was the agency's responsibility to negotiate financial matters: of Rule's correspondence with Doubleday, she urged, "don't talk money to them yourself!"[150] More important was a letter she wrote on 6 July 1972 in which she articulated her views on the subject with great clarity and, in so doing, distinguished between the markets for American versus Canadian magazines:

> I may say that in principle we are very much opposed to *any* free use of any of our authors' writings whatsoever. Our position is that these magazines have to pay their rent, their paper bills, their telephone bills, etc., and there is consequently no reason why they should not pay their authors, even if the sum is only nominal ... I was shocked beyond words to discover that a magazine like the *Canadian Forum* has never in its entire existence paid for any contribution, and I consider this a very poor indication of the regard Canada has for its writers and for literature and cultural life generally. If Canada wishes to develop its own strong and honored literature, it had better do something about that. Their attitude is back in the 18th century in the days of the poor scrivener without any rights whatsoever.[151]

Macomber offers an interesting perspective on Canada's approach to literature and writing in general in the period, and, moreover, on how an agent might identify to what a writer was entitled. Still, the different pay scales for the different markets were a minor difficulty at this point in Rule's career. By the late 1970s, Rule would meet a series of challenges, one of them the ill health of Macomber, which in 1977 obliged her to take a leave from the Borchardt agency.[152]

Another challenge evolved after Macomber left the Borchardt agency, when Rule decided to negotiate somewhat independently her novel *Contract with the World* with Talon, and specifically with David Robinson and Karl Siegler. Rule had two reasons for voicing protest. First, Talon had paid her royalties only once per year, when the contract stipulated that she was to receive these twice a year. Second, she believed that Robinson's and her editorial "tastes [were] different" and, as she observed, "taste has a great deal to do with editing": "If you think it doesn't, I am the more depressed at the notion of working with you as an editor." Perhaps her previous experiences with her agents and with *Redbook* led her to conclude that she did not want to work with Robinson "as an editor because I don't feel you have the insight or experience to be helpful to me."[153] To this letter, Siegler rather than Robinson responded. He first addressed the publisher's "lack of borrowing power," which would end in its "demise" if it paid royalties with greater frequency. To the question of editing, he was less patient: he charged her with "playing the role of prima dona [*sic*]" and ridiculed her demand that she be "met with an appropriate degree of fawning acquiescence." In short, he felt that Talon's "editorial competence" had been impugned.[154] When Rule responded on 21 April 1979, she suggested that perhaps there was a lapse of communication between her agent and herself, for she had never been informed that the terms of the contract would be so ignored. She announced with a sense of finality that, although she would consider doing a mass paperback of *This Is Not for You* with Talon, she would offer *Contract with the World* to another publisher.[155]

A third challenge was that the content of her books met with renewed resistance. Whatever her position may have been with Talon, *Contract with the World* had already been refused by Collins because, as a shamefaced editor who "mumbled something about Canadian provincialism" noted, "their marketing people felt that a book with such explicit homosexuality could not work and they would only be able to sell 2,000 copies."[156] Perhaps this was a sign of a renewed conservatism, a shifting socio-political climate. Certainly it was a portent: the greatest challenge of her career as an author lay ahead of her and was to have far-reaching and public consequences – and her agents would not be able to negotiate or intervene in the matter.

The Little Sisters Trial

In December 1986, a shipment of books en route to the Little Sisters Book and Art Emporium in Vancouver was detained by Canada Customs. The reason given for this seizure, the first in a series, was the same as that given for the earlier seizure of the GLM Archives: the material was deemed to be obscene. Two books "arrested" in the series of shipments were Rule's *The Young in One Another's Arms* and *Contract with the World*, the former stopped in 1990 and the latter in 1994. In essence, whether novels and texts by Canadian authors were deemed "fit" for Canadian consumption might be determined not by publishers or even agents, but by other prescriptive forms of authority – more precisely, customs agents. In response to Canada Customs' "practice of seizing materials destined specifically for a gay and lesbian bookstore," Little Sisters bookstore, its owners Jim Deva and Bruce Smyth, and the BC Civil Liberties Association issued a constitutional challenge in which they questioned "the federal government on the issue of freedom of expression" (Rule 1995, 3). They also challenged "Canada Custom's power to seize a book at the border and force the bookstore that was ordering it to prove that the publication was not 'obscene,'" and argued that its practices were discriminatory (3).

The *Little Sisters* case has generated considerable scholarship given its ramifications for the issue of censorship, but it is also important for the way in which Rule was affected: in spite of her efforts to work through agents to protect her moral commitments and literary material, her career as respectable author was impugned by the proceedings at the trial.[157] The case reinforces how both papers and books might be involved in acts of legal arrest intended to prevent the circulation of ideas that threaten the national imaginary. The "arresting" of Rule's books, moreover, directly opposed the cause to which she had committed her life: disseminating ideas about and creating space for the queer and feminist communities. The case would surely have called to mind the precedent related to the GLM Archives and reinforced why it was important to preserve for posterity documentation related to the trial and also, more largely, to her career.

The *Little Sisters* case began to unfold in October 1994. During the first trial, Rule was one of the key witnesses to address the understanding of the process by which one determined a book's status as "art," and the consequences of stopping an author's novels at the border, as Customs had done with hers. On 24 October 1994 she expressed her concern that those exercising judgment about the literary merit of such novels might have missed "the cultural context of the book": "books," she noted, "are not born out of nothing. They live inside the traditions of our culture" (1995, 6). The result of writing within that context might be "very troubling," including and especially writing related to human sexuality, but, she added, "if we don't finally come to understand [it] in all its complexity, we are in great danger of not knowing how to live our lives" (6). Aside from observing the importance of cultural context, Rule added that someone evaluating the literary merit of novels must develop a sensitivity to its tone: "let the book dictate how we deal with it" (5). She called attention to the fact that those who were making such judgments at the border may not have been well equipped to make such decisions. She had one former student in a remedial English class at the University of British Columbia, she recalled, who had later become a customs official for Canada – ironically, Rule had written his letter of recommendation, albeit without having been "aware at that time that such a person would be given the responsibility" of detaining books destined for Canada (9). Given her painstaking dealings with agents, editors, and publishers over the course of her career to allow for the unhindered consideration of ideas related to the queer and feminist communities, it is obvious why this lack of care in selecting those responsible for censoring books coming across the border might have deeply troubled Rule.

Her insistence upon viewing books in this context also demonstrated that locking up books was ultimately futile, if not naive. If books do inhabit the traditions of a culture, preventing others from reading certain books would not eradicate the ideas contained in their pages. Still, the seizures' material implications for Rule's career were obvious: two of her novels were prevented from being sold in Canada because of their "lesbian" – or, to borrow the terminology employed at the time, "obscene" – content. Rule also identified repercussions beyond the practical: at stake was her carefully constructed reputation as a writer, one she had so carefully managed through her interactions with her literary agents and publishers. The kind of attention she secured during the trial was antithetical to her literary persona and to the kind of writing to which she had devoted herself: that of a higher literary value, rather than popular, erotic material. So she observed at the trial:

> It's the kind of attention that would very possibly cut me off from the general audience for whom I write. It is the kind of statement or implication that does not simply last for that week or that month, but labels me for the rest of my professional life as someone who is probably a pornographer because, you know, if they held the books, there must be something in them that they don't like. (18)

The banning of her books and the subsequent federal trial called into question her status and reputation as a "Canadian author," and obliged her to renegotiate her place within the Canadian literary canon.[158] *The Young in One Another's Arms* may have won the Canadian Author's Association Award for the best novel in 1978, but to her mind, the notoriety of the trial would overshadow the distinction, particularly because of her sexual orientation: "I bitterly resent the attempt to marginalize, trivialize and even criminalize what I have to say because I happen to be a lesbian" (18). She concluded that the state of political affairs in Canada had erased her status as "good Canadian citizen" and configured her as "sexual creature" instead. Her legitimacy as a citizen was threatened and her authorial voice within the nation diminished.

Rule consistently valued protection from limitations to freedom of expression over the pursuit of lucrative financial contracts in her interactions with publishing figures, especially with her agents, and in the eventual development of her archive at the University of British Columbia. The breakdown of her relationship first with Wing and then with Hellmer was rooted in their inability to meet her expectation that they as agent would protect her work from unauthorized editing, and thereby protect the moral vision of her work and the space she struggled to cultivate for the articulation of queer and feminist concerns. In Hellmer's case, it was also rooted in his apparent unwillingness to locate or develop such space in the market for her sometimes "ill-fitting" fiction, and his failure to negotiate an appropriate venue for Rule's longer fiction. Even when she tried more conventional routes or popular markets, Rule was adamant about pushing the boundaries of what was deemed acceptable.[159]

As she herself discovered in her subsequent publishing negotiations, her literary freedom was circumscribed by both overt and implicit expectations about who could make claims to being an author, what interests would govern the shaping of written material (economic and otherwise), what public spaces sanctioned literary material, and what an author might be authorized to write about. The *Little Sisters* case and the seizure of documents from the GLM Archives demonstrated that even agents could not protect her from the larger national or even international powers that imposed their own criteria for publication and circulation of books. These competing expectations and interests affected knowledge and literary production in the period, and Rule would consistently challenge those expectations and interests throughout her literary career. The legal entanglements related to the GLM Archives, however, taught her that she could create a legacy that promised to extend the activist work to which she committed herself during her lifetime.

But there are larger implications as well. Rule understood at the outset of her career that she was "homesteading" a territory that was largely heteronormative and patriarchal. She knew that her work – literary and otherwise – had the potential to turn into either "a ghost town" or "a city." In a December 2006 interview, I asked her if she had succeeded in turning that territory into a city. She replied with characteristic firmness: "No. It became a nation." The archive she established would attest to her response: it enriches understanding of how an author negotiates professional structures, and the means by which Rule engaged agents to establish greater literary credibility, to access mainstream and predominantly heteronormative markets, to challenge national orthodoxies that assumed a heteronormative literary canon, and to extend her activism well beyond her lifetime. Her archive thus sustains and nourishes academic scholarship that will only continue to grow and enrich the "nation" – the imaginative space that Rule had so assiduously endeavoured to expand for herself and for others and that has its physical instantiation or parallel in her fonds. Rule thus offers an example of how archives, institutional and material, may be used to subvert official narratives and circumvent those policing measures that shape the politics of remembering and the cultural production of the past. Her struggle for this imaginative space, her legal entanglements, and her creation of a sanctioned archive to evade the dominant and restrictive ideologies of the period would, in some ways, bear resemblance to the later efforts of M. NourbeSe Philip, the subject of the next chapter. Like Rule, Philip would use an archive to extend her activism and to protest against discriminatory practices; however, she would do so by deliberately withholding her papers from mainstream institutions. Philip's case serves as a reminder that even a carefully constructed archive, like that of Rule, is sometimes an insufficient means to express one's agency or represent one's concerns.

5 The Minor Archive: M. NourbeSe Philip and Mediations of Race and Gender in Canada

On 7 September 1995, M. NourbeSe Philip (1947–) was denounced in a radio broadcast by Michael Coren, a journalist for CFRB 1010 radio, for the recognition bestowed upon her as the recipient of the 1995 Toronto Arts Award in writing and publishing.[1] At the time of his remarks, Philip was already a celebrated poet, academic, essayist, activist, playwright, and novelist, nationally and internationally renowned for her literary endeavours as much as her attention to issues of social justice and her pronouncements against discrimination.[2] Coren's scathing broadcast, in part informed by an article by Joey Slinger that had appeared two years earlier in the *Toronto Star*, was a response to a press announcement on 6 September in which the Arts Foundation of Greater Toronto declared that it would host the tenth-anniversary Toronto Arts Awards and formally celebrate that year's winners, including Philip, at Roy Thomson Hall in Toronto on 23 October 1995.[3] Philip engaged in a series of protests related to Coren's broadcast, first by refusing to appear at the awards ceremony and then by contacting Richard Ouzounian, president of the Arts Foundation, to engage support in the matter; she also asked CFRB for a retraction and, when that proved fruitless, turned to the Canadian Radio-Television and Telecommunications Commission (CRTC) for redress. When neither Ouzounian nor CFRB nor the CRTC supported these appeals, she sought legal recourse, which finally culminated seven years later, in May 2002, when a legal settlement was reached.[4]

Thereafter, no significant media account addressed the matter, nor could it do so, since a requirement of the settlement was that its terms be kept in the strictest confidence. However, during and well after the years of these critical entanglements, Philip preserved a substantial cache of papers related to events in what might be called a private archive, which to date she has deliberately withheld from deposit in an official institution. Her papers need to be viewed as unarrested, that is, as part of the agencies and political strategies she would employ to represent herself, to challenge Coren's broadcast, and to critique the discourses that informed that broadcast. Philip and Coren thus called upon, were invested in, or generated radically different forms of archives for their respective purposes: hers were legal and private, whereas his were media based.

As Burman observes about the media, it renders hypervisible those who are discursively exiled from national interests: "internal 'Others'" are "usefully mobilized in political and media discourses as foreign elements so as to subtly outline the ideal citizen of a particular geopolitical movement" (179).[5] Such hypervisibility involves recirculating media images to forge "spaces of removal," or spaces that demarcate the boundaries of citizenship, and then casting certain subjects as deviant (180). The fact that the Coren-Philip matter became quite high profile is thus of relevance, as is the grammar by which Coren criticized her: his discourse may be seen to have positioned her as deviant by virtue of her gendered and racialized body. Erikson notes that "deviant offenders and the agents of control have always attracted a good deal of public attention," but whatever public forum was used to generate such negative attention in the past, a change was effected in the eighteenth century that "coincided almost exactly with the development of newspapers as a medium of mass information" (13). Unaccounted for by Jürgen Habermas's notion of public space, contemporary media are a kind of social form that is not as easily monitored or precisely controlled as the legal system. In the period of this particular conflict, institutional and media representations of African Canadians – favourable or not – were scant at best (Mackey 417). When they were represented, African Canadians were often conceptually positioned as outside the nationally imagined community or, as Paul Gilroy notes, located as victims or as sources of the problem. In this instance, Coren proved that this social form could thus be wielded as a "discourse of chaos" that both suppresses and subjugates black women and locates them as exiles (McKittrick 232).

In turn, Philip would effect a reversal, the first through the institution of the law, that is, through a court case. Her actions eventually led to a legal settlement. Although its terms cannot be disclosed, the fact that there was one at all remains a remarkable victory given historical, legal reiterations of racialized immigrant subjects: previously "staged battle[s]" framed its participants as "unscrupulous and degenerate immigrants" struggling against "noble and civilized white state representatives" (Burman 179; see also Razack). The settlement thus effectively shifts this paradigm and demonstrates how these legal encounters might be restaged; yet it also operates as a powerful mechanism of silencing by forbidding disclosure of its details. Indeed, as Philip noted, she only agreed to these terms because otherwise the legal process demanded she provide her private journals for scrutiny.[6] Rather than subject her private life to such violation, she accepted the terms of the settlement.

Philip thus effected a second reversal through the cultivation of her own personal, unarrested archive, which contains materials well beyond those on which this chapter draws. As I noted in the introduction, one form of the unarrested archive is that which is deliberately withheld from the institutions that have both wielded control over and disciplined national subjects. In this case, Philip's papers carefully document the exchanges between the key players in the narrative, the discrepancies that manifested themselves between such exchanges, and the stories that were rehearsed in the popular media. It is clear, from perusing her papers, that she refused to be positioned as "foreign element." Instead, her efforts might be read as essential to the formation of a "counter-archive," what Arjun Appadurai observes, like Wendy W. Walters, is a form of "aspiration" as much as "recollection" (17). At the same time, Philip challenged the construction of the "ideal citizen" and associated socio-spatial regulation, "which is underwritten by racial-sexual mappings on and of the body" (McKittrick 179). Indeed, Philip's personal archive suggests how racialized identities are socially produced and how a body of knowledge – or rather, assumptions – underpinned a collective imaginary that appeared and reappeared in the media and that was called upon so as to overwrite and silence her own narrative. In the preservation of these papers, she presented what Walcott would call "a self-assured Blackness" and also other forms of "creative insubordinations" to resist enforced narratives of deviance by which Coren and others tried to circumscribe her (7, 9).

Philip's decision to preserve her papers by withholding them from a formal institution in Canada, then, were to work against not one but two forms of archives: first, official archives that were apparently meant to represent a nationally imagined collective, and second, media and public or popular archives. Unlike Rule, who found a means of agency by protecting the legacy of her life and work through formal repositories, Philip located a sense of agency outside such repositories. Even as she and Coren became locked in a struggle over the boundaries of legitimate expression and over the right to protect the boundary of the cultural integrity of the African Canadian community, Philip strategically used this moment to transform a source of discrimination into a source of empowerment. The creation of her personal, unarrested archive thus offers a powerful counterbalance to Coren's broadcast and the media archive upon which he called to legitimate his remarks because it reveals the socio-political investments – hers and that of hegemonic culture – at work over a protracted span of time. In this instance, a scholar's reading practices extend from the archival records themselves to the institutions and the context in which they appear. As this chapter will show, her legal battle, her impetus for writing and for retaining her own papers, and the status of the papers themselves, when taken together, stage a complicated response to a political and cultural environment that was inimical to any sense of stability as citizen or claim to be an author in Canada.

Theorizing the Minor Archive

It is clear that it is not simply the content of Philip's papers that is of significance, nor the possibility for future alternative readings that they offer. Rather, her act of preserving and withholding her papers from an official Canadian and purportedly "multicultural" institution in order to forge her own archive provides a context: it shows how such caches of archive materials may be created as a response to unequal power relations.[7] As I outline in the introduction, interpreting archival material does not simply mean reading the documents housed within an institution or a collection; it involves a set of reading practices that are applied beyond the documents, that involve consideration of their context – the very location and naming of the archive – which shapes our understanding of what we may find. In this instance, Philip constructs a peculiar form of the unarrested archive, what I call a "minor archive" that, as Françoise Lionnet and Shu-mei Shih argue about minor transnationalism, accomplishes far more than simply "critiquing the centre": the latter enhances an archive's central status by reifying its place "as the main object of study" (3), whereas the minor archive offers a "space of exchange and participation where processes of hybridization occur ... without necessary mediation by the center" (5).

Lionnet and Shih call upon "minor transnationalism" as a means of circumventing limited understandings of power relationships, in which dominant groups oppress and minority cultures react. They suggest that critics instead move beyond strict vertical readings of such relationships, which characterize the dynamic as only consisting of "action and reaction," to acknowledge how "other forms of participation in the transnational ... may be more proactive and more creative even while economically disadvantaged" (7). However uneven these power relations may be, they note, the "minor and the major participate in one shared transnational moment," which calls upon "transversal movements of culture" (8). Cultural transversalism, they add, involves

> minor cultural articulations in productive relationship with the major ... as well as minor-to-minor networks that circumvent the major altogether. This transversalism also produces new forms of identification that negotiate with national, ethnic, and cultural boundaries, thus allowing for the emergence of the minor's inherent complexity and multiplicity. (8)

This formulation of the minor, its engagement with the major, opens up space for understanding how the minor's agency might be manifested and demonstrates the range and multidimensionality of those manifestations; it also recognizes how the minor might work with existing parameters of citizenship when "the nation-state remains the chief mechanism for dispersing and regulating power, status, and material resources" (8). As this chapter shows, rather than simply waiting to be recognized as a "citizen," the minor subject adopts a "horizontal approach" that brings "minor cultural formations across national boundaries into productive comparisons" (11). If there are minor cultures, then there are also minor archives that bear witness to and are the products of multiple encounters, that are hybrid and relational, that restage and animate the possibilities for minor-to-minor engagements, that showcase the range of agencies available to the minor subject, and that are inflected by transnational processes and discourses. This kind of unarrested archive demonstrates its elasticity, its kinetic value.

In this instance, Philip's archive is positioned to bypass the claims of a national identity that had previously excluded her from representation because of her race and gender. The location of her papers, the space she constructs away from mainstream Canadian institutions, calls attention to the materialities of racial exclusion and the processes by which citizenship does (or does not) work in the nation – as it also demonstrates the engagements and agencies to which she has access and calls upon the larger African Canadian community of which she is a part. As McKittrick and Woods argue, spatial relations are tangible manifestations of racial ideologies and demonstrate to what extent they are deeply imbedded. The processes of normalization, they argue, "are worked out in our geographic system: a broader, and ongoing, history of segregation ... often concealed by partial perspectives and a disregard of the unknowable and unseeable; these processes come "clearly into view alongside the spatial, and lived, limits of democracy and citizenship" (3). That partial perspective or understanding is expanded by bringing into view the existence of another space, in this case, that which Philip's papers occupy and the papers themselves, which she deliberately withholds from the clutches of a formal institution. In this sense, her archive is unarrested, or deliberately kept from organizational centres of power. In selecting those to whom she would show the papers, however, she permits another form of the unarrested archive to emerge: she allows her papers to be released into the hands of selected persons, those whom she sanctions as appropriate to the conversation she wishes to have. In engaging with institutions and persons thus, she first challenges the disregard for the unknowable; second, she suggests how legitimate spaces cannot always be forged *within* officially sanctioned institutions; and third, she shows how she resists being passively situated (3). She creates a minor archive that is located "elsewhere" of her own volition. Her minor archive is thus an expression of her agency and takes on entirely different permutations in its potential to undermine hegemonic spatial practices and ideologies.

Philip's legal and archival agencies are especially important when located within larger legal discourses and archival practices in which Black Canadian women are featured, in Canada and abroad. It is this kind of minor-to-minor network to which Lionnet and Shih gesture. In this instance, Philip's development of a minor archive must be read as part of a larger phenomenon. Vernon critically assesses why Black women in Canada would refuse to give their papers to national institutions, tracking Library and Archives Canada's creation of its "Multicultural Mandate" in recognition that the papers stored therein had reflected only historically dominant cultural groups; she suggests that silences or absences in archives are not necessarily a "sign of marginalization and exclusion – a silence that belies the nation's and the archives' state-legislated multicultural policies" (197). Rather, the LAC's mandate was undercut, since "'multicultural' identity and legitimacy" are achieved only insofar as the LAC managed to institutionalize and represent difference: "the racialized silences in the archive 'must' be filled" (197).

In trying to redress its past exclusions, LAC encountered resistance when it tried to solicit papers from members of racialized and ethnicized groups: it encountered those who refused to fill silences and gaps that had been institutionally sanctioned for decades. Their need to "see themselves" in the LAC was not as urgent as that institution had anticipated. Racialized and ethnicized communities were already occupied in creating their own, independent archives. Some were also simply "reluctant to speak candidly about sensitive issues" with an "an archive employee, an outsider" (Vernon 198). Vernon notes that donating Black archival material is at times perceived as "equivalent to 'giving it over to white people'" (201); as well, there are real concerns that professional archivists would not "appreciate the memorial, spiritual, sentimental and cultural values clinging to objects that might at first appear odd and unimpressive" (200). Withholding papers from public institutions or strategically mobilizing them are means of enacting a political agenda at the forefront of such concerns. In the latter case, the newly formed archives themselves – not entirely the materials they house – are constructed as spaces of empowerment that work to impede or intervene in national or transnational agendas that would otherwise silence Black women.

Absences or silences in the form of withholding papers from formal, institutional archives are a manifestation of the unarrested archive. They call attention to a former exclusion, as well as being an expression of agency and self-recognition: this is a significant gesture, since it serves as a refusal of the material relations of power re-enacted by institutions that formally include and exclude papers and yet that purport to be representative. Employing Derrida's notion of "archive" as a register of power, Richards argues that an archive, specifically an imperial one, is "not a building, nor even a collection of texts, but the collective imagined junction of all that was known or knowable, a fantastic representation of an epistemological master pattern" (100). Even a collectively imagined archive, however, may be challenged by those who both preserve and withhold papers to protest epistemological master patterns – this archive, in "tone and temper," may "convey the rough interior ridges of governance and disruptions to the deceptive clarity of its mandates" (Stoler 2009, 2).[8] In this case, Philip's unarrested archive serves as a disruption of the holdings of national institutions, while the papers themselves and the causes for their unique preservation illuminate the politics or "rough interior ridges" of a nation that had racially determined her place – or lack thereof – in its political imaginary. In effect, Philip creates the minor archive as a means of mobilizing power and resisting the "domiciliation" that Derrida addresses in *Archive Fever*. The very need for its construction identifies the social location and subjectivity to which Philip might have been consigned, but refused, as it also highlights the failures of an imagined multicultural community in Canada.

Derrida's renowned formulation of domiciliation is useful here, both for its suggestion of how papers are kept "under house arrest" in a concrete and official institution and for its idea of a more general and abstract cultural heritage of which the institution is an emblem. The principle of domiciliation – that is, the structure and political motivations to which the archive subscribes – that underlies the mandate for the nation or other public institution would obviously differ from that subscribed to by a person who refuses to have his or her papers governed by the state. If we approach Philip's archive as a response to national domiciliation, her documents may be read as offering, as McGregor argues about those by filmmaker Nelofer Pazira, a site of negotiation that challenges the social boundaries by which she was stigmatized and then ostracized. These social boundaries are largely constructed by the "official Canadian archive of publicly disseminated information" and the popular media (109). As McGregor notes, neither of these archives is "exclusively material," and they include "various discursive components," even if they are "shaped by the material conditions of production and dissemination" (109). It is these very forms of archives – the popular media and publicly disseminated information – that Philip's also resists. Her minor archive offers a critical disruption and a more radical interpretation of a Canadian literary scene that popularly valorizes and promises the imminent achievement of the multicultural ideal; it likewise becomes a means of expressing autonomy as a writer and a political activist, a way of wresting power from mainstream institutions and responding to a media-based discursive archive that would operate as a colonizing force to render her in "other" terms.

Finally, the minor archive may be seen to forge space – geographical, psychological, and imaginative – for others who have been marginalized by political experiences, who have been comparably excluded (Buss 5). If a media-based archive resituates and even silences Black women's voices, a personal archive such as Philip's might be used to re-imagine, rewrite, and restage narratives and histories, by engaging with media representations and widening the fields of knowledge and possibilities for engagement between involved parties. The formation of her archive may thus be read in both specific and general formulations: as an expression of self-agency and the source of a larger counter-narrative. It is a means of reshaping the ideological terrain and responding to a hegemonic account of national identity in Canada that, especially in the 1990s in Toronto, prevented her from receiving proper recognition or dignity; more forcefully, that account endeavoured to characterize her and her writing as violating social protocols. The preservation of her papers thus serves as a sharp contrast to the propensity of mainstream, popular rhetoric – and perhaps of mainstream institutions – to valorize multiculturalism as the identifying hallmark of Canadian culture and to be self-congratulatory about its purported socio-political achievement in Canada. In retaining her papers, Philip is investing them with the "kinetic quality," a radical potential, that she elsewhere attributes to memory.[9] Her decision to preserve these papers allows her to confront the national narrative, as her minor archive provides the space for her and others to work: Philip uses her papers effectively to resist both the official institution and the more general and abstract cultural heritage that would sanction the two media-related events we consider below, the first involving Joey Slinger of the *Toronto Star* and the second Michael Coren of CFRB radio.

Philip's Minor Archive

Philip's written response to my inquiry about her papers demonstrated how she had been profoundly affected, even impeded, by the exclusion of a nationally imagined history for African Canadians, by the racism in a country that would pretend it has achieved its multicultural ideal. The papers clearly mapped out the repercussions within her own life. For reasons that this chapter explores, Philip refused York University's offer in 1996 to house her papers with them; instead, she began to regard the United States as providing her a more relevant national imaginary, a source of writerly nourishment. "I felt I had disappeared as a writer in Canada," she noted in an untitled statement she sent to me: "My continued work in the United States confirmed for me that my work remained relevant and significant." The conclusions she reached about her place – and therefore the place of her papers in Canada – were not what I and other academics might have expected. Indeed, she herself observed that

> as someone who came to Canada from elsewhere and came to writing in Canada, I have thought that this particular space – a colonising and racially inflected space for First Nations and other peoples of colour – provided an opening from which to fashion a particular voice.[10] … [But] Canada does not have a similar and easily traceable genealogy of writers of African descent, although it has been argued persuasively that there was a literary history of the publication of sermons by African Canadians in the Atlantic Provinces – in particular Nova Scotia.[11] In other words, I would have had to engage with these traditions in a conscious way. In the space that is Canada, I confronted a sense of there being an absence of tradition, of being on the margin, whose meaning includes frontier, and all that that entails.

Rather than discovering, then, that this "absence of tradition" allowed for space for her creative expression, Philip realized that, ironically, it represented "a sort of death for me as a writer": "it is for this reason that I decided that I could not allow my papers to be held here in Canada." This remark almost seems a rejoinder to her epigraph in *Frontiers*, a book she dedicates to Canada "in the effort of becoming a space of true be/longing." That space for "true belonging," it seems, did not manifest itself. Lack of imaginative and psychological space mirrored lack of physical space, at least for her documents and where she believed they might be housed.

I had reasons, then, for trepidation when I asked Philip about her unarrested archive and then about access to the documents therein.[12] She granted me permission to view five boxes of what she had preserved. In my attempt to reconstruct the narrative of dissent I interpreted as embodied in her minor archive, I had concerns about undermining or impeding her own archival or authorial agency, which she had so assiduously struggled to preserve, and about issues related to voice and appropriation. In an attempt to sidestep such issues, we agreed that anything I wrote must meet with her approval and that she had the right, at any moment, to withdraw that approval. Any exchange, and any means by which I recorded what I found in her documents, she would monitor and ultimately sanction. After spending some time in an office rented in Toronto for the purpose of looking through her private boxes of papers, I appreciated the full gravity of what I had asked to examine.

It is, first and foremost, a rich archive. Like Rule's materials, those of Philip attest to her commitment to her activist pursuits and literary endeavours, but also to the patterns of racism in Canada and to the means and forms of advocacy Philip adopted to challenge such discrimination. The papers also showcase the range of requests she received from various quarters to speak out or write against racism.[13] Of the five boxes that Philip allowed me to peruse, three contained documents such as newspaper articles, letters, court transcripts, and other such materials that focused on media representation related to Philip, from 1989 to 2002. The newspaper articles addressed two incidents. The first of these was a supposed altercation between Philip and June Callwood, the outgoing president of PEN.[14] During the World Congress of PEN International held at Roy Thomson Hall in Toronto on 24 September 1989, protestors, among them Philip, gathered outside the hall to voice concerns about PEN Canada's lack of representation of writers of colour. The demonstration seems to have escalated, such that Callwood was allegedly accosted by the protestors when she seemed ready to ignore their objections. Media coverage about the demonstration, and specifically that which appeared in the *Globe and Mail*, described Philip in particular as having "tormented" Callwood, although she had merely approached her with a leaflet.[15]

Some four years later, Joey Slinger of the *Toronto Star* revived the incident, claiming to have been present when two protestors handed a pamphlet to Callwood, and then he named Philip as one of the two who "harangued [Callwood] with the accusation that PEN Canada didn't have enough black members." Callwood, he reported, told "a black woman to f— off."[16] In his column, Slinger added that Philip herself greatly embellished the incident by increasing "the number of f— offs to three," a form of artistic licence, he added, "attributable to her having been transformed in that moment from a writer hardly anybody had [ever] heard of" (A2). Slinger's article seems to imply that Philip, in heightening the conflict, was involved in a scheme of shameless self-promotion, although by that point she had already published no fewer than ten books. It did not seem to matter that *both* Callwood and Philip stated that Philip had said nothing provocative.[17] Nor did it seem to matter that the Ontario Press Council had taken up the matter for resolution.[18] Afterward, the *Toronto Star* printed a correction stating that Slinger's account "unfairly and inaccurately portrayed Ms. Philip's behaviour": "The *Star* did not intend to suggest that Ms. Philip was and is anything other than a respected author of poetry, fiction, and nonfiction and the recipient of a number of writers' awards" (Correction, 5 May 1990).

Thereafter, however, Philip would be repeatedly reconfigured in popular media discourse as a central figure in this conflict. Various newspaper journalists would call upon Slinger's initial column as a primary source of information and as a means to frame and legitimate the veracity of their own stories. Even years thereafter, journalists insisted on portraying Philip as directly fuelling the conflict. One article, by Don Sellar, appeared in the *Toronto Star* on 12 June 1993 and dealt directly with Slinger's article. Sellar noted that both Philip *and* Callwood said Philip had not "harangued" Callwood with accusations and that "the Ontario Press Council accepted Philip's version of the incident." However, he then noted that Slinger's article "fed new oxygen to [Philip's] smoldering quarrel with writer June Callwood" – although no such quarrel existed. Several articles appeared during this period and well after: one article appeared in *Toronto Life* in March 1993 and another by Judy Stoffman appeared in *Saturday Night* in April 1993. In the latter the author highlighted that "not since PEN-member June Callwood told Marlene NourbeSe Phillips [*sic*], a writer of color, to f— off has the organization found itself at the centre of such controversy." Still another appeared in *Now* magazine, penned by Enzo di Mathes in the 1–7 February 1996 issue, in which he featured the incident involving June Callwood. And again, on 12 November 2003 Martin Knelman of the *Toronto Star* wrote an article on the subject. These articles suggest the formation of a media-based discourse about Philip's person, one that legitimated the characterization of her as antagonistic and aggressive. This hypervisibility demonstrates how the media becomes another form of the unarrested archive: a self-generating one, along the lines of Jean Baudrillard's definition of a simulacrum, by which the media presents its own truth without recourse to other documents or facts. It is this proliferation of images that ultimately gave rise to Coren's attack on Philip, to which we now turn.

The vehicle of this second media-related incident was a radio broadcast several years later, on 7 September 1995; it used as a springboard the first media incident perpetuated by Slinger, borrowing his tactic of identifying her as a woman rather than a writer to create leverage for a public attack – but it was to have more severe repercussions. In his CFRB broadcast Coren made a number of caustic remarks about Philip's receiving an award from the Arts Foundation of Greater Toronto, singling her out although there were many other winners (Sandra Shamas, Peter Smith, Dennis Lee, John Scott, Peter Herrndorf, the Garys [Gary Cormier and Gary Topp], Atom Egoyan, and Olivia Chow were fellow recipients).[19] The press release about the award recipients had been picked up by several newspapers, including the *Globe and Mail* and the *Toronto Star*,[20] and by a number of television networks, among them Citytv, Global, CFTO, and CBC.[21] The Arts Foundation of Greater Toronto had only been registered as a non-profit charitable organization the year before, in 1995, and existed to provide support for various disciplines of art. That year, as one newspaper article indicated, there was no monetary value attached to the award, as funding for the arts had become scarce.[22] By contrast, two years prior each winner received five thousand dollars; in the year of Philip's win the award bestowed only social recognition for artistic efforts in a particular category.

The awards were designed to "focus public attention on the superb artists who have helped make the arts and culture of Greater Toronto a treasured national resource" and to generate "community-based recognition of individual artistic achievement." They were given in the fields of visual arts, performing arts, music, media arts, writing/publishing, architecture/design, and lifetime achievement.[23] The event attracted high-profile community members; the year before Philip won, approximately seven hundred guests attended, most of whom worked in the arts, from art administrators and publishers to "people who work in the film and music industries."[24] The unpaid jury members who decided on the recipients changed from year to year and were also drawn from a "broad cross section of the local arts community."[25] Those on the jury the year that Philip was given the award included Dionne Brand, Ian Pearson, Sharon Fernandes, and Kate Elliott.[26]

A typed transcript of Coren's broadcast about this press release was retained in Philip's papers – to strategic effect when situated among her own papers that showcase her distinguished literary career.[27] Positioning the transcript within the archive of Standard Broadcasting,[28] otherwise known as CFRB, would have invited a global perspective on the station's broadcasts rather than showcasing how Coren's broadcast is informed by a series of previous media reports and what the repercussions might have been. Indeed, in its current context within Philip's archive, Coren's broadcast throws the implicit racial polarization in Canada into stark relief in even the recent past, and, specifically, heightens the means by which Philip was working through the stigmatization imposed by a form of popular culture that positioned her as a transgressive figure. It is worth examining that broadcast in its entirety because its contents also refer to another mediation – a discursive archive by which Coren could legitimate his attitude towards and assumptions about Philip and engage in a polemics that positioned her as a shameful figure, as "inadequate or diminished" (qtd. in Bouson 2). Rather than approaching the archive as a tangible institution or repository that holds documents or material evidence, we might view the documents themselves as a combination of popular and official publicly disseminated information about social events and persons of the period, by which Philip's activism was contextualized.

Michael Coren's Broadcast

Coren opens his broadcast by identifying himself as a writer, perhaps to generate legitimacy and position himself as an authority for the remarks that were to follow: "I've written seven books now and that's actually how I got into media, I suppose, by being a biographer and a writer. I know about the literary community." He thus draws a direct link between his position as radio host and his own literary productivity, but suggests that the former was sanctioned by, if not secondary to, his status as writer. That status, he implies, was the source of his knowledge and right to speak about "the literary community." This claim, however, is not persuasive given the nature of his work, which largely focused on biographies of British and American writers rather than those of Canada – that is, his understanding of the community did not necessarily encompass the Canadian literary scene nor, microscopically, that of Toronto. He had, however, just published a book with Stoddart titled *Setting it Right*, a collection of his columns and articles printed in newspapers such as the *Globe and Mail*. His self-proclaimed status as writer might be seen to have been deployed to generate leverage for the remarks that followed.

In his broadcast, he quoted Philip speaking on the award she was about to receive, saying that she had not expected such an honour because of her previous work as an activist: "I'm well aware I've taken positions in cultural issues that have not endeared me to some people" (qtd. in Mietkiewicz). This point was foundational to Coren's remarks, although he would also focus on the monetary gain he believed Philip was to receive from the award. He argued that Philip

> has received through taxpayers' money the Toronto Arts Award. That means she's contributed a great deal to the Toronto arts scene. *This is a woman* who came here in 1968 and has done nothing but defecate upon this country and this city and the Canadian culture since she came here.

> *This is a woman* who tried to get Show Boat banned because it was racist. *This is the woman* who accused June Callwood, the social activist, of racism.
>
> *This is a woman* who boycotted, protested, demonstrated vehemently outside the ROM, the Royal Ontario Museum, when they had their exhibition, this showing about colonial Africa. So harsh was Marlene NourbeSe Philip and *her people* that the director of that exhibit, in fact, even left the country because the woman in question had graffiti spread on her wall and she was threatened. I'm not saying NourbeSe Philip directly did that, but she was part of the demonstration. (1; italics mine)

In these remarks he might be seen to invoke a disciplinary discourse, inviting open punishment for Philip as he positions her first as an "outsider," whose "people" are not part of the Canadian socio-political fabric, and second, as "woman" rather than writer. He consistently refuses her the name and status of a writer, the effect of which is to reinforce anonymity, especially since, as he claimed, he "knows" the literary community. The emphasis on her race and gender might be interpreted as a tactic. In terms of the latter, women are critiqued primarily for their "category membership – as females first and foremost" because femaleness carries a "devalued status" (Schur 6–7). His tactic here seems similar to that of Slinger, who also referred to her status as a woman rather than a writer, and suggested that scarcely "anybody" had heard of her. In highlighting her status as a woman, Coren seems to configure her as an illegitimate saboteur, someone who agitates for the sake of self-advancement rather than for a cause to which she is deeply committed. Yet the article from which Coren drew his quotation of Philip states that she was being "recognized for an impressive body of work that includes a children's novel, three books of poetry, an adult novel … and two collections of essays" (Mietkiewicz G9); these collections of essays directly tackle issues related to racism in Canada.

Coren also attempted to create a series of dichotomies that located Philip as a transgressive figure who cooperates with "her people" rather than with "the Canadian culture," one that he characterized as monolithic, as racially white, with normative cultural values and standards of behaviour outside of which she presumably operated. He endeavoured to render "the Canadian culture" as a source of legitimacy that required protection from the assaults rendered by her and "her people." He thus "construct[ed] the minority group as the oppressor" and those "in power ... as victims," strategies that "deny the legitimacy and autonomy of 'other (black) subjectivities and struggles'" (Mackey

423). He insinuates that her activism on behalf of the African Canadian community is illegitimate, which claim extends beyond her person: it is a means of undermining activism in general and racially denigrating a collective.

In so doing, he sidesteps the racist undercurrents of two prominent moments in Toronto history: the *Into the Heart of Africa* exhibition displayed at the Royal Ontario Museum in 1989, and the musical performance of *Show Boat* that premiered in Toronto in 1993. Criticism is replete with analyses of both the ROM exhibition and *Show Boat.*[29] The debates largely revolve around issues of race and cultural appropriation, but also representations of race and multiculturalism in Canada. In criticism, these two events are also largely approached as landmark sites of activism, and Philip was one of several who registered protest against both the exhibit and the musical production, especially for their investment in the production of attitudes that undermined racial minorities.[30] In particular, the former was challenged for its stereotypical representations of African people, the latter for "its depiction of 19th century imperialism in Central Africa" (Mietkiewicz G9). Philip herself addressed the controversy related to *Show Boat* in *Showing Grit* (1993), in which she explored the implications of Garth Drabinsky's production, that is, "the historical and cultural milieu of the musical and what it meant for the African Canadian population in Toronto."[31] The African Canadian community in Toronto became involved in these events as a means of "mobilizing against racism in contemporary multicultural Canada" (Mackey 412).

Two points are relevant here. First, the Royal Ontario Museum had, until *Into the Heart of Africa*, not represented the Black community in the seventy-seven-year history of its exhibitions. This lacuna highlights its complicity with official and national archival institutions, which had also neglected such representation. The second point of relevance is more specific and stems from what Coren implied: when he referred to Philip's public interventions and social activism, he positioned her as *the* spokesperson for these two sites of activism, rather than as one member of a collective who regarded the exhibit and musical as racially denigrating. He rendered her hyper-visible when he pitted her against Callwood, whom he identified as the sole "social activist" of the two. He exacerbated that indignity by invoking the terms of the abject – social protest as "defecation." Via these strategies, Philip's social activism is stigmatized and her public interventions constructed as a narrative of deviancy. He also calls into question Philip's contribution to the

Canadian literary scene by identifying that she was not born in Canada. The implications of this extend well beyond Philip, encompassing all those who are not Canadian by birth. (Ironically, Coren immigrated to Canada and was not himself a citizen by birth.) His remarks reveal his belief that Canadian citizenship is determined by one's race.

In short, Coren's polemical broadcast hinges on three key aspects of Philip's identity: her status as a woman, as a diasporic subject or immigrant, and as racially other. As McKittrick notes, the "black female body" is often regarded as "a sexed, (dis)located and anywhere New World subject" (224), for it is "on the body that the complexity and ambiguity of history, race, racism and place are inscribed" (225). His emphasis on her body encapsulated these attitudes. He defined Philip as a (dis)located and improper immigrant whose place in the nation was foreclosed. His anaphoric repetition of "This is a woman" also highlighted her gender, as it simultaneously detracted from her status as writer or artist: "This woman, to win the Toronto Arts Award, is an insult to every other artist, to the people of Toronto."

According to Bouson, shaming rhetoric is often deployed in a patriarchal culture to subject the female body to regulation and control: "Conceived of as defective or deficient from male norms and as potentially diseased, women have long been embodiments of shame in our culture, and, indeed, the female socialization process can be viewed as a prolonged immersion in shame" (2). Held up against a "clean and proper [male] body" (4), a woman's body is thus "associated with out-of-control passions and appetites and with something dirty and defiling" (3); however, to showcase a woman as such and to invoke disciplinary shame, she must suffer "exposure" of her deviancy (5). Coren made use of such rhetoric to "expose" Philip: he deployed the terms of the abject by "uncovering" the purportedly unjust, even perverse, process of awarding such a distinction to a "scheming" or "unscrupulous" woman rather than to an artist.

The process of cultural, intellectual, and physical devaluation was extended when he identified her as immigrant. Indeed, that process shifted beyond her person to African culture itself, as he highlighted and demeaned the African dress she had selected for two publicity photos. As a diasporic subject, Philip would destabilize the homogeneous national ideal to which Coren seemed to hold fast. He thus reinforced the "binaries of colonial discourse" that characterize immigrants "as being in exile from a singular nation home" and that deny them the possibility of taking "up confident residence" (Page 2). He invoked this discourse in his choice of the photograph he discussed during his broadcast. There were two photographs of Philip in circulation at the time of the award announcement: one was a group publicity photo that appeared in the Toronto Arts Award Foundation newsletter on 6 September 1995, and the other was a photo of her alone that accompanied a 7 September *Toronto Star* article.[32] Coren focused on the latter photo, the effect of which was to heighten her isolation from the other winners of the award. He remarked that in this photo she is "wearing, you know, the compulsory nanny glasses and with something looking like a dirty tea towel wrapped around her head. I don't know, maybe that's African costume. I don't know what it is." His dismissive remark about her "African costume" was amplified when he likened her headdress to a "dirty tea towel." That image, first, associated her with female domesticity rather than artistic endeavour, and, second, disparaged her in its implication that she was unkempt. Indeed, Coren's indictment suggested she was culturally confused: she used a "tea towel," arguably a symbol of Western civilization and domesticity, as part of a costume related to her African ancestry. As Philip was to argue elsewhere, these references to her and her attire were demeaning not just to her person, but also to African culture – she considered them a seemingly deliberate attempt on his part to diminish her status as writer and to demean a larger class of people.[33] His comment on her "compulsory nanny glasses" also subtly identified her age – another source of shame for women (Bouson 11). As Bouson notes, the process of shaming involves "de-forming and re-forming of bodily and social spaces" to turn others away from the person being shamed (14). As well, Coren's use of the definite article regarding her glasses – "the" nanny glasses, not just any pair – seems to suggest her deviousness: she was apparently adopting a pose, posturing for the sake of effect.

He concluded his remarks by, at last, naming her, but only while incorrectly observing that she was to be the recipient of an award that involved money:

> Anyway, Marlene NourbeSe Philip has been given money and the Toronto Arts Award for defecating on the arts in Toronto and on the Canadian people. And you know what? It doesn't surprise me. It's the way things are going.
>
> … I, for one, am sick and tired of people like this looking at us with such contempt and saying: I'll take your money, I'll call you every name under the sun and I'll laugh all the way to the bank.

The production of race relations in Canada – its multicultural contours and the corresponding deep racism against which that multiculturalism is upheld – is restaged in these remarks. One ideological strain clearly sanctions her role as social activist and author, as is evidenced in the fact that the Arts Foundation of Greater Toronto was valorizing her in the form of an award. As Philip herself was later to observe, "this kind of attack goes to the heart of what this city is supposed to be about."[34] The other strain, upon which Coren was relying, characterized her as abject, someone whose perverse behaviour was being irrationally rewarded. His reference to "the way things are going" may reference the popular rhetoric of multiculturalism and the imputed rewarding of those of visible difference – or "outsiders" rather than "true Canadians," only the latter of whom are worthy of public honours. In other words, he employed a discourse that suggested newcomers to Canada were either ungrateful or disloyal when they pointed out injustices in the political framework of the country. Although it is not clear to what group Coren referred when he makes reference to "people like this" – those of a different race, those who criticize race, or those who immigrated to Canada – what is key is his positioning of Philip outside of the Canadian community: "people like this" regard "us" – the *real* Canadian community – with contempt. In making such a remark, Coren maps the lines for who might be considered a Canadian citizen and who might not. Evidently, Philip did not meet his terms.

Philip's minor archive reanimates these questions about citizenship, as it also demonstrates the disjunction between his broadcast and her life's work. Her papers extend well beyond this particular typescript of Coren's broadcast. Of the boxes of material that Philip retained, there are many other documents related to her publication history, to public talks she gave, to her efforts related to social activism. There are a considerable number of papers that concern this incident – a strategically ironic commemoration of an event that would have denied her dignity and repressed her but for her own voiced protest and her diligence in keeping records that collectively serve as a form of dissent. These papers also show that her refusals to be "disciplined" were not easily accomplished. The dispute with Coren would be resolved in a legal settlement approximately seven years later; during those years Coren would offer a half-hearted retraction, and Philip would marshal support from various quarters, especially from others whose own protests might have registered some effect in denouncing Coren's statements. Indeed, the proliferation of documents that followed these media events attests to the effects his public disparagement had upon Philip and the African Canadian community. They also reveal that Coren himself participated in a system that would endeavour to deny Philip and African Canadians a place in the Canadian imaginary.

The Aftermath

Philip's archive contains many documents that trace events after Coren's initial broadcast and the largely inadequate response rendered by institutions at local, provincial, and federal levels. One of these documents is a transcript of Coren's rather ambiguous public retraction, on 20 October 1995, in which he identified some components of his broadcast statement that might have been erroneous; Philip noted in a letter to Richard Ouzounian that he claimed he had "no evidence on which to base certain 'factual' statements about [her] activities."[35] Still, he did not publicly apologize for the remarks he made about Philip's race or about her career as a writer; his lack of a proper retraction and apology, Philip argued, was a way of reiterating the original "thrust of his statements."[36] He noted that, to the "extent that my comments could be misunderstood" regarding her supposed antagonism towards Callwood, he wished to "retract any such erroneous impression." He then recontextualized his remarks about her alleged participation in the protests outside the Royal Ontario Museum that eventually led to the resignation of its curator, Jeanne Cannizzo. Rather than retract the statement, he suggested that he did not have "any information to contradict her claim" about her lack of involvement in the protests, and pointed out that she had published several articles on the subject. He did not withdraw his belief that the award should not have been bestowed upon Philip; in fact, he reiterated his "sense of revulsion" at the award.[37] Roughly six weeks later, on 6 December 1995, he offered another on-air statement in which he suggested that the references to her use of a "dirty tea towel" as an "African costume" were warranted because it was "an integral part of the persona she has chosen to present to the public as a social activist."[38]

Several surviving letters reveal that Philip did not thereafter attend the awards ceremony and suggest the reasons for that decision. (Her husband, Paul Chamberlain, went in her stead to thank the audience and collect the award.[39] The remarks she asked to be conveyed that evening included the expressed hope that people had, as the result of her work, "found new and more liberatory ways of seeing the world" – perhaps an indirect, ironic thrust at Coren's radio broadcast.) A letter to Judith Thompson, a former recipient of the award, on 23 October 1995 declared her intention not to attend, and her regret that she was unable to, but did not offer details about the reasons for her decision. A letter from Philip dated 18 February 1996 sheds more light on her decision. Julia Howell, executive director of the Arts Foundation of Greater Toronto, had written to Philip on 6 October 1995, a month after Coren's broadcast, that the foundation would "probably write a letter to the station manager" about the incident; on 27 October 1995 Philip wrote to Richard Ouzounian, president of the foundation, to point out that no such letter had yet been issued. As of 18 February 1996, when she wrote again to Howell, Ouzounian had yet to acknowledge her letter. The letter reveals that Philip was evidently perturbed by the foundation's lack of support, and not only by Ouzonian's lack of response but also by Howell's "lackadaisical" reaction:[40]

> I waited and waited but your letter was only forthcoming after the Awards dinner. It is hard not to conclude that the Foundation's response to Coren's attack on me and on the Foundation was not a priority.[41]

For good reason, Howell was not immune from Philip's suspicions about lack of proper support, although Philip was to contextualize the actions of Howell within the policies of the foundation. As she pointed out to Howell, it was the foundation that decided to give her the award; and it was the foundation that failed, when the situation with Coren arose, to address the matter swiftly and to clarify the nature of the award publicly. The foundation remained silent until after the awards ceremony, and consequently Philip felt "hung out to dry";[42] not to respond, she had earlier observed, would appear as a form of "collusion."[43] She had reason to approach the foundation in this manner, the same reason that may have played a role in the foundation's delayed response: CFRB was one of the "founders" of the event, a major media sponsor of Arts Week, of which the awards were a featured event.[44]

There were measures the foundation might have taken. As Philip noted, it could have "written to the President of CFRB promptly and copied it to the CRTC" and then "issued a press release affirming confidence."[45] Howell had also apparently asked Philip for a copy of the remarks she was planning to make at the awards ceremony, what she later claimed was "standard practice" for "a production of this kind." Philip's letter, dated 1 November, suggests that, as a result, she felt "singled out" and "controlled" by the process. The foundation did not issue a statement the day or the evening of the awards. As Philip observed, no great disruption would have been occasioned by some statement, even "a motherhood and maple syrup statement about the need to respect and tolerate differences, particularly given the fact that the Awards have to do with Toronto – a city of many races and ethnic groups."[46] She suggested, moreover, that the foundation lodge a complaint with the CRTC to control "this sort of gutter journalism that passes as commentary and analysis."[47]

In her letter of 3 November Howell suggested that the delay in responding to the radio broadcast was due to the fact that she wished to consult "with board members with whom I have confidence." On behalf of the foundation, she did write to CFRB, addressing many facets of Coren's virulent attack upon Philip. One key point Howell raised in her letter was the fact that Philip did not in fact receive any money from the award and that, moreover, the Arts Foundation that conferred such awards operated independently of taxpayers:

> If [M. NourbeSe Philip] had [received such money] it would not be coming from the public purse. Had Mr. Coren done his research he would know that tough times have prevented the Arts Foundation from presenting cash Awards these past two years. He would also know that the Arts Foundation raises close to 95% of its funds from the private sector and that corporate and individual donors have confidently and supportively respected jury decisions.

The awards had been designed to bestow honour rather than money – or shame – and, as Howell noted, to "thank artists in our city for their contributions." The honour was not one for which artists could apply, and, Howell added, his "mean-spiritedness" was vented at the expense of "one of our more thoughtful, devoted and courageous citizens." Howell was, of course, trying to effect a reversal by conferring dignity upon Philip – and, by extension, the awards program – and by emphasizing her status as both artist and citizen, two of the three foundational aspects of Coren's attack.[48]

Philip tried to find recourse in other quarters as well, in one instance sending a letter to Gary Slaight, vice-president and general manager of CFRB, in which she noted the ironies about Coren's referencing his status as an author while not "commenting on a fellow author's merits" or even making "a passing reference to that author's work." On

20 October she sent a letter to Barbara Hall, who was at the time both the mayor and chair of the Mayor's Committee on Racism, questioning the principle of freedom of expression that authorized Coren's making unfounded remarks and correcting Coren's misstatements: nothing in the broadcast was "accurate or true except for the fact that I came to this country in 1968."[49] She sent other letters to the CRTC, the Federal Human Rights Commission, and the Urban Alliance. Others rallied to support her, including Beverley Daurio, and Gillian Morton of the Women's Centre of the University of Toronto.[50] In response to Philip's letter to CFRB protesting Coren's broadcast, the station defended Coren's broadcast (letter dated 8 November 1995), a position they reiterated when they wrote to the CRTC on 5 January, 23 February, and 21 March 1996, and again when they wrote their report on 2 July 1996 and sent it to Allan J. Darling, secretary general of the CRTC. On 7 March 1996, Philip wrote again to Darling[51] to suggest that a station such as CFRB, the "largest private broadcaster in Canada," was "in a position to do great damage to individuals like myself and groups which are marginalized in this society." In CFRB's letter of March 1996, however, the station contended that Coren had not made "abusive comments on the basis of race" and that he had gone on air, in the first instance, "to retract and apologize for several inaccuracies made in his initial broadcast," and, in the second, to "express regret for his reference to [her] headdress" but also to affirm that "his comments were not actuated by race."[52] They argued that his remarks were focused upon her role as a social activist.[53] Indeed, they maintained, Coren was "distressed" when he discovered he had "misspoken."[54] Nonetheless, since the station had already made an investigation into the broadcast and Coren had made on-air retractions, they were satisfied. For the report for the CRTC, under the subheading "Relatively Small Number of Complaints," the station indicated that their programming was intentionally created to generate both "comment and controversy."[55] The CRTC did little beyond inviting a response to the allegations of racism and asked for accountability in terms of CFRB's own policies promoting "high standards" of broadcasting.[56] In the end, CFRB would defend Coren, and the CRTC would defend CFRB.

Philip would discover this when she took other serious measures to address the incident with Coren, initially by registering an official complaint with the CRTC (on 20 October 1995) and then by contacting other organizations, including the federal Human Rights Commission, the Urban Alliance on Race Relations, the Mayor's Committee on Racism,[57] the League for Human Rights of B'nai Brith Canada, and the Media Coalition. Maxwell Yalden of the Canadian Human Rights Commission issued a letter to Keith Spicer, chair of the CRTC, on 16 November 1995 to ask for "prompt attention" to the matter.[58] Shortly thereafter, the Mayor's Committee on Racism agreed to request that both CFRB and Michael Coren issue a public apology, a letter they sent on 1 February 1996,[59] and then struck a subcommittee to monitor and assess this issue.[60] The League for Human Rights also sent a letter to Allan Darling of the CRTC in which they argued that Coren's program violated the CRTC radio regulations and asked that "corrective action" be taken.[61] The Urban Alliance on Race Relations wrote to the CRTC that they understood CRFB's operating license was "up for renewal" and to request that "the station be required to provide programming that reflects the attitudes, opinions and values of all races and cultures across Canada."[62] All of these organizations, as well as Philip, argued that Coren had breached section 3(b) of the Broadcasting Act, which prohibits broadcasts of "abusive comment that, when taken in context, tends or is likely to expose an individual or group or class of individual to hatred or contempt on the basis of race."[63] This act was invoked in CFRB's own policies for open-line programming: "CFRB will not permit the broadcast of any abusive comment contrary to section 3(b) of the *Radio Regulations, 1986*."[64] Under a separate section, titled "Abusive Comment," the document stipulated that

> a licensee shall not broadcast any abusive comment that, when taken in context, tends or is likely to expose an individual or a group or class of individuals to hatred or contempt on the basis of race, national or ethnic origin, colour, religion, sex, sexual orientation, age or mental or physical disability.

The letters charged that Coren's comments had application well beyond Philip and the persona she "chose" to present to the public as an African Canadian.[65] The question was thus whether or not Coren had indeed "tested" or "breached" the limit of what was permissible over the airways, whether his remarks could be justified under Charter provisions regarding freedom of expression, and whether or not the ideals of pluralism, multiculturalism, and democracy had been violated.

The letters had some impact: although the CRTC did not accept Philip's complaints as legitimate reasons for preventing the renewal of CFRB's license, which was indeed extended to 31 August 1999, they did so only for three years rather than the customary seven. This shortened period would allow the CRTC to reconsider the station "in accordance with the Commission's regional plan."[66] It had indeed reviewed the comments sent in by the Media Coalition, MediaWatch, Philip, and the African Canadian Legal Clinic, but determined that, "while testing the limit of what would be seen as permissible," Coren's remarks did not in fact breach the terms of the act or the Radio Regulations, 1986.[67] In a letter dated 8 May 1996 Darling also responded to letters from Philip's solicitors and from the groups and individuals who had written in support of her. Although he acknowledged that "some very harsh statements" had been made, he pointed out that Coren had denied that his comments had "any racial connotation" and that, on the whole, "broadcasters perform an important public service in a democratic society in dealing with public issues."[68]

On 11 June 1996 Philip wrote to then-MP Jean Augustine because, she argued, it "appear[ed] that the CRTC [had also] exonerated Michael Coren and CFRB."[69] In the interim, in February 1996, CFRB hired Cecil Foster, a Barbadian-born author and broadcaster, as a full-time radio host to contribute to the recognition of visible minorities in the City of Toronto.[70] He had already made a series of guest appearances in the fall of 1995. Augustine took up the matter with Clifford Lincoln, the chair of the Standing Committee on Canadian Heritage, whose response indicated the chord that Philip had struck. She counted on the support of such key individuals to gain traction in her struggle with Coren: the unfortunate situation, Lincoln wrote, "clearly underscores the need for standards of civility in public debate in a multicultural society such as ours."[71] Still, he could offer no direct line of action, since the Standing Committee did not intervene in individual cases. He nonetheless contacted the Canadian Human Rights Commission and the International Centre for Human Rights and Democratic Development, both of which replied that the matter fell outside their jurisdiction.[72] Just after the end of the three years of CFRB's license renewal, in 5 January 2000, Philip tried again: she contacted the CRTC's successor to Darling, Ursula Menke, to call into question the record CFRB had with African Canadians and other minority groups and to suggest that it had shown a "certain animus towards the African Canadian communities."[73] The license was renewed again from September 1999 to 31 August 2006.[74] No apology from Coren to Philip was yet forthcoming.

Philip had already been actively involved in calling upon various policing agents in an attempt to draw attention to the discriminatory practices at play. Coren had endeavoured to characterize her conduct and writings as occasioning a rupture in the cultural integrity of the nation; yet, as Philip strove to prove, his activities caused a rupture by violating the apparent terms and values of the multicultural ideal – those called upon by Jean Augustine and at the core of the national imaginary. Eventually, she found recourse: she engaged at her own expense legal counsel to take up the cause, a necessary form of redress when CFRB continued to maintain that it was "a good corporate citizen" and that the complaints levelled against the station might serve as a check but not "as an absolute barrier."[75] Philip called upon the Arts Foundation of Toronto to protest, to express its disapproval, and to support initiatives she suggested as a form of redress: "anti-racist workshops for CFRB staff and broadcasters; anti-racist announcements and commentaries about the contribution of African Canadians to Canada, and an annual Award for a young writer in the area of human rights."[76] CFRB considered these remedies, however "laudable," "inappropriate and totally unwarranted" for the situation at hand.[77] In making these requests, Philip wanted to show that, although Coren's attack seemed to be directed specifically at her, the issues that attack raised concerning race had larger implications: they were the very ones against which Philip had a history of agitating, that she had placed at the forefront of her social activism, and that were of larger concern to the African Canadian community in Toronto.[78] Perhaps more importantly, these were purportedly the same issues upon which ideals of Canadian multiculturalism and racial tolerance had been founded.

The Court Case

The confrontation between Philip and Coren eventually found its way into the judicial system, at Philip's initiative: she brought a libel action against Coren and CFRB. By November 1995 she had engaged the legal services of Bellmore and Moore to address several issues that arose out of the alleged violations of CFRB's own policies.[79] Philip and Coren thus employed two different boundary-making devices to determine the lines for behaviour and citizenship (Erikson 12): he used the media in the form of public broadcasting and she the legal system. Coren might be seen as using his talk show to stage a form of public punishment and to suggest that she was a transgressive figure who was engaged in activities "outside the margins" of ideal citizenship. At the same time, he may have seen himself as the "policing agent" whose duty it was "to guard the cultural integrity of the community" (Erikson 13). She, however, endeavoured to locate some form of exoneration through the legal system while calling attention to his conduct as fostering a climate of racial intolerance. As she herself noted in a letter to Allan Darling, "an integral part of regaining one's dignity and self-respect and healing is engaging one's self in correcting the injustice."[80] Certainly, Coren's broadcast seemed to have had some kind of effect upon her career: Philip did more than forty public readings in the five years leading up to the broadcast; in the six years that followed, she did only eleven.[81]

Because of the drawn-out nature of the legal process, Philip was obliged to change lawyers twice. Although there was a legal settlement, in March 2002, she still felt that "something in me was not honoured in that process." As Beth Symes, her lawyer, observed, legal cases are not necessarily "good vehicles to do good," whatever the outcome: they still do not "provide the closure you are seeking."[82] Three years thereafter, on 30 November 2005, CFRB fired Michael Coren – apparently not because of the conflict with Philip, but for verbally abusing a caller who claimed to be obese. (The call-in had been set up in advance; Coren claimed to have been trying to expose North American hypocrisy and to challenge "the sort of people who routinely blame starvation in African and Asia.")[83] If the settlement with Philip had some kind of bearing on this decision, it was never declared as having been a factor. Whatever the reasons for his termination and whatever the terms of the settlement, it was still difficult for Philip to resume the routine of her former life in the literary community of Toronto and, more generally, in Canada.[84] Confidentiality over the terms of the settlement was legally enforced, and therefore the details could not be released to influence media presentations about her thereafter. There was some sense that justice had prevailed in that Coren was terminated from his position at CFRB, albeit for a different cause. Yet Philip suffered from the "misrecognition" that attached to her via the flurry of media attention.

It is her unarrested archive that serves as a second and perhaps more powerful recourse, another form of redress; it demonstrates how a second strategy in the form of an archive might be used to guard the boundaries related to questions of race and identity. In this instance, Philip's minor archive thus becomes extraordinarily charged, a way of remediating these events and a means by which to bypass the stigma of the immediate context that bore upon her identity as an African Caribbean woman in Canada. She forged a space that is private and withheld, which suggests that the lines of demarcation related to citizenship might be negotiated by several different agents and in vastly different ways. Therein, she points out how cultural difference – what has often been defined as politically benign rather than as emanating from manifestations of power – is instrumental to generating exclusive practices and hierarchal formations (see Mackey 417). The media responses to Philip demonstrate that the "place of black femininity rests outside modern conceptions of rationality, citizenship, and belonging," and that a Black woman is perceived "outside modernity (disenfranchised, speechless, irrational, (un)definable, all flesh), and inside modernity (thus signifying what proper modern subjects are: not her, not black, not black and female)" (McKittrick 226).

Philip has thus used a minor archive to effect something "major": it reveals the larger struggles related to citizenship, the means by which to create space for identities and belonging, as it also exposes the instances and "discourses of chaos" that subjugate Black women and their bodies (McKittrick 232). Her archive is replete with documents that offer a defence against the writing over of her subjectivity by the media – she is social activist rather than social outcast, legitimate protestor rather than public parasite. Indeed, her records perform a counter-discursive function that showcase the kinds of interventions Philip made to engage with and locate herself within the African Canadian community and to protect that community and other races from the effects of racism. Although there is, of course, no "guarantee of recovery" – of facts, or representations – such an unarrested archive at least in its specificity provides a means of complicating powerful discursive formulations holding that the political fabric of Canada is conducive to multiculturalism and is close to an ideal from which it is actually very far indeed. Even in its current private state, Philip's minor archive contains the very kinetic, radical potential to remediate and contest those media images in circulation, to challenge the boundaries of idealized citizenship, and perhaps most importantly, to offer creative insubordinations that counteract official narratives about the nation-state and about its citizens.

Conclusion

This book began by considering how Michel Foucault characterizes the archive, in its broadest sense, as determining what is articulable in a given period. Using his formulation about "the law of what can be said" as the starting point, I employ a more narrow sense of his definition to suggest that what can be enunciated in and about a given period related to women authors has traditionally been limited by what a repository holds. I observe that women authors, who could initially make only tenuous claims to authorship, have increasingly worked to expand that principle in terms of the visibility of their publications and their literary records. As a result, they are being increasingly recognized for their contributions and have secured greater prominence over the course of the twentieth century. For various reasons related to the growing socio-political value attributed to women's achievements, their status has indeed shifted, as this mounting attention to their records demonstrates. Established institutions have since expanded and continue to develop their holdings to include the literary records of women writers.

In spite of a shifting socio-political climate that is more conducive to safeguarding the papers of women writers, it does not follow that women authors will ultimately decide to deposit their records in official institutions; however, when they do so, it is clear they have learned to select the respective institution with great care. How and where they safeguard their papers becomes an articulation of the socio-political framework within which they are working, and showcases how women's expressions of self-agency in relation to their literary records have shifted over time. It is crucial to assess not only the reasons for their safeguarding of their papers – if they did retain them – but also where they housed those papers and what materials they decided to retain. It is further revealing of women writers' agencies to consider with whom they negotiated to set up their respective archives and to advance their writing careers: the literary materials they retain are as significant as the institutions in which their papers are preserved. Indeed, both the materials and the decision about where to house them may serve as registers of how to expand spaces for women writers, to challenge the very structures in which they are housed, and, sometimes, to thwart the circulation of discourses that would limit or threaten women authors' agencies.

To that end, I postulate that we may characterize the different approaches to and modes by which both archives and women's agencies are defined. In this book, I offer five types of arrested and unarrested archives: the archive of embodiment, the archive of kinship, the archive of imminence, the archive of activism, and the minor archive. These are certainly not exhaustive, but offer a preliminary range researchers might employ to approach or analyse women's records and their means of expressing self-agency through or against established repositories. *Unarrested Archives* thus focuses on questions related to how the literary archives of Canadian women writers come to be forged within, against, or outside centralized repositories of official records; it considers what political engagements these women writers represent and what form their agencies assumed as they negotiated directly or indirectly with those who assisted in the publication process and then with established institutions to preserve their records – unless, as was the case with M. NourbeSe Philip, they decided to forego the process altogether.

In *Unarrested Archives*, I have also argued in support of extending researchers' explorations of materials, from those under house arrest in centralized institutions to those that are located in more unconventional sites: women's literary records are sometimes unarrested, located beyond the purview of formal institutions, or embedded in archives that do not focus intentionally or exclusively on their work or accomplishments. These records hold the potential to generate a range of socio-political effects, including meaningful insights about sites of epistemological privilege, and perspectives from which to view that privilege. This potential also allows unarrested archives to complicate the "arrested" or static nature of more formal holdings, even when women writers' papers do find their way into such centralized repositories. To call up another definition of "arrested," "fixing" critical attention on women's papers and archives, in whatever form they are manifested, does not thereby produce a static body of scholarship. Instead, this book is designed to show, first, that there are multiple forms of archives; second, that scholarly attention might yet be directed towards locating new avenues and approaches to women's archives; and third, that researchers can continue to shift the process by which women writers have been critically neglected.

Indeed, gaps in women's records still exist, and these gaps sometimes speak volumes in relation to the law of "what could *not* be said"; they also invite researchers to locate renewed research perspectives and methods. As Rodney G.S. Carter notes, archival silences are often the "manifestation of the actions of the powerful in denying the marginal access to archives," a process that occludes the ability of marginal groups "to form social history and memory" (215). Even so, no archive is ever complete. Absences in archives are occasioned for a variety of reasons, from the archival practices of institutions, to individual concerns about privacy, to familial interventions made on behalf of authors. Sometimes, these gaps are wilfully constructed by the authors themselves because, as we saw in the chapter on Sheila Watson, authors wish to shape the interpretive lenses that are thereafter applied to their records and that generate narratives about their lives; or because, as the chapter on M. NourbeSe Philip illustrates, institutions may not show themselves responsible to particular communities and authors are thus reluctant to house their papers with them. These absences from official establishments gesture towards archival records that are "unarrested" – that is, literary records that are withheld by authors from institutions that would not only preserve such records, but perhaps also construct a meaning in relation to them that is not consonant with an author's own agenda and her socio-political objectives. Such an author would therefore avoid depositing her literary records with an institution to express self-agency. At other times, however, absences in the record are created as established repositories misplace, accidentally destroy, or discard materials when they are no longer deemed relevant to contemporary collecting practices. Some government-sanctioned institutions that are not devoted to archival practices also intentionally try to create such gaps in knowledge when the materials are regarded as threatening to the state. So it is in the chapter on Jane Rule, in which I explore how the state intervened in two separate ways to detain papers and books that it regarded as detrimental to the national imaginary. In generating new perspectives, researchers can better respond to such absences and chart the lives of women as writers and their cultural productions, even when centralized repositories are silent on the subject. Implicitly in this chapter, I consider transnational archives and the implications for papers that cross national boundaries, although it is not a focus of the argument.

Unarrested Archives is thus oriented towards, first, expanding the definition of archives in relation to Canadian female authorship; second, reorienting critical approaches to archival materials; and third, assessing what materials we do have and how to use these in order to evaluate how Canadian women authors expressed various forms of self-agency. Although I begin with a more traditional understanding of archives – first, as a material collection of papers housed in (or outside of) an institution, and second, as the institution, which is authorized by the state and given over to the preservation of such materials – I also work towards enlarging critical scholarship about what constitutes the archive and about our approaches to literary records. Researchers may reconsider how to expand their methods from arrested to unarrested archives, the paradigm I set up in the introduction to this book. An expansion of such methods, it should be noted, is not meant to disparage current archival practices, institutions, or archivists who have worked diligently in troubling socio-political conditions to preserve what they can. Rather, the book is meant to serve as invitation to researchers to enlarge and develop approaches to women writers' records in order to compensate for past losses.

This study is also not meant to be comprehensive or definitive, but rather to offer a series of possible readings of arrested/unarrested archives. Indeed, one possibility for further study is related to questions of digitization. Some materials from the Pauline Johnson fonds housed at the McMaster University archives, for example, have already been digitized, one of the first such initiatives in Canada, undertaken around the mid-1990s. Discussions are underway regarding digitization of materials – some of her letters to her husband – from the Sheila Watson fonds at the University of Toronto. Digitization opens up further questions related to access: the "unarresting" of such literary records may take on new forms and extend, and possibly impede, the objectives of authors who choose certain archival establishments to correspond to particular socio-political and even personal concerns. As Kate Eichhorn has shown in *The Archival Turn in Feminism* and elsewhere, "contemporary feminist collections may be most effectively animated when read in the context of their historical collections on feminism and women's lives and … this is something that would be difficult, if not impossible, to achieve through the development of a digital collection" (17).[1]

Unarrested Archives ultimately invokes the paradigm of "arrested" and "unarrested" archival materials to showcase the range of women authors' contributions, as it also highlights how their literary and performative contributions and their records act as expressions of self-agency and forms of social action. This book also reveals the means by which some Canadian women authors were regulated by state interventions and how they cultivated both professional independence and imaginative space for the articulation of their ideas; it remaps the means by which women writers' agencies were enacted through their negotiations related to both their literary performances or publications and their archives and, in so doing, recalibrates scholarly perspectives about Canadian archives and Canadian women writers' agencies in relationship to the archive in the twentieth century. Thus, *Unarrested Archives* reminds researchers that there are several ways by which women's records might be recovered and preserved – but that researchers too are necessarily and significantly involved in the "unarresting" and legitimating of women's literary records for posterity, and in expanding the "law" of what might be said about them.

Notes

Introduction

1 Examples of women authors whose fonds are exceptionally voluminous include L.M. Montgomery and Susanna Moodie. See also Gerson, who discusses the proliferation of women authors in the nineteenth century, although she does not minimize the difficulties they encountered in their literary pursuits. Alongside a volume I co-edited with Jessica Schagerl, *Basements and Attics, Closets and Cyberspace*, Gerson's *Canadian Women in Print* provides some of the foundations for this book, which focuses on the twentieth rather than the nineteenth century. With women's enfranchisement by the early twentieth century, the means by which they approached authorship and their status as authors changed in response to evolving notions of citizenship. Yet, as Gerson notes, at the turn of the century even the most accomplished Canadian woman writer "could be haunted by a sense of deviancy" when embarking on a literary career, the evidence for which emerged in the series of justifications a female writer felt obliged to make (63). Assuming the role of a writer, with all its public inflections, meant that a woman was both "valorized" and "violated," that she was both given an "enduring identity and subjecting herself to discomfiting public scrutiny" (68). If writing has been implicitly understood as part of the male domain and a masculine medium, assuming authorship has been perceived in comparable terms.

2 Sometimes, such emotional lives are not meant for public access. As Maryanne Dever, Ann Vickery, and Sally Newman remind us, examining such emotional lives is problematic when perusing materials that may not have been meant for public dissemination.

3 Authorship has also been consistently viewed in relation to formulations of national belonging and citizenship. In their assessment of "authorship" in nineteenth-century Canada, Micheline Cambron and Gerson add that, although a "precarious profession" for both men and women, it was "increasingly valued for [its] contribution to the nation's growing 'national imaginary'" (134). Roy MacSkimming posits that, in the absence of a means by which the country could define itself, writing and publishing "became vital to [the] process of self-definition" (2). The Canadian publishing industry thus developed, as Paul Litt notes, "along classic National policy lines": those who invested their interests in the Canadian market were "good corporate citizens moved by nationalist ideals" rather than good businessmen (35–6). By the late nineteenth century, men at least could assume their place as authors with some confidence in a developing Canadian market (Golick 210). By contrast, Canadian women writers were sometimes slow to take up the role of author, editor, or critic; they produced genres regarded as of lesser significance to a culture envisioned in national terms; or they expressed deference or apologized for their presumption if they wrote at all because literary production was not "traditionally sanctioned for 'proper ladies'" (Gerson 2010, 68). Most of Canada's early women writers thus "couched their entry into the public sphere in rhetoric that combined the familiar tropes of authorial apology and female modesty" (Gerson 2010, 47). "Authorship," deemed a "valuable and viable occupation" by the late nineteenth century in Canada, had different implications for women than for men (Cambron and Gerson 120).

1. The Archive of Embodiment: Pauline Johnson's "A Cry from an Indian Wife"

1 Bodley Head was famous for being "the producer of avant-garde literature by cultivating unknowns and rebels who had manuscripts that had already been rejected on the grounds of risqué subject matter" (Strong-Boag and Gerson 2000, 144). That Johnson's poetry would be published by such a company suggests the kinds of limits she was approaching in both publication and performance, in this instance in terms of identity and convention.

2 Email from Jean Rose, library manager, Random House Group Archive and Library, to author, "Re: Bodley Head Papers," 1 July 2008, 12:45 p.m.

3 Email from Andi Gustavson to author, "Re: John Lane Papers," 13 July 2011, 5:28 p.m.

4 Email from Gustavson to author, "Re: John Lane Papers," 13 July 2011, 5:28 p.m.

5 The papers that were part of that collection were renamed the John Lane papers (see http://www.reading.ac.uk/special-collections/collections/sc-bodley-head.aspx, 7 June 2012). See also Gerson's "Postcolonialism Meets Book History," in which she examines Johnson's forays in London and her early contact with John Lane. She addresses Lane's other publications and how "Lane's 1895 Catalogue, titled 'List of Books in Belles Lettres,' is bound in with [*The White Wampum*]," such that her book is "listed on the same page as Lane's sexually adventurous Keynote series" (2004, 427; see also 437n1). I approached Gerson about the missing papers – and she too had no knowledge of their whereabouts. Finally, we do know that Johnson herself negotiated the publication of *The White Wampum*. Both its title and dedication suggest the manner in which she was striving for the coexistence of two nations, Native and Canadian: the book was dedicated to her parents (her father was Mohawk, her mother British), and the title, as she explains in the preface, served to connect the two cultures: "As wampum is to the Redman, so to the Poet are his songs" (Gerson xviii). Such ambivalence also characterizes the prefaces used to introduce her collections of poetry and prose.

6 Some of Johnson's papers have been preserved in the Edith and Lorne Collection of Canadiana at Queen's University, and elsewhere. See Sandra Campbell for more information about Pierce's dedication as a collector. See also Gerson, who suggests that although Johnson's poetry "aligns her with the major male Canadian poets of her generation," her identity "as Iroquois excluded her from these other categories" (2004, 432).

7 Nurse adds that Marius Barbeau, a significant cultural anthropologist of the period, was frustrated by how Indigenous persons insisted on donating "things to the Anthropology Division for inclusion in its collection that, in his view, were clearly not authentic. His solution was to accept material so as not to offend informants, but not include it in the Museum's collections" (47).

8 There is only one document, a photograph taken of her house by ethnographer Marius Barbeau. See "Pauline Johnson's house, Six Nations Indian Reserve, Ontario" (Canadian Museum of Civilization Archives Catalogue, 8 June 2012). Also note that the Canadian Museum of Civilization has no Johnson material because Evelyn Johnson gave her family collection to the Royal Ontario Museum (see Nicks, in press).

9 See Rak for more information about this process of digitization.

10 Such confusion was apparent in her lifetime, although a "pattern of overdetermination" was to follow for some time after her first publication; the anthropologist Horatio Hale observed that the "first

inclination of the reader will be to look in her poems for some distinctive Indian traits, and to be disappointed if these are not strikingly apparent" (qtd. in Gerson 2004, 429).

11 Current trends in performance theory, which has been influenced by postmodernism, are "inherently political" in character; as such, the theory "revises, challenges, rewrites, interrogates, and sometimes condemns received meanings" (Reinelt and Roach 2, 3). As Michael Shapiro notes, performance theory is useful in Indigenous Studies for offering another way to read the "confrontation between state nationalizing initiatives and critical, deconstructive reactions" (53): a text, after all, is "different on the stage than it is on the page" (Reinelt and Roach 3). That confrontation may also highlight how state nationalizing initiatives occasioned the archival absences addressed in this chapter. Theories of performance then become especially useful in showcasing how political motivations have a bearing on what is preserved *and* how we read what has been preserved. We can query existing categories that have determined not only what was worthy of preservation but also the interpretative lenses adopted.

12 See, for example, Collett.

13 Anonymous, "Brantford Abroad" (n.d.), Pauline Johnson Fonds, McMaster University, box 4, file 1.

14 In *Paddling Her Own Canoe*, Strong-Boag and Gerson note that the three primary concerns in Johnson's poetry were Native Canadians, nature, and love (139).

15 See also Francis, who is less tolerant of the Indigenous outfit she adopted and of the compromises she was obliged to make.

16 As Marshall notes, Johnson had few options: there were "no writers' grants, no positions as Poet in Residence at prestigious universities, no teaching jobs in creative writing at the local community college as there are for modern native writers. The recital circuit was therefore a welcome and exciting solution" (27).

17 Johnson would later promote her identity with all North American Indigenous nations, but initially she regarded the Iroquois as superior.

18 See also Gray 147.

19 Johnson's stories written for *Mother's Magazine* appeared in this collection and were "largely tales of struggle and triumph with Indian women as their heroines" (Sonneborn 102).

20 Strong-Boag and Gerson add that Johnson "interpreted ties between the periphery and centre as essentially those of kin and she anticipated tangible family benefits" (203).

21 Strong-Boag and Gerson note that, as a "path-breaker who both upheld and transgressed cultural codes and structures of a society in transition," Johnson was "highly mediated ... by her own various self-representations" (2000, 102).
22 A telling indicator of these cultural tensions is that none of the Johnson children would remain at Six Nations after the death of their father (xv).
23 The latter form of dress was as strategic as the former, given the fact that "elites competed with each other to display wealth and status" (Burman and Turbin 2). Margo Lukens notes that she "even attempted on one occasion early in her performing career to deliver some of her readings in Mohawk [...] but the audience 'booed [her] from the stage'" (45).
24 As Devereux notes, Indigenous women were "central to the construction and occupation of white colonial space as objects of exchange and as sexual and reproductive commodities" (30). See also Jean Barman.
25 See Gerson and Strong-Boag for an assessment of how settler audiences were "educated to recognize what represented Indianness on stage" (111).
26 Nellie McClung's memoirs provide evidence that this change was not strictly from "Indian" to Victorian dress; she recalls that the audience was initially surprised to see Johnson in Native dress. Johnson reassured her audience, however, that she would adopt Victorian dress in the second half of her performance (as qtd. in Marshall 30).
27 Rather than arguing that Johnson was participating in nostalgic desires, one might interpret her "backward gaze" as "proprietary, seeking to maintain possession of the flow of history in one's own terms": indeed, Johnson may be seen to be engaged in a "forward-looking, utopian desire to get beyond the terrible alienations and deprivals of existing aboriginal modernity" (Willmott 2004, 75). As Morgan argues, it is also possible to read her efforts as underscoring how "these racially charged categories of womanhood were as artificial as the forms of dress that represented them" (331).
28 Morgan argues that she developed "a class-based aura of refinement that helped domesticate her status as an 'exotic colonial'" (331).
29 Johnson didn't always select her performance venues; see McRaye (65–8) for descriptions of their makeshift performance spaces when they toured Western Canada.
30 She also had associations with women such as Nellie McClung, however, which "helped sustain a performer who brought her advocacy of Natives and New Women to potentially unfriendly audiences in North America and England" (Gerson 2002, xix).
31 This term is key when we contextualize it within the fact that Goldwin Smith gave a talk the year (2 February 1891) devoted entirely to the subject.

32 In "The Pilot of the Plains," for example, Johnson explores the fidelities expressed between a male white figure and an Indigenous woman.

33 Elsewhere, they note that the poem "highlights the perspective of the tormented Native wife and mother" and is significant for its "attribution of moral leadership to women" (Gerson and Strong-Boag 2005, 51).

34 Anonymous, "Brantford Abroad," n.d., box 4, file 1, Pauline Johnson Fonds. See Leighton for a fuller treatment of Johnson's reception. One review suggested that she had not quite been successful in conveying the emotional force of the poem: "The Cry of the Indian Wife Before the Battle requires much more force than the reader was capable of imparting to it" (*The Herald*, 1 March 1892, box 4, file 1, Pauline Johnson Fonds). The reception unevenly shows that she was successful in registering protest rather than in reinforcing the "vanishing race." One review, which appeared in the *Globe*, praised her for stealing "the show from the more experienced readers" (as qtd. in Sonneborn 101). The review was also revealing, however, for its emphasis on the importance of Canadian literature, for its designation of Indigenous literature as the cultural legacy of a vanishing race, and for its conflation of all Indigenous nations as a homogeneous group (see Leighton 3). Many reviews, therefore, were more interested in her performance than her attack upon European hegemony (Strong-Boag and Gerson 115). These two strategies evidently informed Yeigh's decisions thereafter: he urged her to include several poems about Indigenous persons in her subsequent performances because they were considered "crowd-pleasers"; that is, they appealed to the tendency to romanticize Indigenous persons. Indeed, he hailed her success as "a Canadian Indian Poet" and thereafter advertised her as a "Mohawk Princess" (Leighton 9). As a number of critics have observed, Yeigh's advertisement had no such basis in Mohawk culture, but rather was designed to "appeal to non-Indians' romanticized views of Indian women" (101) and exploit the exotic fascination she would have held for her audiences. When accused of "catering to popular taste," she admitted that perhaps she "played to the public," but it was in the service of "educating" the public (as qtd. in Hoefel 114). In "limiting her sphere of action to the performance venues of the state and the page," she could "utter political statements without threatening to alienate her readers and her audience" (Hoefel 118).

35 *The Daily Tribune*, 23 March 1892, box 4, file 1, "Reviews: Performances, 1892," Pauline Johnson Fonds. See also the untitled article in *The Sun*, dated 7 April 1892, in which she is described as having "thrilled the audience" (box 4, file 1, "Reviews: Performances, 1892," Pauline Johnson Fonds).

36 As qtd. in Strong-Boag and Gerson 107.

37 Keller notes that a witness to one of her performances fought against the Riel Resistors in 1885 and experienced regret thereafter (6).

38 See, for example, "A Red Girl's Reasoning."

39 It is likely that Johnson deliberately used "the sexual and titillating representations of the female Indigenous body that were associated with twentieth-century advertising culture" (see Devereux 36).

40 Johnson was never described as an actress, but rather as an elocutionist. Her letterhead from 1899 describes her more generally as "The Indian Poet-Reciter." In 1906, she was advertised to Londoners as "The Iroquois Indian Poet-Entertainer" and a late poster labels her as "The Mohawk Author-Entertainer" (see Gerson and Strong-Boag 2002, 105).

41 If she aligned herself with such authors in order to have her work publicly sanctioned, she also associated herself with male touring partners to "assert her respectability." From 1901, McRaye became a fellow stage performer who became responsible for raising funds for her in her last year of ill health. McRaye specialized in rendering the poetry of William Henry Drummond, whose anecdotes of French Canada were approached as light humour. His role would be akin to that which Ira Dilworth played for Emily Carr after she died: McRaye joined forces with Vancouver's "feminist and press elite" to produce *Legends of Vancouver* in 1911 as a means of raising funds to support her. He also assisted in the posthumous publication of two other collections of prose in 1913, *The Moccasin Maker* and *The Shagganappi*; these he followed with his own account of Johnson's life, *Pauline Johnson and Her Friends* (1947), which was published a year after he died.

42 I am grateful to Professor David Bentley for suggesting I consult this text.

43 This tendency would have been further underscored by the attribution of moral superiority to Indigenous persons: "Native society," Strong-Boag and Gerson note, "constituted a moral resource offering redemption to a European civilization compromised by capitalist excess" (194).

44 See Goldie/Francis. In adopting a costume informed by popular conceptions of what constituted Native dress, as Carole Gerson and Veronica Strong-Boag have observed, she demonstrated how the logic of her public identity as an Indigenous woman was in part derived from Eurocentric notions, or how assimilationist tendencies were at work; in changing costumes, she arguably demonstrated how she might disrupt received codes or dislodge those attempts to make nostalgic claims or identifications with Indigenous persons. It is possible, as Fiamengo observes, "that her performances caused many to read or reread her

poetry with a heightened attention to questions of race, sympathy and national justice" (98).

45 Just as suffragists "mapped new meaning" onto the female body by their politically charged spectacular forms, so Johnson might have been seen to do something similar with the Indigenous subject.

46 Carpenter would hold that this voiced protest, her engagement in "complex negotiation of late nineteenth-century scripts of anger" (55), would have been regarded as characteristic of her race – rather than of her talent, as was the case of such peers as Sarah Bernhardt. Johnson was otherwise "limited to conventional sentimental scripts that were not necessarily conducive to Indigenous anger" (80). Her emotionality may have been sexualized and therefore subject to "white men's desire" (55). Yet the anger evoked by Johnson in her performance was only one note she struck in a far more complex and various range of emotions. As Forte adds, "verbally expressing pain is a necessary prelude to the collective task of diminishing pain," which "crucially depends on getting others to listen and secondarily on eliminating the tendency to doubt the reports" (252).

47 Taylor argues, calling upon Foucault, that confession is "a ritual where articulation alone, independently of its external consequences, produces, in the person who articulates it, intrinsic modifications: it makes him innocent, it redeems him, purifies him, promises him salvation" (8).

48 See Leighton 9. Also, see also the newspaper article titled "An Indian Maiden Delights a Large Audience with Her Dramatic Recital" that speaks of how she mourned "her brave" in her performance of "A Cry from an Indian Wife" (Undated article, no author, box 4, file 1, "Reviews: Performances, 1892," Pauline Johnson Fonds).

49 See also Fiamengo, who suggests that the poem "was to provide a model of empathy and recognition that some listeners might embrace" (104). Her positioning as wife would have also been unique because she was able to express desire, love, and passion "from a woman's perspective" at a time when most love poetry was written from the point of view of men (Gerson 2010, 188).

2. Her "Eye" Was Her "I": Emily Carr, Autobiography, and the Archive of Kinship

1 See Rubin's "The Traffic in Women." I am grateful to my student Zöe Costanzo for reminding me of this essay.

2 All citations of *Klee Wyck* in these pages are to this edition; quotations from the 1951 edition are drawn only from the foreword by Dilworth.

3 Provincial Museum, Curatorial Files, Carr to Young, n.d.

4 As other examples, see Stephanie Kirkwood Walker and Susan Elderkin.

5 Emily Carr to Ira Dilworth, 15 December [1944], British Columbia and Archives Records Service (BCARS), Victoria, Emily Carr Fonds 1905–46, MS 2181. In another letter to Dilworth dated 10 October 1942 she wrote that W.H. Clarke, her first publisher, had mentioned that "he'd like to publish it. And I told him it was *yours right now* and always and that *you knew* I did not want it published till after I was dead. & he said he understood" (2006, 155).

6 Dilworth to Clarke, 14 February 1944, BCARS, Parnall Collection, MS 2763, box 3, file 2.

7 As Egan argues, Carr "seems to construct her selves along a variety of tangents with varying degrees of satisfaction" and if these "selves" in book form show "formal weaknesses," it must be remembered that Dilworth had reshaped her manuscripts into the more coherent wholes that at long last found publication and that were then made available to the public (174).

8 It is also a pursuit that evidently contradicts her firm belief that all things Canadian are thoroughly superior to those British.

9 Undated letter, BCARS, Emily Carr Fonds 1905–46, MS 2181, box 2, file 5. In another letter dated 20 March 1932 he offered some suggestions "with a certain amount of timidity"; these were largely suggestions related to punctuation.

10 All letters from Harris are deposited with BCARS, Emily Carr Fonds 1905–46, MS 2181, box 2.

11 He wrote that "those people who can help us are they that can participate in our ideas, what we are trying to do, and further our ideas, clarify our expression, not their own." Undated letter, MS 2181, box 2, file 9.

12 Undated letter.

13 See his letter dated 1 January 1933, in which he invites Carr to join the "new society" with its initial twenty-six members. Such attitudes explain why she may have been less disposed to work cooperatively with women. This unwillingness suggests that she found her relationships with men far more effective, meeting the purposes she had in mind. Even though Harris later works to establish the nationally oriented Canadian Group of Painters in 1933, which includes other women aside from Carr, she herself thereafter remains disinclined to work with women. Indeed, she would often dismiss those women who were close to the men with whom she allied herself. Bess Harris, Harris's second wife, was for example a woman with whom she occasionally sparred (see

Lawren Harris to Carr, letter dated Thursday, c. August 1942, in which he states "your last letter seemed a bit snappy but my guess is that Bess was partly spoofing you or else, or in the other part, being protective of my sensibilities,"). In one letter, Harris mediates between Carr and his wife, and argues that the latter did indeed understand her "isolation from helpful contacts and friendships ... the isolation [she] live[d] out on Victoria Island." Such isolation, however, was not to be addressed by women, nor by their attempts to collaborate with Carr in her artistic endeavours.

14 Brown anticipates the support in his correspondence that Dilworth would later and more consistently provide; as in her later and frequent letters to Dilworth, she was writing to Brown to express gratitude for his support, for "hauling me out of the slough of despair and setting me to work again" (Carr to Brown, 19 October 1934, National Art Gallery Archives, Emily Carr Papers).

15 Undated letter, BCARS, Emily Carr Fonds 1905–1946, MS 2181, box 2.

16 Autobiography has been regarded – however problematically – as either a genre or a mode once characterized by its masculinist bias: it was thought to be a genre that was representative not only of a person, but of a period, and to be inflected by a special "'relation' between the author and the public" that demonstrated how the author's involvement in contemporary *public* life might have been representative or exemplary for his readers (see Smith 1993, 7); women, however, could not have been "representative" of an order that was patriarchal, especially when their taking up of the pen was an act that in itself was considered transgressive. As Smith observes, "patriarchal notions of woman's inherent nature and consequent social role have denied or severely proscribed her access to the public space; and male distrust and consequent repression of female speech have either condemned her to public silence or profoundly contaminated her relationship to the pen as an instrument of power" (7). A woman who attempted to lay claim to the form, therefore, contravened patriarchal definitions of female nature by trying to enact "the scenario of male selfhood" (8).

17 See Humphrey, p. 120 (letters to Humphrey, 31 January and 6 February 1938, both of which address the manuscript). Ryerson Press subsequently lost the manuscript, and it was almost a full year before the stories were recovered.

18 See also Carr's letter to Humphrey, 8 May 1938 (Humphrey 129). Burns also published two articles on Carr, "Emily Carr" and "Emily Carr and the Newcombe Collection."

19 Carr to Flora Burns, 16 February 1940, BCARS, Flora Alfreda Hamilton Burns Collection, MS 2786, box 1, file 5.
20 Carr to Burns, 21 February 1941, BCARS, Flora Alfreda Hamilton Burns Collection, MS 2786, file 5, in which Carr discusses the copy of the "Wild Flowers" manuscript she is sending to Burns.
21 Carr to Dilworth, 24 December 1941, BCARS, Emily Carr Fonds 1905–1946, MS 2181.
22 BCARS, Parnall Collection, MS 2763.
23 26 October 1941, BCARS, Emily Carr Fonds 1905–1946, MS 2181; italics mine.
24 See her letter to Dilworth, in which she describes how she has lost his ring, 11–12 October 1944 (Carr 2006, 280).
25 See Carr 2006, 9–10.
26 J. King Gordon to Carr, 26 June 1940, BCARS, Parnall Collection, MS 2763, box 3, file 10.
27 Gordon to Carr, 26 June 1940, BCARS, Parnall Collection, MS 2763, box 3, file 10.
28 Ira Dilworth to Flora Burns, 22 November 1942, Flora Alfreda Hamilton Burns Fonds, BCARS, box 1, file 15.
29 In a letter dated 29 February 1940 he wrote to her about the reception of her broadcast stories in a manner that demonstrates his support and enthusiasm (Carr 2006, 26–7).
30 Nellie McClung to Carr, 27 February 1943, BCARS, Parnall Collection, MS 2763, box 4, file 14.
31 21 November 1941, BCARS, Emily Carr Fonds 1905–1946, MS 2181.
32 6 November 1941, BCARS, Emily Carr Fonds 1905–1946, MS 2181.
33 29 March 1942, BCARS, Emily Carr Fonds 1905–1946, MS 2181.
34 28 December 1941, BCARS, Emily Carr Fonds 1905–1946, MS 2181.
35 Carr to Ruth Humphrey, letter postmarked 29 October 1943, *University of Toronto Quarterly* (146).
36 Critics hold different perspectives about Carr's relationship with Dilworth. One of her biographers, Maria Tippett, for example, sees Carr as "defer[ring] to Dilworth more and more about her writing" (1979, 269). Paula Blanchard, another biographer, determines that, although Carr "insisted that she could not write without him, and that by itself her writing was just 'a flout of drift,'" Dilworth was indeed far from aggressive in his editing style: "many of Dilworth's written comments survive, and there is nothing in them to suggest that he overstepped the bounds of editor. He corrected spelling and punctuation and helped her organize and polish her material, and he was firm about judicious cuts.

But the style is entirely Emily's, easily recognizable to anyone familiar with her letters and journals" (275). Blanchard here separates *style* from *content* and, in so doing, suggests that Carr might retain her "essential" manuscript – her essential self – in spite of Dilworth's interventions. Dilworth employed similar terms: "during Emily's lifetime no word in anything she had written was changed without her full consideration. The changes that I made were changes simply that any editor would make – changes in punctuation, changes in paragraphing ... [Her] style was her style, never mine, and I had nothing to do with this magnificence of expression that she possessed, apparently from the time she was a child" (see interview with Elspeth Chilsolm, "Canadian Pioneers," [Acc. 7110073] 29 October 1969, CBC Archives, Toronto). It is this kind of appraisal that undoubtedly earned her trust. Whatever perspective is adopted, it is clear from Carr's surviving letters that, towards the end of her life, she came to rely upon him. As she noted in a letter dated 24 April 1942, "Having the biog: & knowing all my corners intimately better than anyone else[,] I just naturally lean on you[,] hoping I'm not too heavy" (2006, 137).

37 Unless she means that she embodies the nation and thus the kiss is *given to* Canada.
38 See Dilworth to Carr, c. 25 March 1940, BCARS, MS 2763, Parnall Collection, box 2, file 23.
39 Carr suggests in a letter dated 23 December 1941 that the book is "my Christmas present to you[.] Accept [it] as your *very own* with my love" (2006, 77).
40 28 December 1941 (2006, 82).

3. "It's What You [Don't] Say": Sheila Watson, the Imminent Narrative, and the Archive of Displacement

1 Sheila and Wilfred died a month apart, she in February and he in March 1998.
2 Watson recounts her father's stern rebuke when she had casually remarked to one of her father's patients that he was "crazy"; although she had "meant it in a general sense," her father corrected her by replying, "It is not what you mean, it is what you say" (qtd. in Flahiff 2005, 14).
3 Fictional autobiography, as for example Charlotte Brontë's *Jane Eyre*, is an exception to this pattern.
4 Radical challenges were made to the notion of a unified self (Smith and Watson 123), especially with the developments of Freud and Lacan.

Sidonie Smith and Julia Watson observe that the "universal 'self'" became "in the wake of multiple theoretical challenges of the first half of the century, a 'subject' riven by self-estrangement and self-fragmentation" (124). But this would have already been the case for a woman taking up the autobiographical form – she would have been regarded as an embodied subject whose attempts at disembodied rationality were greatly circumscribed. Rather, she would become involved in the act of "enshrin[ing] consciousness" – consciousness of consciousness – "the ability to reflect upon oneself through the autobiographical process" (Smith and Watson 125).

5 At the time of writing this book, another collaboration is underway, an initiative led by Paul Hjartarson at the University of Alberta to digitize significant portions of both Wilfred Watson's and Sheila Watson's archives. Hjartarson and Neuman are also working with the University of Alberta to create a digital archive for Wilfred Watson – but not for Sheila Watson. Even if a digital archive is created, however, Hjartarson noted that "the letters themselves ... would be available in the same way they currently are": "[primary scholars] might apply online for access to selected documents" (Paul Hjartarson, email to author, "Re: Archive futures: Draft Programme etc.," 2 July 2013, 6:10 p.m.).

6 See, as examples of important scholarship on Watson, the edited collections by Diane Bessai and David Jackel, Stephen Scobie, and George Bowering.

7 See Watson to Wynn Francis, 14 April 1976, Sheila Watson Fonds, John M. Kelly Library, University of St Michael's College, University of Toronto (henceforth SWF), Correspondence, Letters from Sheila Watson, Series 3, Subseries I, Outgoing Correspondence. All subsequent references to letters from Sheila Watson share the same series and subseries.

8 Watson was far from relying on any person in the publishing process. Indeed, in a letter to Phyllis Wilson, who worked in the Editorial Division of Oxford University Press, Watson wrote to ask about the possible inclusion of her story "Antigone" in an anthology being proposed by Rosemary Sullivan: "I am not sure," she noted, "whether the phrase 'world distribution rights' refers to the distribution of the anthology or to republication rights for the story itself." She added that should it mean the former, she expected "to receive pro rata payment for its inclusion in the anthology. At the moment, I would be reluctant to relinquish control of the rights." No agent could have responded with greater clarity or firmness (SWF).

9 Sheila Watson to Wilfred Watson, letter dated "Monday," Wilfred Watson Archives, University of Alberta.

10 She was likely referring to the inclusion of an epigraph to *The Double Hook*, with which she had been uneasy (Flahiff 2005, 198).

11 Sybil Hutchinson to Sheila Watson, 26 January 1949, Series 4.0, Publishing Records and Business Correspondence, SWF. All subsequent letters from Hutchinson share the same series.

12 Such resistance had little to do with lack of merit, since many praised the novel's sophistication, and had little or nothing to do with her gender. She first considered sending the manuscript to the London-based publisher Rupert Hart-Davis in December 1953 (Sybil Hutchinson to Sheila Watson, 26 January 1949, SWF); eventually she did so, but the publisher returned the manuscript because it had "too many characters and themes, all insufficiently explored, too much motion and dust" (qtd. in Flahiff 2005, 81). A journal entry dated 21 October reveals that she sent Chatto and Windus a copy of the manuscript thereafter, which, she notes on 15 November, is quickly returned (as qtd. in Flahiff 2005, 116, 124). She reported to her friend Anne Angus that they appreciated the work's "writing and the intuition behind it" but found it "difficult to understand the motivation" (Watson to Angus, 17 December 1953, St Michael's College). Ultimately, it was rejected because it lacked economically viability: "the book would stand no chance in the British market" (qtd. in Flahiff 2005, 196). Timothy Seldes, senior editor at Doubleday & Company at the time, also rejected the novel because "our readers felt that this particular book was not successful enough for us to do well with" (Series 4.0, Publishing Records and Business Correspondence, SWF). Like his counterpart at Chatto and Windus, he did not believe he could locate a large enough audience to make it a lucrative endeavour. Canadian publishers gave similar responses. Macmillan expressed reluctance because its editor, John Gray, had not received positive consensus among his editors, something he required before deciding in favour of publication. When Watson submitted it to Macmillan, only "Dobbs admired it, but other in-house readers found the novel too difficult or obscure" and so, ultimately, Macmillan turned it down (MacSkimming 59).

13 McClelland to Watson, 8 August 1958, SWF.

14 McClelland to Watson, 8 August 1958, Series 4.0, Publishing Records and Business Correspondence, SWF. All subsequent letters from McClelland & Stewart share the same series number.

15 A surviving letter from Sheila Watson to Cleanth Brooks, 30 September 1960, indicates that, upon his recommendation to McLuhan, she would write (as she did) to McClelland to attempt to interest Random House

and Harcourt Brace (SWF, Correspondence, Letters from Sheila Watson, Accession 2006.01, box 35, I).

16 Jack McClelland to Helen Martin, on staff at Wellesley College, McMaster University Papers.

17 McClelland notes in a letter dated 8 August 1958 that he was undecided about using Salter's foreword. SWF.

18 McClelland to Salter, Department of English, University of Alberta, 9 March 1959 (McClelland & Stewart Fonds, McMaster University, Hamilton).

19 McClelland to Salter, 13 December 1957, SWF.

20 Note from Mathers to Watson, SWF.

21 Watson to Anne Angus, 9 January 1958, SWF.

22 Foreword by Salter, SWF.

23 April 23, SWF.

24 Salter to Watson, SWF. Watson also received considerable support from Malcolm Ross, the editor of *Queen's Quarterly* at that time. See Ross to Watson, 22 December 1953. Ross was sufficiently pleased with the story "Brother Oedipus" that he was willing to publish it after some editorial changes he suggested to Watson: he invited her to "reconsider what seemed to him certain 'over-literary' and 'self-conscious' references" (Flahiff 2005, 80). In particular, he asked her to "work over your introductory section." Watson agreed with these changes, and Ross, who thought her revisions "improve[d] the story considerably," published the story in the summer edition of 1954 (Ross to Sheila Watson, 27 April 1954). He was thereafter encouraging, in one letter noting that "I hope that you will let me see more of your work" and in another informing her that her story was "being very well received" (6 July 1952). As she notes in her journal on 21 October, she sent him her second story, "The Black Farm," which was to appear two years later in *Queen's Quarterly*. That he supported her writing is also clear in his decision to send the latter story to Robert Weaver of the CBC to see "if a double acceptance [could] be arranged." Watson's telling response to her friend Angus suggests the effect of such efforts: "There is something about the way in which Dr Ross has handled my work that cuts straight to the heart" (12 December 1955).

25 See Watson's letter, envelope marked 10 September 1954, SWF.

26 Letter dated 22 March 1955, SWF.

27 Watson had been "making a collection of magazine covers for a Canadian art editor who is preparing a section of one of the issues of his magazine on the design of little magazine covers"; such work would have prepared

her and rendered her more sensitive to the selection of the image for her own book (letter to Mr William Cookson, Editor of *Agenda*, SWF). Subsequent covers were not so successful. A letter from McClelland to Watson reveals that she had disclosed her displeasure with another cover, to which McClelland responded with agreement. A new cover was designed (9 November 1981).

28 Watson to Flahiff, Outgoing Correspondence, SWF.

29 Flahiff to Watson, Bloomsday 1993, Series 4, Subseries 3.2, Incoming Correspondence, SWF., John M. Kelly Library, University of St. Michael's College, University of Toronto. All subsequent incoming personal letters share the same series and subseries.

30 See letters from Claire Pratt to Sheila Watson, dated 20 October 1961 and 22 December 1961, and that by S.J. Totton, editor-in-chief, 3 December 1963, Series 4.0, Publishing Records and Business Correspondence, SWF.

31 McClelland to Watson, 24 October 1964, SWF.

32 Letter to Watson, 8 August 1989, SWF.

33 Seligman to Watson, 22 July 1991, SWF.

34 Gibson to Flahiff, 20 April 1992, SWF.

35 Further correspondence reveals the logic behind her reluctance to part with her second manuscript. In an undated letter to Angus, she commented on how the process of correcting proofs for her book was "a humbling experience ... everyone has taken so much trouble with the manuscript." That response suggests a certain degree of modesty. In another, dated 6 April 1959, she observed again that "McClelland and Stewart has taken a great deal of trouble with the 'production,' as it is called. I hope the firm is not disappointed" (Watson to Angus, SWF). She was to reiterate that sentiment in almost precisely the same terms in a letter dated 10 September 1991, when she submitted *Deep Hollow Creek*. These kinds of misgivings or doubts extended well beyond *The Double Hook*, for in yet another letter to Angus, dated 8 January 1961, Watson commented on how she had written "with some trepidation" to the editor of the *Herald Tribune*, which had published an article by Edith Sitwell on Wyndham Lewis. In spite of her own expertise on the subject, she noted that she experienced mistrust in her "ability to speak publicly on any topic." This diffidence would also likely inform her reservations about publishing. In a letter to Angus dated 13 July 1959 she addressed the "responsibility of publishing one's thoughts": "I don't think of a writer as 'priest' or even acolyte but (as you say) I do think of him as 'responsible'" (Watson to Angus, SWF).

36 Flahiff to Watson, Labour Day 1997. In another letter dated 20 June 1997 he wrote to suggest that St Michael's might be the most appropriate archive: they were "pleased by the prospect that the papers, books, etc. might reside in our library. It is a fitting place – for all the reasons you know." Flahiff began to sift through the material and "sort out the contents of [her] boxes," as he also put the papers in acid-free containers. He initially used three-by-five-inch index cards and worked by hand, rather than by computer, to organize the material until he realized that "a more economical method" was required and purchased a laptop (SWF).
37 Flahiff to Watson, 20 June 1997, SWF.
38 Flahiff to Watson, Labour Day 1997, SWF.
39 Flahiff to Watson, Labour Day 1997, SWF.
40 Even so, as Anna St. Onge, the archivist who later came to work on Watson's papers, observed, "in practice, especially with private papers, archival work can be an emotional activity" (5).
41 Flahiff to Watson, 22 October 1997, SWF.
42 Flahiff to Watson, 20 June 1997, SWF.
43 Flahiff to Watson, 22 October 1997, SWF.
44 F.M. Salter to Sheila Watson, 4 December 1957, SWF.
45 The other two entries that are published in Flahiff's biography appear on 26 September, when Watson refers to Dull, the "actor who trained Jean-Louis Barrault," and on 1 October, when she mentions that she has tickets to see Baurrault's *Aeschylus* (Flahiff 100, 102).
46 Journal, 25 October, SWF.
47 The reference to the Aristotelian custom of walking while teaching is modified here – she is walking and teaching (her readers), but also seeing and learning while walking.
48 See also Wood (2004) and Salzini (2008).
49 See, for example, Willmott (2004) and his assessment of her second novel, "The Nature of Modernism in *Deep Hollow Creek*" (1995).

4. Jane Rule and the Archive of Activism: Negotiating Imaginative – and Literal – Space for a Nation

1 Christopher Hives, email to author, "Rule Material," 30 May 2013, 11:36 a.m.
2 Box 39, file 57, Jane Rule Fonds, University Archives, University of British Columbia (hereafter "JRF").
3 I will use "queer" rather than "gay," following Peter Dickinson's terminology.

4 "Come from the Raid?," typescript by Michael Lynch, box 21, file entitled "The Body Politic," JRF. "Four officers of the Metropolitan Toronto Police and one Ontario Provincial Police officer" were involved in the raid. The warrant they provided cited "the charged under Paragraph 164 of the Criminal Code": "use of the mails for the purpose of transmitting or delivering anything that is obscene, indecent, or scurrilous." These items included two books, *The Joy of Lesbian Sex* and *The Joy of Gay Sex*, that had already been admitted to Canada by customs officials.

5 Box 21, file "The Body Politic," JRF.

6 Laurenda Daniells, email to author, "Jane Rule Fonds – Inquiry," 30 May 2013, 6:46 p.m.

7 Laurenda Daniells, email to author, "Jane Rule Fonds – Inquiry," 30 May 2013, 6:46 p.m.

8 See Linda Morra, "Autobiographical Text, Archives, and Activism," forthcoming.

9 Interview with Lisa McCullough, *The Washington Blade*, 18 April 1986, box 33, file 5, JRF.

10 Rule decided to stop writing after 1990, although some of her work was published posthumously. See, for example, *Loving the Difficult* (Sidney, BC: Hedgerow, 2008). The reasons for her retirement seem to be related to her debilitating arthritis (see Schuster 6).

11 Rule to Margaret Hollingsworth, 4 September 2001, file 8.11, box 02/03/76, acc. 2005-008, Archives and Special Collections, University of Victoria.

12 See letter by Rosemary Macomber (of the Borchardt agency) to Rule, 6 July 1972, in which she praises the Canada Council and deplores how *Canadian Forum* does not pay its writers: "I consider this a very poor indication of the regard Canada has for its writer" (box 21, file titled "Copies of Other Stories," JRF).

13 See M.D. Smith, who notes that "Canadian pulp magazines existed within a cultural hierarchy that proved itself to be trans-national, and the lack of difference between the production of pulp fiction in Canada and its production in the United States suggested that the two nations shared many social and cultural characteristics that prompted political anxiety in Canada on a national scale" (262).

14 Mass-market magazine fiction flourished in post-war Canada.

15 Even in 1952, when George H. Doran wrote *Chronicles of Barabbas, 1884–1934*, his chapter titled "The Exotics" is revealing of how he and others in the publishing industry might have approached queer culture:

he remarked on the "exotics [who] profit[ed] by the decadence of an overstimulated and blasé social order" (267).

16 Rule's book *Lesbian Images*, for example, was commissioned by Doubleday in the 1970s.

17 See also George Fetherling's entry titled "Literary Agents" in *Encyclopedia of Literature in Canada* (668).

18 Russell & Volkening to Rule, 25 June 1954, box 19, file 7, JRF.

19 A.P. Watt claimed he had "invented the business when he established A.P. Watt & Co" (Tebbel 130). He represented writers such as Rudyard Kipling and Conan Doyle (Tebbel 131).

20 In a letter from Rule to Ellen Kay, dated 23 October 1963, she discusses how she reached an agreement with Leresche "only about three weeks ago to have her handle my work in England and on the continent while Kurt Hellmer dealt with the States and Canada" (box 19, file 4, JRF).

21 Hellmer fled Nazi Germany in the 1930s and settled in New York, where by the 1940s he had become a literary agent (http://en.wikipedia.org/wiki/Kurt_Hellmer. Accessed 4 April 2010).

22 http://en.wikipedia.org/wiki/Georges_Borchardt. Accessed 4 April 2010. At the time of writing, his agency continued to represent Rule's work.

23 Opportunities for publishing in Canada had also increased by the early 1970s as a result of some government support, both federally and provincially. See Robert Farr's "Government Looks All Around."

24 See Willis Kingsley Wing's letter to Rule, 30 April 1957, box 19, file 7, JRF.

25 See Robert Weaver's letter to Rule, 21 January 1959, vol. 4, file 27 (1957–1982), MG31 D162, Library and Archives Canada.

26 The letters exchanged between Rule and Weaver do not clearly indicate which story was taped for consideration for *Anthology*, but in a letter in August 1957, Weaver makes reference to "A Walk by Himself," that "earlier" story she had submitted for his consideration.

27 Rule to Weaver, 1 April 1957, vol. 4, file 27 (1957–1982), Robert Weaver Fonds, MG31 D162, Library and Archives Canada.

28 In an undated letter that follows, Rule speaks of how two-thirds of the story was read over the air before it was "censored by a lord high someone or other ... The CBC accepted the story, asked for a rewrite, which was also accepted, broadcast it over two thirds of Canada, then cut it off. I want to know why." There is no letter of response in the archives (vol. 4, file 27 [1957–1982], MG31 D162, Library and Archives Canada). The story was subsequently published in *Klanak Islands* (see Jane Rule Fonds Catalogue, box 13, file 4, JRF).

29 See Korinek. Also see "Chatelaine: We're Celebrating 80 Years," http://en.chatelaine.com/english/celebration/article.jsp?content=20080225_154938_6272.

30 Rule to "Mrs. Chatelaine Contest," 15 September 1968, box 23, file 1, JRF.

31 Rule to "Mrs. Chatelaine Contest," 15 September 1968, box 23, file 1, JRF. It is unclear whether or not Rule also submitted a story with her entry form; the fonds hold her five-page response, but there is no indication of an accompanying story.

32 Winthrop Watson to Rule, 30 April 1979, box 21, file titled "Georges Borchardt," JRF.

33 Rule's stories appeared in April 1969 ("The List"), August 1972 ("The Secretary Bird"), December 1976 ("The Delicate Balance"), August 1977 ("Joy"), December 1979 ("A Migrant Christmas"), and May 1981 ("Seaweed and Song") (box 37, file 7, JRF).

34 "Jane Rule, Winner Fiction Competition," *Miss Chatelaine* 15.2 (March 1978), box 37, file 10, JRF. This article addresses Rule's role as judge in the 1978 competition.

35 Carol Meyer to Rule, 21 December 1979, box 21, file titled "Harcourt Brace," JRF.

36 Rosemary Macomber to Rule, 19 August 1975. Macomber writes that "Kate loves [*The Young in One Another's Arms*], but she has to marshal enough support from other editors to put it through their editorial committee" (box 19, file 9, JRF).

37 Anne Borchardt to Rule, 6 August 1979, JRF.

38 Meyer to Rule, 31 August 1979, box 21, file titled "Harcourt Brace," JRF.

39 Meyer to Rule, 26 February 1980, box 21, file titled "Harcourt Brace," JRF.

40 Anne Borchardt to Rule, 17 July 1980, box 19, file 9, JRF.

41 Willis Kingsley Wing to Rule, 22 July 1958, box 19, file 7, JRF.

42 Wing to Rule, 11 April 1957, box 19, file 7, JRF.

43 See also his letter dated 25 November 1958, in which he suggests that "in my judgment what you ought to do is focus on the novel and not dissipate your energies into other areas of writing" (box 19, file 7, JRF).

44 As for the apparent lack of speed in dealing with her manuscripts, he noted: "If you take your responsibilities to your authors seriously, careful reading and evaluation of manuscripts added to all the business activities that involve us, the time factor becomes a somewhat different thing" (Wing to Rule, 6 January 1958, box 19, file 7, JRF).

45 Wing to Rule, 28 February 1958, box 19, file 7, JRF.

46 Wing to Rule, 8 April 1957, box 19, file 7, JRF.

47 Wing to Rule, 16 December 1957 and 25 November 1958, box 19, file 7, JRF.
48 *Housewife* was a monthly glossy magazine produced by Hulton Press in the 1950s.
49 A copy of the typed manuscript is housed in the Rule archives, box 13, file 5. I have not yet been able to locate a copy of the story as it was printed in *Housewife* magazine.
50 Wing to Rule, 1 September 1961, box 19, file 7, JRF.
51 Rule to Wing, 9 September 1961, box 19, file 7, JRF.
52 It is not clear whether or not Rule sent both of these letters to Wing.
53 Wing to Rule, 3 October 1961, JRF.
54 Rule to Leresche, 21 September 1962, box 22, file 1, JRF.
55 Wing to Rule, 4 August 1961, JRF.
56 Wing to Rule, 4 August 1961, box 19, file 7, JRF.
57 Dobbs adds that as of 1 December 1961 he would be employed as an associate editor at *Saturday Night* magazine (Dobbs to Rule, 14 November 191, box 19, file 9, JRF).
58 Wing to Rule, 30 August 1961, box 19, file 7, JRF.
59 See Rule's letter to Hope Leresche, 21 September 1962, box 22, file 1, JRF.
60 Wing to Rule, 16 August 1962, JRF.
61 Leresche and Steele took over the Sayle Literary Agency (founded by J.B. Pinker) in the 1970s and renamed it after themselves (http://britishbookstoday.com/literaryagents.html, 10 April 2010).
62 Leresche to Rule, 18 September 1962, box 22, file 1, JRF.
63 Rule to Leresche, 23 October 1962, box 22, file 1, JRF.
64 Leresche to Rule, 19 October 1962, JRF.
65 David Farrar to Hope Leresche, 17 December 1962, box 22, file 1, JRF.
66 Rule to Leresche, 16 October 1963, box 22, file 1, JRF.
67 Leresche to Rule, 18 September 1962. In another letter, dated 6 July 1966, Leresche essentially described Rule as naive: "I do really think Hellmer takes authors for a ride, but few of them I suspect are as willing or gullible (forgive me!) as yourself in these matters" (box 22, file 1, JRF).
68 Rule to Leresche, 21 September, 2 October 1962, box 22, file 1, JRF.
69 The relationship was harmonious despite the fact that Rule's manuscript "Permanent Resident" had received rejections from twenty-one publishers. For example, on 25 July 1963 Hellmer wrote that Harper, Pantheon Books, and Funk and Wagnalls had all refused the book. Their grounds for refusal are revealing. Pantheon wrote that it fell "short of our expectations" because it "is difficult to write about the subject without propagandizing" and that it was "only in the better women's magazines

that this kind of writing can truly succeed"; Funk and Wagnalls wrote that, "aside from the resistance I think I would meet as to basic content, the book is – in my final judgment – a bit suffocating. [Rule] tries hard to fill her novel with sensuality, but it is rarely erotic, and after all, with a subject like this it would have to be erotic at least some of the time to be convincing" (box 19, file 7, "Correspondence with Agents and Publishers re: 'Permanent Resident' [Desert of the Heart]" JRF). On 2 May 1963 Hellmer had relayed this report from Houghton Mifflin: all five of its editors had "exercised considerable restraint in the treatment of that most difficult of delicate themes – Lesbianism" (box 19, file 7, JRF). They added, however, that "the novel's appeal necessarily rests on its sensational theme, and we feel we are not the house to capitalize on the kind of exploitation the book would need in making it a commercial success."

70 31 October 1962, box 19, file 7, JRF.

71 Rule to Hellmer, 21 November 1963, box 19, file 7, JRF.

72 Benjamin La Farge, associate editor, to Rule, 18 February 1965, box 19, file 7, JRF.

73 Rule to Hope Leresche, 16, 21 October 1963, box 22, file 1, JRF.

74 Leresche to Rule, 12 December 1962, box 22, file 1, JRF.

75 Wright and McTaggart, Barristers and Solictors, to Frank Upjohn, Macmillan Company of Canada, 4 January 1963, box 22, file 8, JRF.

76 Rule to Leresche, 17 December 1962, box 22, file 1, JRF.

77 Rule to Leresche, 21 October 1963, box 22, file 1, JRF.

78 "Jane Rule: The Woman behind *Lesbian Images*," *Body Politic* 21 (December 1975): 14. She also mentioned this incident during an interview with the author, December 2006.

79 "Censorship," typescript, box 25, file 6, JRF.

80 Leresche to Rule, 12 October 1963, box 22, file 1, JRF.

81 As one example, in the opening line of the story the protagonist, Kate, is described as wakening from a "damp, guilty dream"; the final printed story removed the words "damp, guilty." See typed ms. of "No More Bargains" in "Short Stories & Essays – Published and Unpublished," box 12, file 14, JRF. The passage about juice and coffee to which Rule refers reads: "Les came into the kitchen, clean-shaven, in his uniform, and drank his juice and coffee standing up." Box 37, file 7, JRF.

82 Rule to Hellmer, box 19, file 7, "Correspondence re: Desert of the Heart," JRF.

83 Rule to Leresche, 16 October 1963, box 22, file 1, JRF.

84 This quotation and the account of the censoring of the story that appeared in *Redbook* have been taken from an essay by Hofsess titled "Jane Rule's Wisdom of the Heart," box 21, file 32, JRF.

85 Leresche to Rule, 12 September 1963, box 22, file 1, JRF.
86 Leresche to Rule, 12 October 1963, box 22, file 1, JRF.
87 Rule to Ellen Kay, 8 November 1963, box 19, file 5, JRF.
88 In fact, in the December 2006 interview, she claimed to know nothing of markets but to write for herself – markets, she asserted, belong to the agent's field of knowledge.
89 Leresche to Rule, 12 September 1966, box 22, file 1, JRF.
90 The New American Library had been bought by the *Times Mirror* of Los Angeles, then by Odyssey Partners and Ira J. Hechler, and then by Penguin Publishing Company.
91 Rule's initial contact at New American Library was with David Brown, whose wife had authored *Sex and the Single Girl* (1962), an advice book for women that sold over two million copies when published. Brown resigned only a few short months after his initial contact with Rule (see his letter dated 16 April 1964, box 19, file 8/9 (incoming correspondence), JRF).
92 Rule to LaFarge, 31 January 1965, box 19, file 7, "Correspondence re: Desert of the Heart," JRF.
93 Box 19, file 7, "Correspondence re: Desert of the Heart," JRF.
94 Rule to Roy D. Chennells, 20 February 1965, box 19, file 7, "Correspondence re: Desert of the Heart," JRF.
95 Hellmer to Rule, 23 February 1965, box 19, file 7, "Correspondence re: Desert of the Heart," JRF.
96 Hellmer to Chennells, 19 April 1965, box 19, file 7, "Correspondence re: Desert of the Heart," JRF.
97 Redding to Hellmer, 3 May 1965, in which he writes that New American Library had sent Rule's novel to World's production department with her approved corrections: "No additional changes were made at World" (JRF).
98 See Hellmer to Rule, 26 July 1965, box 19, file 7, "Correspondence re: Desert of the Heart," JRF.
99 Hellmer to Rule, 1 February 1966, box 19, file 7, "Correspondence re: Desert of the Heart," JRF. Leresche confirms this parting of ways earlier, in a letter dated 9 October 1965 (box 22, file 1, JRF).
100 Rule to Borchardt, 29 May 1966, box 19, file 9, JRF.
101 There is evidence that he sent the story to *Redbook, Saturday Evening Post, McCall's, Woman's Day, Family Circle, Cosmopolitan*, and *Mademoiselle*, all of which declined it. Eventually, it was sold through the Borchardt agency in 1977. See Macomber to Rule, 19 January 1977, box 19, file 9, JRF.

102 Macmillan would remainder *Desert of the Heart* in 1975. See Finn Bay to Rule, 26 May 1975, box 30, file 3, JRF.

103 As F.A. Upjohn, manager of the Trade Department of Macmillan, noted in a letter dated 1 November 1962, "We had hoped that Willis Wing would find an American publisher from whom we could buy stock." When the British-based Secker and Warburg made the offer, however, Macmillan made a similar arrangement: Secker and Warburg agreed to supply Macmillan with "copies from their first printing" (cf. letter dated 9 November 1962).

104 Press release for *Desert of the Heart*, MacMillan Company of Canada, 12 February 1964, box 30, file 3, JRF.

105 Gray to Rule, 12 July 1966, box 19, file 8/9, JRF. He was referring to a letter dated 6 July 1966, in which he noted that the novel was yet "below what I'm sure you can do" and that therefore he and the other readers could not be "unreservedly enthusiastic." She assured him that she "didn't find [his] comments either facile or insensitive." Her letter is dated October of the subsequent year, surely an error on Rule's part, since the contents of the letters clearly correspond and they are placed in otherwise chronological order in the file.

106 Rule to Gray, 23 February 1966, JRF. The dating of these letters is somewhat skewed, because her manuscript did not arrive for evaluation until June 6 and then the reader's report was mislaid

107 Rule to Leresche, 11 July 1966, box 22, file 1, JRF.

108 By contrast, on 6 May 1974, Jane Rotrosen, Hellmer's associate, had brought the novel to the attention of a couple of Hollywood film producers who had expressed interest. They were obliged to withdraw their offer as the result of "financial complications" only two months later.

109 13 December 1972 and 6 May 1974.

110 Rosemary Macomber took over and, on 26 September 1975, confirmed that the contract with Arno applied only to US hardcover rights (Macomber to Rule, box 19, file 9, JRF).

111 Leresche to Rule, 14 April 1966, box 22, file 1, JRF.

112 Macomber, Borchardt's assistant, wrote that "therefore whatever arrangement is made with Wieser & Feeley really must emanate from [Leresche] rather than from us" (Macomber to Rule, 6 August 1975, box 19, file 9, JRF; see also Leresche to Rule, 10 May 1966, box 22, file 1).

113 Rule to Borchardt, 29 May 1966, box 21, file 6, JRF.

114 Rule to Borchardt, 29 May 1966, box 21, file 6, JRF. In the same letter, she stipulated that the newly acquired agent was to look into the World Publishing Company with which she had placed her first novel, *Desert of*

the Heart, and advise her about what do with her manuscript "This Is Not for You": "World's handling of the book ... doesn't give me a great deal of confidence in their efficiency. What I need is the advice of someone who does know what would be wisest to do with this new book."

115 Borchardt to Rule, 2 June 1966, box 19, file 9, JRF.

116 Leresche to Rule, 11 June 1966, box 22, file 1, JRF. She had two reservations: first, that the narrator did not evolve, and second, that the narrator was "all-powerful" – that is, her observations so dominated that it was difficult for a reader to assess other characters independently of the narrator's observations.

117 Borchardt to Rule, 23 June 1966, box 19, file 9, JRF.

118 Borchardt to Rule, 3, August 1967, box 19, file 9, JRF.

119 Borchardt to Rule, 19 October 1967, box 19, file 9, JRF.

120 Borchardt to Rule, 13 July 1967, box 19, file 9, JRF.

121 Borchardt to Rule, 3 August 1967, box 19, file 9, JRF.

122 Mrs Neal G. Stuart to Macomber, 30 October 1967, box 19, file 9, JRF.

123 Macomber to Rule, 10 November 1967, box 21, file "Copies of Other Stories," JRF. See also her letter to Rule dated 14 October 1968 in which she discusses the proposed manuscript – an early version of *This Not Quite Promised Land* – for *Redbook*, but dismisses the idea because the protagonists are too old for *Redbook*'s readership. Macomber concludes that they "want 'young mammas' and very little else. However, this does not preclude you from writing a simply wonderful novella about young marriage and motherhood. I know you could do it strictly within the confines of their restrictions."

124 Macomber to Rule, 25 February 1970, box 19, file 9, JRF.

125 Macomber to Rule, 30 November 1967, box 19, file 9, JRF.

126 Macomber to Rule, 26 April 1968, box 19, file 9, JRF.

127 Macomber to Rule, 5 June 1968, box 19, file 9, JRF.

128 Macomber to Rule, 29 December 1967, box 19, file 9, JRF.

129 Macomber to Rule, 24 April, 3 May 1968, box 19, file 9, JRF. See also her letter to Rule about the change in title, dated 11 June 1969.

130 Macomber to Rule, 1 November 1971, box 19, file 9, JRF.

131 Macomber to Rule, 12 April 1976, box 19, file 9, JRF.

132 Macomber to Rule, 30 January 1975, 22 March 1976, box 19, file 9, JRF.

133 Macomber to Rule, 12 November 1976, box 19, file 9, JRF.

134 Macomber to Rule, 22 August 1968, box 21, file "Copies of Other Stories," JRF.

135 Macomber to Rule, 7 June 1976, box 19, file 9, JRF.

136 Macomber, quoting Mrs Neal to Rule, 16 September 1968, box 19, file 9, JRF.

137 Macomber to Rule, 20 August 1969, box 19, file 9, JRF.
138 Macomber to Rule, 12 March 1974, box 21, file "Copies of Other Stories," JRF. See also her letter dated 10 January 1974, in which she claims that she "never dreamed that the book was going to turn out to be a stunner."
139 Leresche to Rule, 3 May 1973. Part of this response, however, had been based on Leresche's notion that there were fundamental differences in "attitudes, behaviour and mores on the two sides of the Atlantic," which would render the book unappealing to those in Britain. However, a letter dated 15 August 1974 suggests that Lereseche must have relented, since the publishing firm Peter Davies agreed to and provided a contract for *Lesbian Images* (box 22, file 1, JRF).
140 Macomber to Rule, 9, 25 February 1970, box 21, file "Copies of Other Stories," JRF.
141 Macomber to Rule 23 February 1972, box 21, file "Copies of Other Stories," JRF.
142 Macomber to Rule, 29 September 1969, box 21, file "Copies of Other Stories," JRF.
143 Macomber to Rule, 21 October 1969, box 21, file "Copies of Other Stories," JRF.
144 See Macomber to Rule, 27 April, 14 December 1970, box 19, file 9, JRF.
145 Macomber to Rule, 22 February 1973, box 21, file "Copies of Other Stories," JRF. See also Leresche to Rule, 14 July 1971, box 22, file 1, JRF.
146 Macomber to Rule, 15 February 1972, box 21, file "Copies of Other Stories," JRF.
147 Macomber to Rule, 6 February 1976. The novel was then serialized by *Redbook*; see Macomber to Rule, 13 May 1976, box 21, file "George Borchardt." For the Collins agreement see Lisa Adams to Rule, 23 August 1978, box 19, file 9, JRF.
148 See Anne Borchardt to Rule, 13 September 1977, box 19, file 9, JRF. See also Rule to Louise Dennys, 16 March 1982, box 113, file 30, JRF. Anne also had to use this occasion to remind Rule that she should not make agreements with others without consulting the agency first: "We promise not to do anything not in your best interest!" (27 August 1979).
149 During this period, Leresche relinquished direction of the literary agency, which was taken over by Tessa Sayle, who had worked alongside Leresche for seven years (Leresche to Rule, 4 November 1976, box 22, file 1, JRF).
150 Macomber to Rule, 2 March 1973, box 21, file "Copies of Other Stories," JRF.
151 Macomber to Rule, 6 July 1972, box 21, file "Copies of Other Stories," JRF.

152 Anne Borchardt to Rule, 13 September 1977. See also Macomber to Rule, 7 November 1977, box 19, file 9, JRF.

153 Rule to David Robinson, 4 April 1979, box 30, file 3, JRF.

154 Karl Siegler to Rule, 18 April 1979, box 30, file 3, JRF.

155 Rule to Siegler, box 30, file 3, JRF.

156 Anne Borchart to Jane, 6 December 1978. Rule received a like response on 30 April 1979, when Winthrop Watson of the Borchardt agency quoted Barbara West of *Chatelaine* as claiming that "we have a very conservative readership that would not readily accept a story with a theme of this kind. Many of our readers would not understand it, and those that did would probably be offended." She was referring to Rule's story "Home Movie" (box 19, file 9, JRF). Other stories were rejected for more banal reasons. Darlene Madott was obliged to return "Home Movie" because it was set in Greece – and, perhaps oddly, "a lot of short-stories, none of this quality, with Greek settings" had been submitted, but *Toronto Life* preferred stories with a local setting (Madott to Winthrop Watson, 6 July 1979, JRF).

157 See, for example, Ryder, who argued that "the extent to which the Little Sisters decision will foster a new era of restrained Customs censorship, or make it possible for Customs to continue the same 'appalling level of over-censorship,' remains to be seen. The Court's ruling is disappointing because it does not do enough to reduce the risk that over-censorship will simply recur" (207–8).

158 Rule changed her citizenship from American to Canadian in the 1960s after careful deliberation because she preferred the politics of Canada over that of the United States; she subsequently declared herself to be a "Canadian author."

159 When Hellmer argued that popular magazines conventionally had the last say in publishing material, Rule disproved him by eliciting a completely different response from *Redbook*'s editor Barbara Blakemore. As Schuster notes, her struggles "enable[d] her to devise strategies of resistance and subversion" (2).

5. The Minor Archive: M. NourbeSe Philip and Mediations of Race and Gender in Canada

1 Coren's broadcast did not come to Philip's attention until 23 September ("Chronological Outline of Events," document in Philip's private archive).

2 Her essays often serve as a form of activism and reconceptualizations of national identities, as is the case with *A Genealogy of Resistance* (1997)

and *Frontiers* (1992), collections that tackled issues related to racism and culture. In "Echoes in a Stranger Land," for example, she reflects upon the "racism permeating the institutions of Canada" and laments the fact that "little has changed over the years" (11): "It matters not a jot that an African Canadian person may think herself very much integrated within Canadian society and a part of it ... if the dominant society continues to see them – us – as alien, different and Other, they cannot truly belong to the society" (18). Some of her work has been anthologized and taught in universities across North America and abroad: her young adult novel *Harriet's Daughter* was adopted in school boards across Ontario and became "required reading across the Caribbean for the CXC (secondary-leaving) exams" (Casas 43). Much of her work has won literary awards and prizes, and in 1990 she was awarded a Guggenheim Fellowship. Perhaps most famously, her collection of poetry *She Tries Her Tongue, Her Silence Softly Breaks* (1989) won the prestigious Casa de las Americas prize – while still in manuscript form.

3 Letter from Julia Howell, executive director, Arts Foundation of Greater Toronto, to Philip, 14 June 1995, private archive.

4 As part of the settlement, Philip is unable to disclose its terms.

5 Lionnet and Shih refer to such exiles as "the object of interior exclusion" or the "exclusion of the minoritized other" (12). See also Mariana Valverde and Anna Pratt, and Sherene Razack.

6 As disclosed to me in conversation with Philip on 26 October 2012.

7 See also Burman 2007.

8 See also Garay and Verduyn 9.

9 Philip had already provided a literary precedent for this strategy: she had published *Looking for Livingstone: An Odyssey of Silence*, a "pseudo-artifact," which had been "found" in an archive (Kaye 155). Elsewhere, she also commented on the importance of memory, which bears direct significance to the function of archives: "I am ... arguing for a subversive role for memory, that memory is more than nostalgia – it has a potentially kinetic quality and must impel us to action" ("Echoes in a Stranger Land," 20).

10 She added, "Had I emigrated to the United Kingdom or the USA, I would have had to confront, in both places, a long history of writing by Africans. In the former case, I am referring to the long history of writing by citizens of the former empire and present Commonwealth – Africa, Asia and Caribbean; in the latter, published writing by African Americans goes back at least to the enslaved African poet Phyllis Wheatley."

11 See the work of poet George Elliott Clarke.
12 In January 2010, when Philip came to Bishop's University and then to l'Université de Sherbrooke to read from her poetry, I asked about and discovered that she had retained a private cache of papers – in her basement. She allowed me to look through the papers in an office in downtown Toronto; I was able to read through the documents that bear witness to the events I will narrate in this chapter.
13 Various materials provide examples of her activism: a letter to Guy Gervais, Department of External Affairs (27 April 1988); her initiative in attempting to establish a productive link between the Black Secretariat and the Harbourfront Reading Series (26 February 1988); an undated letter from David Lobdell to Philip, in which he asks her to speak on behalf of a neglected book, titled *Mother Solitude*, by the Haitian novelist Emile Ollivier; her letter to the editor of the *Toronto Star*, 23 September 1994, in which she points out that in the paper Maya Angelou is listed along with such women as Margaret Atwood and Margaret Thatcher but is the only woman who is not identified in terms of her career; another letter to the editor (10 November 1998) about Gwynne Dyer's article "An African Scourge Cries Out for Action," which appeared on 6 November 1998 in *The Toronto Star* – Philip lists the various sloppy aspects of the article, including Dyer's suggestion that "Africa barely figures in the global economy"; and her letter to the *Toronto Star* about Douglas Gibson's remark that there is an absence of racism in Canadian publishing (30 May 1989). All of this material is found in Philip's private archive.
14 PEN is an international organization of writers who promote intellectual co-operation and the right to freedom of expression, and defend writers who are persecuted, imprisoned, and sometimes killed for their views.
15 The same is said in Philip's letter to the editor, *Globe and Mail*, 27 September 1989 (private archive).
16 In response, in the May 1998 issue of *Now Magazine*, Sheelagh Conway and Philip wrote an article, "Profanity from PEN," demanding Callwood's resignation as president.
17 See Sellar. I also found in her private archive an article by Philip, which appeared in *FUSE* 13.3. Her letter to the Ontario Press Council, dated 7 November 1989, states that she "merely approached Ms. Callwood as she came out of the Hall and held out a pamphlet to her. I engaged in no conversation with Ms. Callwood … There was no heated altercation and I certainly do not consider that I was a tormentor of Ms Callwood" (private archive).

18 Callwood, president of International PEN, to Philip, dated 27 November 1989, private archive. Callwood expresses "regret" for what she had uttered outside Roy Thomson Hall; although she notes that she felt "provoked by the unreasonableness of your leaflet," she also suggests that "we could have done better." A letter from Mel Sufrin, executive secretary of the Ontario Press Council, to Philip, dated 18 December 1989, announces that there will be a formal investigation into her complaint about misrepresentation in the *Globe and Mail* (private archive).
19 *Arts Foundation of Greater Toronto News* (newsletter), fall 1995, private archive.
20 See Crew.
21 Julia Howell, executive director, Arts Foundation of Greater Toronto, to Philip, 12 September 1995, private archive.
22 "TVO Chief Herrndorf Receives Inaugural Kilbourn Prize," *Globe and Mail*, 7 September 1995.
23 Arts Foundation of Toronto fact sheet, April 1995.
24 Howell to Philip, 18 August 1995, private archive.
25 See Crew.
26 Greater Arts Foundation of Toronto to Philip, 6 October 1995, private archive. Philip confirmed these jurors in a telephone conversation with me on 26 October 2012.
27 Transcript of broadcast by Michael Coren, 7 September 1995, private archive.
28 It is worth noting that Standard Broadcasting purchased a minority interest in Milestone Radio Incorporated during the period when Philip was involved in a legal battle with the former. Milestone Radio was the *only* broadcasting company in Canada that was owned and operated by Black Canadians.
29 Philip wrote a letter to the editor of the *Toronto Star* in which she addressed the "disturbing implications" of the title of the exhibit and the means by which elements – "booty" from Africa – of the exhibit had been accrued (23 August 1989, private archive). As other examples, see also Philip, "Museum Could Have Avoided Culture Clash" and "MINING 'The White Soul of Canada'"; Mackey; Da Breo; and Butler.
30 At no time did Philip demonstrate outside of the Royal Ontario Museum, a fact she corroborates in an email sent to me ("From nourbeSe," 12 November 2012, 2:02 a.m.). Instead, Philip's protests took the form of writing about and against the exhibition.
31 See also the essay by Todd Decker and those that appear in Walcott; and Philip, "Museum Could Have Avoided Culture Clash."
32 Titled "Author and Activist" and written by Henry Mietkiewicz.

33 Philip to Mayor Barbara Hall, 20 October 1995, private archive.
34 Philip to Howell, 1 November 1995, private archive.
35 Philip to Richard Ouzounian, president, Arts Foundation of Greater Toronto, 27 October 1995, private archive.
36 Philip to Howell, 1 November 1995, private archive.
37 Broadcast transcript for program "Corenucopia," 20 October 1995, private archive.
38 Document titled "Chronological Outline of Events," private archive.
39 Philip to Howell, 23 October 1995, private archive.
40 Philip to Howell, 1 November 1995, private archive.
41 Philip to Howell, 18 February 1996, private archive.
42 Philip to Howell, 1 November 1995, private archive.
43 Philip to Ouzounian, 27 October 1995, private archive. The Foundation did have a copy of the transcript. A handwritten letter survives from Philip to Howell, 29 September 1995, in which Philip mentions an enclosed copy of the radio transcript. It did not seem to have been sent, which is confirmed by another letter, dated 6 October 1995, to Philip from the foundation that discusses approaching the radio station manager about "the Michael Coren thing" and mentions an enclosed copy of the transcript.
44 "1995 (Tenth Anniversary) Program of Toronto Arts Awards," brochure, private archive.
45 Philip to Howell, 1 November 1995, private archive.
46 Philip to Ouzounian, 27 October 1995, private archive.
47 Philip to Howell, 1 November 1995, private archive.
48 Subsequent letters from the foundation show their continued involvement with Philip; Howell asks her, for example, to select a candidate for the Protégé Award, a practice in which Toronto Arts Awards recipients select a "work of art from a younger artist to serve as a permanent memento." Philip chose Gordon Owen. (Howell to Philip, 12 November 1995, private archive.)
49 Philip to Mayor Barbara Hall, 20 October 1995, private archive; see also Moloney.
50 Beverley Daurio to Allan Darling, secretary general, CRTC, 12 November 1995; Women's Centre at U of T to CRTC, 13 November 1995; Heather Murray, New College, University of Toronto, to Gary Slaight, president, CFRB Radio, 28 November 1995 (all copied to Philip), private archive.
51 She had written to Darling on 17 January and 19 February 1996.
52 Slaight, CFRB, to Darling (copy sent to Philip), 21 March 1996, private archive.

53 Slaight, CFRB, to Philip, 8 November 1995, private archive.
54 Slaight, CFRB, to Philip, 8 November 1995, private archive.
55 Slaight, CFRB, to Darling, CRTC, 2 July 1996 (copied to Philip), private archive.
56 Darling, CRTC, to Slaight, CFRB, 21 December 1995 (copied to Philip), and Jennifer Wilson, Public Affairs, CRTC, to Philip, 1 November 1995; private archive.
57 A memo from the Toronto Mayor's Committee on Community and Race Relations, dated 31 January 1996, notes that, since a libel action had been commenced in the courts, the committee could not appropriately discuss "any allegations pertaining to the libel action" (private archive).
58 Copy of letter, private archive. A letter was also sent by Charles Caccia, MP, to the CRTC, but, as it arrived three days after the deadline for written interventions, on 21 June, the letter was returned to Caccia (Peter Cussons, manager, Ontario Region, CRTC, to Charles Caccia, House of Commons, 5 July 1996 [copied to Philip], private archive).
59 Janice Dembo, coordinator, Mayor's Committee on Community and Race Relations, to Coren, 1 February 1996 (copied to Philip), private archive.
60 Dembo, coordinator, Mayor's Committee on Community and Race Relations, to Darling, CRTC, 31 January 1996, private archive. See also Small, "Panel Calls for Probe of Radio Host's Remarks," 5 March 1996, *Toronto Star*.
61 League for Human Rights of B'Nai Brith Canada to Darling, CRTC, 15 June 1996 (copied to Philip), private archive.
62 Antoni A. Shelton, executive director, to CRTC, 20 November 1995 (copied to Philip), private archive.
63 Philip to Darling, CRTC, 13 June 1996, private archive.
64 "CFRB Policies on Open-Line Programming," p. 1, private archive.
65 Philip to "Friend/Colleague," 7 March 1996, private archive.
66 Canadian Radio-Television and Telecommunications Commission, decision CRTC 97-372, Ottawa, 7 August 1997 (license renewal for CFRB). There were a couple of short-term renewals in the process, which the CRTC suggested was the result of not being in a position to rule on the license by the date of its expiry. See "CFRB Licence [*sic*] Renewed Short Term," *Toronto Star*, 3 December 1996. In a letter dated 7 March 1996, Philip notes that the license was renewed for a short-term period several times and interprets these series of short-term renewals as the effect of the protest being registered by letters of support (private archive).
67 MediaWatch, submission regarding Public Hearing CRTC 1996-6, Number 6 – Application (199603569) by Standard Radio Inc., CFRB 1010

AM Licence Renewal, 18 June 1996, and their letter to Darling, CRTC, 30 April 1996; African Canadian Legal Clinic's intervention, sent to Darling, CRTC, 18 June 1996; Philip to Darling, 13 June 1996; private archive.

68 Darling, CRTC, to Philip. 8 May 1996, private archive; see also Barnes.

69 Philip to The Honourable Jean Augustine, House of Commons, 11 June 1996, private archive.

70 See Goddard, 17 February 1996.

71 Clifford Lincoln, chair, Standing Committee on Canadian Heritage, to Jean Augustine, MP for Etobicoke-Lakeshore, 19 August 1996 (copied to Philip); also Augustine to Philip, 31 May, 3 July 1996 (private archive).

72 In a letter to Philip dated 16 November 1995 Maxwell Yalden, chief commissioner, Canadian Human Rights Commission, states that "the Canadian Human Rights Commission does not have the authority to deal with complaints about the content of radio broadcasts."

73 Philip to Ursula Menke, secretary general, CRTC, 5 January 2000, private archive.

74 CRTC, Decision CRTC 99-336, Ottawa, 26 August 1999 (license renewal for CFRB and its short-wave transmitter CFRX), private archive.

75 Slaight, president, CFRB, to Darling, secretary general, CRTC, 2 July 1996 (copied to Philip), private archive.

76 Philip to Ouzounian, 27 October 1995, private archive.

77 Slaight, CFRB, to Philip, 8 November 1995, private archive.

78 In one article she wrote for the the *Globe and Mail*, she addressed the issue more generally by pointing out that "to want justice as a black person in this society is to be described as an activist," and that activists were often seen in derogatory terms. In a letter to the editor to the same newspaper on 30 May 1989, she registered her protest against an article by H.J. Kirchhoff featuring statements by Douglas Gibson about the "absence of racism in Canadian publishing"; she cited as an example her novel *Harriet's Daughter*, which had been repeatedly declined by Canadian publishers only to receive two immediate offers when she sent it to England.

79 Philip would retain another two legal representatives, Hilary Linton, and Eberts Symes Street & Corbett, before the trial found resolution in a settlement.

80 Philip to Darling, CRTC, 14 November 1995, private archive.

81 Email from Philip to Barbara Godard, 7 November 2011, private archive.

82 Email from Symes to Philip, 16 February 2002, in response to Philip's email to Symes, dated 16 February 2002, private archive.

83 Greg Quill, "Coren Says He Was Just Being Very, Very Funny," *Toronto Star*, 30 November 2005.

84 As Erikson notes, the reintegration of someone characterized as deviant, however wrongfully, is a slow process; one might be "ushered into the deviant position by a decisive and often dramatic ceremony" and yet be "retired from it with scarcely a word of public notice" (16). The person castigated therefore feels "no proper license to resume a normal life in the community," since "nothing has happened to revoke the verdict or diagnosis pronounced upon him at that time" (16).

Conclusion

1 Eichhorn's article "Beyond Digitization: A Case Study of Three Contemporary Feminist Collections" is forthcoming in *Archives and Manuscripts*, ed. Maryanne Dever and Linda Morra.

Works Cited

Archives Consulted

Acc. 2005–008. Archives and Special Collections, University of Victoria.
Edith and Lorne Collection. Queen's University.
Emily Carr Fonds, 1905–1946. 2181; MS-2763; E/D/C23. British Columbia and Archives Records Service. Victoria, British Columbia.
Emily Carr Papers, National Art Gallery Archives, Ottawa.
Flora Alfreda Hamilton Burns Collection. MS 2786. British Columbia Archives and Records Service, Victoria.
Jane Rule Fonds. University of British Columbia Archives, Vancouver.
McClelland & Stewart Papers. McMaster University, Hamilton.
M. NourbeSe Philip papers. Private archive.
Parnall Collection. MS 2763. British Columbia Archives and Records Service, Victoria.
Pauline Johnson Fonds. City of Vancouver Archives.
Pauline Johnson Fonds. McMaster University, Hamilton.
Robert Weaver Fonds. MG31 D162. Library and Archives Canada (LAC), Ottawa.
Sheila Watson Fonds. John M. Kelly Library, University of St Michael's College, University of Toronto.
Wilfred Watson Fonds. University of Alberta, Edmonton.

Print and Web Sources

Aigner-Varoz, Erika. "Suiting Herself: E. Pauline Johnson's Constructions of Indian Identity and Self." Diss. University of New Mexico, May 2011. Print.

Anderson, Benedict. *Imagined Communities: Reflections on the Origin and Spread of Nationalism.* London: Verso, 1991. Print.

Anonymous. "Brantford Abroad" (n.d.), Pauline Johnson Fonds, McMaster University, box 4, file 1.

Appadurai, Arjun. "Archive and Aspiration." *Information is Alive: Art and Theory of Archiving and Retrieving Data*. Ed. Jake Brouwer and Arien Mulder. Rotterdam: NAj Publishers, 2003. 14–25. Print.

Arondekar, Anjali. *For the Record: On Sexuality and the Colonial Archive in India*. Durham: Duke UP, 2009. Print.

Arts Foundation of Greater Toronto. http://www.torontoartsfoundation.org/. Accessed 25 September 2012. Web.

Ballantyne, Tony. "Re-reading the Archive and Opening Up the Nation-State: Colonial Knowledge in South Asia (and Beyond)." *After the Imperial Turn: Thinking with and through the Nation*. Ed. Antoinette Burton. Durham: Duke UP, 2003. 102–24. Print.

Barman, Jean. "Aboriginal Women on the Streets of Victoria: Rethinking Transgressive Sexuality during the Colonial Period." *Contact Zones: Aboriginal and Settler Women in Canada's Colonial Past*. Ed. Katie Pickles and Myra Rutherdale. Vancouver: UBC P, 2005. 205–27. Print.

Barnes, Alan. "Errors in Coverage but Press Council Rejects Complaint." *Toronto Star* 5 November 1996: A12. Print.

Barriault, Marcel. "Archiving the Queer and Queering the Archives." *Community Archives: The Shaping of Memory*. Ed. Jeannette A. Bastian and Ben Alexander. London: Facet, 2009. Print.

Benstock, Shari. "Expatriate Sapphic Modernism." *Rereading Modernism*. Ed. Lisa Rado. New York: Garland, 1994. 97–121. Print.

Berlant, Lauren. "Intimacy: A Special Issue." *Critical Inquiry* 24.2 (1998): 281–8. Print.

– *The Queen of America Goes to Washington City: Essays on Sex and Citizenship*. Durham: Duke UP, 1997. Print.

Bessai, Diane, and David Jackel, eds. *Figures in a Ground: Canadian Essays on Modern Literature Collected in Honor of Sheila Watson*. Saskatoon: Western Producer Prairie Books, 1978. Print.

Blair, Jennifer, Daniel Coleman, Kate Higginson, and Lorraine York, eds. *ReCalling Early Canada: Reading the Political in Literary and Cultural Production*. Edmonton: U of Alberta P, 2005. Print.

Blanchard, Paula. *The Life of Emily Carr*. Vancouver: Douglas and McIntyre, 1987. Print.

Blavatsky, H.P. *The Secret Doctrine: Collected Writings*. Wheaton: Theosophical UP, 1978–9. Print.

Bouson, J. Brooks. *Embodied Shame: Uncovering Female Shame in Contemporary Women's Writing*. Albany: State University of New York, 2009. Print.

Bowering, George. "Sheila Watson." *Encyclopedia of Literature in Canada*. Ed. W.H. New. Toronto: U of Toronto P, 2002. 1199. Print.

–, ed. *Sheila Watson and* The Double Hook. Ottawa: Golden Dog, 1985. Print.
Bruusgaard, Emily. "Chatelaine Magazine." http://pw20c.mcmaster.ca/case-study/chatelaine-magazine. 21 June 2010. Web.
Burman, Barbara, and Carole Turbin, eds. *Material Strategies: Dress and Gender in Historical Perspective*. Oxford: Blackwell, 2003. Print.
Burman, Jenny. "Deportable or Admissible? Black Women and the Space of 'Removal.'" *Black Geographies and the Politics of Space*. Ed. Katherine McKittrick and Clyde Woods. Toronto: Between the Lines, 2007. 177–92. Print.
Burns, Flora. "Emily Carr." *The Clear Spirit: Twenty Canadian Women and Their Times*. Ed. Mary Quayle. Toronto: U of Toronto P, 1966. 221–41. Print.
– "Emily Carr and the Newcombe Collection." *The Beaver* 293 (Summer 1962): 27–35. Print.
Burton, Antoinette, ed. *After the Imperial Turn: Thinking With and Through the Nation*. Durham: Duke UP, 2003. Print.
– *Archive Stories: Facts, Fictions, and the Writing of History*. Durham: Duke UP, 2005. Print.
Buss, Helen. *Mapping Our Selves*. Montreal: McGill-Queen's UP, 1993. Print.
Butler, Judith. *Antigone's Claim: Kinship between Life and Death*. New York: Columbia UP, 2000. Print.
Butler, Judith, and Gayatri Chakravorty Spivak. *Who Sings the Nation State? Language, Politics, Belonging*. Chicago: Seagull, 2007. Print.
Butler, Shelley Ruth. *Contested Representations: Revisiting* Into the Heart of Africa. Peterborough: Broadview, 2008. Print.
Cambron, Micheline, and Carole Gerson. "Authors and Literary Culture." *History of the Book in Canada*. Vol. 2, *1840–1918*. Ed. Yvan Lamonde, Patricia Lockhart Fleming, and Fiona Black. Toronto: U of Toronto P, 2005. 119–34. Print.
Campbell, Sandra. *Both Hands: A Life of Lorne Pierce of Ryerson Press*. Montreal/Kingston: McGill-Queen's UP, 2013.
Carpenter, Cari M. "'A Woman to Let Alone': E. Pauline Johnson and the Performance of Anger." *Seeing Red: Anger, Sentimentality, and American Indians*. Ohio: Ohio State UP, 2008. 54–86. Print.
Carr, Emily. *An Address by Emily Carr*. Toronto: Oxford UP, 1955. Print.
– *The Book of Small*. Toronto: Oxford UP, 1942. Print.
– *Corresponding Influence: Selected Letters of Emily Carr and Ira Dilworth*. Toronto: U of Toronto P, 2006. Print.
– *Dear Nan: Letters of Emily Carr, Nan Cheney and Humphrey Toms*. Ed. Doreen Walker. Vancouver: UBC P, 1990. Print.
Growing Pains: The Autobiography of Emily Carr. Toronto: Oxford UP, 1946. Print.

– *The Heart of a Peacock*. Toronto: Oxford UP, 1953. Print.
– *The House of All Sorts*. Toronto: Oxford UP, 1944. Print.
– *Hundreds and Thousands: The Journals of Emily Carr*. Toronto: Clarke, Irwin, 1966. Print.
– *Klee Wyck*. Toronto: Oxford UP, 1941. Print.
– *Klee Wyck*. Foreword by Ira Dilworth. Toronto: Clarke, Irwin, 1951. v–xvi. Print.
– "Modern and Indian Art of the West Coast." Supplement to the *McGill News* June 1929: 18–22. Print.
– *Pause: A Sketch Book*. Toronto: Clarke, Irwin, 1953. Print.
– "Picture Gallery." *Victoria Daily Times* 13 December 1932. Print.
Carter, Rodney G.S. "Of Things Said and Unsaid: Power, Archival Silences, and Power in Silence." *Archivaria: Special Section on Archives, Space and Power* 61 (Spring 2006): 215–33. Print.
Casas, Maria Caridad. *Multimodality in Canadian Black Feminist Writing: Orality and the Body in the Work of Harris, Philip, Allen, and Brand*. New York: Rodopi, 2009. Print.
"CFRB Licence [*sic*] Renewed Short Term." *Toronto Star* 3 December 1996: E4. Print.
"Chatelaine: We're Celebrating 80 Years." http://en.chatelaine.com/english/celebration/article.jsp?content=20080225_15493 8_6272. 21 June 2010. Web.
Chilsolm, Elspeth. "Canadian Pioneers." Acc. 7110073. 29 October 1969. CBC Archives, Toronto. Audio recording.
Clay, Margaret. "Emily Carr as I Knew Her." *The Business and Professional Woman* 26.9 (November–December 1959): 1–9. Print.
Collett, Anne. "Fair Trade: Marketing 'The Mohawk Princess.'" *Economies of Representation, 1790–2000: Colonialism and Commerce*. Ed. Leigh Dale and Helen Gilbert. Aldershot, England: Ashgate, 2007. Print.
Cook, Terry, and Joan M. Schwartz. "Archives, Records, and Power: From (Postmodern) Theory to (Archival) Performance." *Archival Science* 2 (2002): 1–19. Print.
Coren, Michael. *Setting It Right*. Toronto: Stoddart, 1996. Print.
"Correction." *The Toronto Star* 5 May 1990: S15. Print.
Cowan, T.L. "'I Remember … I Was Wearing Leather Pants.' Archiving the Repertoire of Feminist Cabaret in Canada." *Basements and Attics, Closets and Cyberspace: Explorations in Canadian Women's Archives*. Ed. Linda M. Morra and Jessica Schagerl. Waterloo: Wilfrid Laurier UP, 2012. 65–86. Print.
Creet, Julia. "Locking Up Letters." *Basements and Attics, Closets and Cyberspace: Explorations in Canadian Women's Archives*. Ed. Linda M. Morra and Jessica Schagerl. Waterloo: Wilfrid Laurier UP, 2012. 313–17. Print.
Crew, Robert. "A Decade of Paying Tribute to People Who Create." *Toronto Star* 7 September 1995: G9. Print.

Cvetkovich, Ann. *An Archive of Feelings: Trauma, Sexuality and Lesbian Public Cultures*. Durham: Duke UP, 2003. Print.

Da Breo, Hazel. "Royal Spoils, Imperialists, Missionaries and the Royal Ontario Museum's African Collection: The Museum Confronts Its Colonial Past." *Fuse* 13.3 (Winter 1989–1990): 27–36. Print.

Decker, Todd. "'Do You Want to Hear a Mammy Song?': A Historiography of *Show Boat*." *Contemporary Theatre Review*. Special issue: *The Broadway Musical, New Approaches* 19.1 (2009): 8–21. Print.

Derrida, Jacques. *Archive Fever: A Freudian Impression*. Trans. Eric Prenowitz. Chicago: U of Chicago P, 1996. Print.

Dever, Maryanne, Ann Vickery, and Sally Newman. *The Intimate Archive: Journeys through Private Papers*. Australia: National Library of Australia, 2009. Print.

Devereux, Cecily. "Finding Indian Maidens on eBay: Tales of the Alternative Archive (and More Tales of White Commodity Culture)." *Basements and Attics, Closets and Cyberspace: Explorations in Canadian Women's Archives*. Ed. Linda M. Morra and Jessica Schagerl. Waterloo: Wilfrid Laurier UP, 2012. 36–59. Print.

Dickinson, Peter. *Here Is Queer: Nationalisms, Sexualities, and the Literatures of Canada*. Toronto: U of Toronto P, 1999. Print.

Dilworth, Ira. "Canadian Pioneers." Interview with Elspeth Chilsolm, Acc. 7110073. 29 October 1969. CBC Archives, Toronto. Audio recording.

– "Emily Carr." *Canadian Art* 2.3 (March 1945): 115–19. Print.

– "Emily Carr: Biographical Sketch." *Emily Carr: Her Paintings and Sketches*. Toronto: Oxford UP for the National Gallery of Canada and Art Gallery of Toronto, 1945. 9–19. Print.

– "Emily Carr – Canadian Artist-Author." *Saturday Night* 57.8 (1 November 1941): 26. Print.

– "Emily Carr – Canadian Painter and Poet in Prose." *Saturday Night* 57.9 (8 November 1941): 26. Print.

– Foreword. *Growing Pains: The Autobiography of Emily Carr*. Toronto: Oxford UP, 1946. vii–ix. Print.

– Foreword. *Klee Wyck*. By Emily Carr. Toronto: Oxford UP, 1941. vii–x. Print.

– Foreword. *Klee Wyck*. By Emily Carr. Toronto: Clarke, Irwin, 1951. v–xvi. Print.

– Introduction. *An Address by Emily Carr*. Toronto: Oxford UP, 1955. v–ix. Print.

– "M. Emily Carr." *Canadian Library Association Bulletin* 3.4 (April 1947): 112–13. Repr. in *Victoria Daily Times* 19 May 1947. Print.

di Mathes, Enzo. *Now* [magazine] February 1–7, 1996: 13. Print.

Doran, George H. *Chronicles of Barabbas, 1884–1934*. New York: Harcourt Brace, 1935. Print.

Downes, David, and Paul Rock. *Understanding Deviancy: A Guide to the Sociology of Crime and Rule-Breaking*. Oxford: Oxford UP, 2011. Print.

Drainie, Bronwyn. "What Kind of Way Is That for Canada's Writers to Talk?" *Globe and Mail* 26 February 1994: C13. Print.

Dyer, Gwynne. "An African Scourge Cries Out for Action." *Toronto Star* 6 November 1998: 1. Print.

Eby, Marek. "Reading Up the Ladder of Privilege: Marginality in Emily Carr's *Growing Pains*." Unpublished paper. 7 April 2013. Print.

Egan, Susanna. "Emily Carr and the Landscapes of Autobiography." *Essays on Canadian Writing* 60 (Winter 1996): 166–86. Print.

Eichhorn, Kate. *The Archival Turn in Feminism: Outrage in Order*. Philadelphia: Temple UP, 2013. Print.

– "Beyond Digitization: A Case Study of Three Contemporary Feminist Collections." Forthcoming in *Archives & Manuscripts*. Ed. Maryanne Dever and Linda Morra. Print.

Elderkin, Susan Huntley. "Recovering the Fictions of Emily Carr." *Studies in Canadian Literature* 17.2 (Winter 1992): 14–27. Print.

"Elocutionary Entertainment. By Miss E. Pauline Johnson." *Emerson Journal* (17 December 1897). Print.

Erikson, Kai T. "On the Sociology of Deviance." *Constructions of Deviance: Social Power, Context, and Interaction*. 4th ed. Belmont: Wadsworth/Thomson, 2003. 11–18. Print.

Evain, Christine. *Douglas Gibson Unedited*. Brussels: Peter Lang, 2007. Print.

Farr, Robert. "Government Looks All Around." *Publishing in Canada: East Looks West*. Ed. John R.T. Ettlinger. Halifax: School of Library Service, Dalhousie University, 1973. 64–84. Print.

Fetherling, George. "Literary Agents." *Encyclopedia of Literature in Canada*. Ed. William H. New. Toronto: U of Toronto P, 2002. 668. Print.

Fiamengo, Janice. "'This Graceful Olive Branch of the Iroquois': Pauline Johnson's Rhetoric of Reconciliation." *The Woman's Page: Journalism and Rhetoric in Early Canada*. Toronto: U of Toronto P, 2008. 89–120. Print.

Flahiff, Fred. *always someone to kill the doves: A Life of Sheila Watson*. Edmonton: NeWest Press, 2005. Print.

– Introduction. *Sheila Watson Fonds*. Special Collections and Archives of the John M. Kelly Library, University of St Michael's College, University of Toronto, 2009. 1. Print.

Forte, Jeanie. "Focus on the Body: Pain, Praxis, and Pleasure in Feminist Performance." *Critical Theory and Performance*. Rev. and enlarged ed. Ed. Janelle G. Reinelt and Joseph Roach. Ann Arbor: U of Michigan P, 2007. 249–62. Print.

Foster, Ann. *The Mohawk Princess: Being Some Account of the Life of Tekahion-Wake*. Vancouver: Lion's Gate, 1931. Print.

Foucault, Michel. *The Archaeology of Knowledge & The Discourse on Language*. Trans. A.M. Sheridan Smith. New York: Pantheon, 1972. Print.

– *The Order of Things: An Archaeology of the Human Sciences*. London: Routledge, 1970. Print.

Francis, Daniel. *The Imaginary Indian: The Image of the Indian in Canadian Culture*. Vancouver: Arsenal Pulp Press, 1993. Print.

Friskney, Janet B. *New Canadian Library: The Ross-McClelland Years, 1952–1978*. Toronto: U of Toronto P, 2007. Print.

Friskney, Janet B., and Carole Gerson. "Writers and the Market for Fiction and Literature." *History of the Book in Canada*. Vol. 3, *1918–1980*. Ed. Carole Gerson and Jacques Michon. Toronto: U of Toronto P, 2007. 131–8. Print.

Garay, Kathleen, and Christl Verduyn, eds. *Archival Narratives for Canada: Re-Telling Stories in a Changing Landscape*. Halifax: Fernwood, 2011. Print.

Garman, Anthea. "Confession and Public Life in Post-apartheid South Africa: A Foucauldian Reading of Antjie Krog's *country of my skull*." *Journal of Literary Studies* 22.34 (2006): 322–44. Print.

Gerson, Carole. *Canadian Women in Print, 1750–1918*. Waterloo: Wilfrid Laurier UP, 2010. Print.

– "Postcolonialism Meets Book History: Pauline Johnson and Imperial London." *Home-Work: Postcolonialism, Pedagogy, and Canadian Literature*. Ed. Cynthia Sugars. Ottawa: U of Ottawa P, 2004. Print.

Gerson, Carole, and Marie-Pier Luneau. "Authors' Careers: Social and Cultural Profile of Writers." *History of the Book in Canada*. Vol. 3, *1918–1980*. Ed. Carole Gerson and Jacques Michon. Toronto: U of Toronto P, 2007. 93–100. Print.

Gerson, Carole, and Veronica Strong-Boag. "Championing the Native: E. Pauline Johnson Rejects the Squaw." *Contact Zones: Aboriginal and Settler Women in Canada's Colonial Past*. Ed. Katie Pickles and Myra Rutherdale. Vancouver: UBC P, 2005. 47–66. Print.

–, eds. *E. Pauline Johnson, Tekahionwake: Collected Poems and Selected Prose*. Toronto: U of Toronto P, 2002. Print.

Gillespie, Diane F. "The Gender of Modern/ist Painting." *Gender in Modernism: New Geographies, Complex Intersections*. Ed. Bonnie Kime Scott. Illinois: U of Illinois P, 2007. 765–77. Print.

Gillies, Mary Ann. *The Professional Literary Agent in Britain, 1880–1920*. Toronto: U of Toronto P, 2007. Print.

Gilmore, Leigh. "The Mark of Autobiography: Postmodernism, Autobiography and Genre." *Autobiography and Postmodernism*. Ed. Kathleen M. Ashley, Leigh Gilmore, and Gerald Peters. Boston: U of Massachusetts P, 1994. 3–18. Print.

Gilroy, Paul. *The Black Atlantic: Modernity and Double Consciousness.* Cambridge, MA: Harvard UP, 1993. Print.

Gluck, Mary. *Popular Bohemia: Modernism and Urban Culture in Nineteenth-Century Paris.* Cambridge, MA: Harvard UP, 2005. Print.

Goddard, Peter. "CFRB Getting a 'Black Voice': New Talk Show 'Shouldn't Just Be About Blacks and Police, Media-Savvy Host Says.'" *Toronto Star* 17 February 1996: J11. Print.

– "Listeners Bash Radio Talk Jock." *Toronto Star* 22 November 1995: D1. Print.

Golick, Greta. "Bookselling in Town and Country." *History of the Book in Canada.* Vol. 2, *1840–1918.* Ed. Yvan Lamonde, Patricia Lockhart Fleming, and Fiona A. Black. Toronto: U of Toronto P, 2005. 210–40. Print.

Goody, Alex. *Modernist Articulations: A Cultural Study of Djuna Barnes, Mina Loy and Gertrude Stein.* Basingstoke, England: Palgrave Macmillan, 2007. Print.

Gray, Charlotte. *Flint and Feather: The Life and Times of E. Pauline Johnson, Tekahionwake.* Toronto: Harper Collins, 2010. Print.

Green, Barbara. *Spectacular Confessions: Autobiography, Performative Activism, and the Sites of Suffrage.* Toronto: Palgrave Macmillan, 1997. Print.

Head, D., and I. Ousby. *The Cambridge Guide to Literature in English.* London: Cambridge UP, 2006. Print.

Hoefel, Roseanne. "Writing, Performance, Activism: Zitkala-Sa and Pauline Johnson." *Native American Women in Literature and Culture.* Ed. Susan Castillo and Victor M.P. Da Rosa. Porto, Portugal: Fernando Pessoa UP, 1997. 107–118. Print.

Huk, Romana. "In AnOther's Pocket: The Address of the 'Pocket Epic' in Postmodern Black British Poetry." *Yale Journal of Criticism* 31.1 (Spring 2000): 23–48. Print.

Humphrey, Ruth. "Letters from Emily Carr." *University of Toronto Quarterly* 41.2 (Winter 1972): 93–150. Print.

Jennings, Michael W., Howard Eiland, and Gary Smith, eds. *Walter Benjamin: Selected Writings.* Vol. 3, *1935–1938.* Cambridge, MA: Harvard UP, 2003. Print.

Johnson, E. Pauline. *Flint and Feather: The Complete Poems of E. Pauline Johnson.* 1912. Reprint. Toronto: Musson, 1913. Print.

– *Legends of Vancouver.* Vancouver: David Spencer, 1911. Print.

– *The Shagganapi.* Toronto: Ryerson Press, 1913. Print.

– "A Strong Race Opinion: On the Indian Girl in Modern Fiction." *The Toronto World.* 1892. Reprinted in Carole Gerson and Veronica Strong-Boag, eds., *Pauline Johnson, Tekahionwake: Collected Poems and Selected Prose.* Toronto: U of Toronto P, 2002. 177–83. Print.

Karr, Clarence. *Authors and Audiences: Popular Canadian Fiction in the Early Twentieth Century.* Montreal/Kingston: McGill-Queen's UP, 2000. 58–79. Print.

Kaye, Frances W. Review of *Looking for Livingstone. Prairie Schooner* 68.2 (Summer 1994): 154–7. Print.

Keller, Betty. *Pauline: A Biography of Pauline Johnson*. Vancouver: Douglas and McIntyre, 1981. Print.

Kirchhoff, H.J., and Isabel Vincent. "Charges of Racism Spark Protest at Writers' Congress." *Globe and Mail* 26 September 1989: A19. Print.

Knelman, Martin. "Toronto's Charismatic Social Fixer: Being Labeled 'Racist' Was Painful." *Toronto Star* 12 November 2003: A3. Print.

Korinek, Valerie J. *Roughing It in the Suburbs: Reading* Chatelaine *Magazine in the Fifties and Sixties*. Toronto: U of Toronto P, 2000. Print.

Leighton, Mary Elizabeth. "Performing Pauline Johnson: Representations of 'the Indian Poetess' in the Periodical Press, 1892–95." *Essays on Canadian Writing* 65 (Fall 1998): 141–65. Print.

Lionnet, Françoise, and Shu-mei Shih, eds. *Minor Transnationalism*. Durham: Duke UP, 2005. Print.

Litt, Paul. "The State and the Book." *History of the Book in Canada*. Vol. 3, *1918–1980*. Ed. Carole Gerson and Jacques Michon. Toronto: U of Toronto P, 2007. 34–44. Print.

Livesay, Dorothy. "Carr & Livesay." *Canadian Literature* 84 (Spring 1980): 144–47. Print.

Lukens, Margo. "'A Being of a New World:' The Ambiguity of Mixed Blood in Pauline Johnson's 'My Mother.'" *MELUS* 27.3 (Autumn 2002): 43–56. Print.

Mackey, Eva. "Postmodernism and Cultural Politics in a Multicultural Nation: Contests over Truth in *Into the Heart of Africa* Controversy." *Public Culture* 7 (1995): 403–31. Print.

MacSkimming, Roy. *The Perilous Trade: Book Publishing in Canada, 1946–2006*. Toronto: McClelland & Stewart, 2007. Print.

Marshall, Christine Lowella. "The Re-Presented Indian: Pauline Johnson's 'Strong Race Opinion' and Other Forgotten Discourses." Diss. University of Arizona, 1997. Print.

McCaig, JoAnn. *Reading In: Alice Munro's Archives*. Waterloo: Wilfrid Laurier UP, 2002. Print.

McGregor, Hannah. "An Archive of Complicity: Ethically (Re)Reading the Documentaries of Nelofer Pazira." *Basements and Attics, Closets and Cyberspace: Explorations in Canadian Women's Archives*. Ed. Linda M. Morra and Jessica Schagerl. Waterloo: Wilfrid Laurier UP, 2012. 107–24. Print.

McKittrick, Katherine. "'Who do you talk to, when a body's in trouble?': M. NourbeSe Philip's (un)silencing of black bodies in the diaspora." *Social & Cultural Geography* 1.2 (2000): 223–36. Print.

McKittrick, Katherine, and Clyde Woods. "No One Knows the Mysteries at the Bottom of the Ocean." *Black Geographies and the Politics of Space*. Ed.

Katherine McKittrick and Clyde Woods. Toronto: Between the Lines, 2007. 1–13. Print.

McLeod, Donald W. "Publishing Against the Grain." *History of the Book in Canada*. Vol. 3, *1918–1980*. Ed. Carole Gerson and Jacques Michon. Toronto: U of Toronto P, 2007. 322–7. Print.

McRaye, Walter. *Pauline Johnson and Her Friends*. Toronto: Ryerson Press, 1947. Print.

Mietkiewicz, Henry. "Author and Activist." *Toronto Star* 7 September 1995: G9. Print.

Milz, Sabine. "'Publica(c)tion': E. Pauline Johnson's Publishing Venues and Their Contemporary Significance." *Studies in Canadian Literature* 29.1 (2004): 127–45. Print.

Moloney, Paul. "CFRB Show Host Urged to Apologize." *Toronto Star* 31 January 1996: A7. Print.

Morgan, Cecilia. "'A Wigwam to Westminster': Performing Mohawk Identity in Imperial Britain, 1890s–1990s." *Gender and History* 15.2 (August 2003): 319–41. Print.

Morra, Linda M. "Autobiographical Text, Archives, and Activism: The Jane Rule Fonds and Her Unpublished Memoir, *Taking My Life*." *Out of the Closet, Into the Archives: Researching Sexual Histories*. Ed. Jaime Cantrell and Amy Stone. New York: SUNY Press, forthcoming.

– Introduction. *Corresponding Influence: Selected Letters of Emily Carr and Ira Dilworth*. Ed. Linda Morra. Toronto: U of Toronto P, 2006. 1–24. Print.

– "'Vexed by the Crassness of Commerce': Jane Rule's Struggle for Literary Integrity and Freedom of Expression." *Canadian Literature. Special Issue: Queerly Canadian* 205 (Summer 2010): 86–106. Print.

Morra, Linda M., and Jessica Schagerl, eds. *Basements and Attics, Closets and Cyberspace: Explorations in Canadian Women's Archives*. Waterloo: Wilfrid Laurier UP, 2012. 1–22. Print.

Neuman, Shirley. "Autobiography: From Different Poetics to a Poetics of Difference." *Essays on Life Writing: From Genre to Critical Practice*. Ed. Marlene Kadar. Toronto: U of Toronto P, 1992. 213–30. Print.

Nicks, Trudy. "Evelyn Johnson and the Chiefswood Collection: Objects and Encounters." *E. Pauline Johnson: "Faithfully Yours."* Ed. Thomas V. Hill. Brantford: Woodland Cultural Centre and Chiefswood National Historic Site. In press.

Nurse, Andrew. "Archives as Narrative: The Politics of Ethnographic Archiving at the National Museum." *Archival Narratives for Canada: Re-Telling Stories in a Changing Landscape*. Ed. Kathleen Garay and Christl Verduyn. Halifax: Fernwood, 2011. 41–55. Print.

O'Driscoll, Michael, and Edward Bishop. "Archiving 'Archiving.'" *ESC* 30.1 (2004): 1–16. Print.

The Oxford English Dictionary. Oxford: Oxford UP, 2009. S.v. "arrested," "kindness." Web. 10 January 2013.

Page, Kezia. *Transnational Negotiations in Caribbean Diasporic Literature: Remitting the Text*. New York: Routledge, 2010. Print.

Panofsky, Ruth. *The Literary Legacy of the Macmillan Company of Canada: Making Books and Mapping Culture*. Toronto: U of Toronto P, 2012. Print.

Philip, M. NourbeSe. "The Disappearing Debate: Racism and Censorship." *Language in Her Eye: Views on Writing and Gender by Canadian Women Writing in English*. Toronto: Coach House Press, 1990. Print.

– "Echoes in a Stranger Land." *Frontiers: Selected Essays and Writing on Racism and Culture, 1984–1992*. Stratford, ON: Mercury Press, 1992. 1–25. Print.

– *Frontiers: Selected Essays and Writing on Racism and Culture, 1984–1992*. Stratford, ON: Mercury Press, 1992. Print.

– *A Genealogy of Resistance and Other Essays*. Stratford, ON: Mercury Press, 1997. Print.

– "Ignoring Poetry." *A Genealogy of Resistance and Other Essays*. Stratford, ON: Mercury Press, 1997. 120–5. Print.

– "MINING 'The White Soul of Canada.'" *Third Text* 14 (Spring 1991): 63–77. Print.

– "Museum Could Have Avoided Culture Clash." *Toronto Star* 14 January 1991: A13. Print.

– *Showing Grit*. Toronto: Poui, 1993. Print.

Podnieks, Elizabeth. *Daily Modernism: The Literary Diaries of Virginia Woolf, Antonia White, Elizabeth Smart, and Anaïs Nin*. Montreal: McGill-Queen's UP, 2000. Print.

Poovey, Mary. *The Proper Lady and the Woman Writer: Ideology as Style in the Works of Mary Wollstonecraft, Mary Shelley, and Jane Austen*. Chicago: U of Chicago P, 1984. Print.

Pratt, Anna, and Mariana Valverde. "From Deserving Victims to 'Masters of Confusion': Redefining Refugees in the 1990s." *Canadian Journal of Sociology* 27.2 (2002): 135–61. Print.

Pratt, Mary Louise. *Imperial Eyes: Travel Writing and Transculturation*. London: Routledge, 1992. Print.

Prince, Gerald. "The Disnarrated." *Narrative Theory: Critical Concepts in Literary and Cultural Studies*. Vol 1. *Major Issues in Narrative Theory*. Ed. Mieke Bal. London: Routledge, 2004. 297–305. Print.

Quill, Greg. "Coren Says He Was Just Being Very, Very Funny." *Toronto Star* 30 November 2005. Print.

Rak, Julie. "Double-Wampum, Double-Life, Double Click: E. Pauline Johnson by and for the World Wide Web." *Textual Studies in Canada* 13.14 (2001): 153–70. Print.

Razack, Sherene. "Making Canada White: Law and the Policing of Bodies of Colour in the 1990s." *Canadian Journal of Law and Society* 14 (1999): 167–70. Print.

Reinelt, Janelle G., and Joseph Roach, eds. *Critical Theory and Performance.* Rev. and enl. ed. U of Michigan P, 2007. Print.

Richards, Thomas. *The Imperial Archive: Knowledge and the Fantasy of Empire.* New York: Verso, 1993. Print.

Ross, Val. "TVO Chief Herrndorf Receives Inaugural Kilbourn Prize. The Toronto Arts Awards, Celebrating Its 10th Anniversay, Added Eighth Honour Despite Looming Funding Crunch." *Globe and Mail* 7 September 1995: C4. Print.

Rubin, Gayle. "The Traffic in Women: Notes on the 'Political Economy' of Sex." *Toward an Anthropology of Women.* Ed. Rayna R. Reiter. New York: Monthly Review, 1975. 157–210. Print.

Rule, Jane. "Anyone Will Do." *Redbook* 133 (October 1969): 108–9. Print.

– *Contract with the World.* Toronto: Insomniac Press, 2005. Print.

– *Detained at Customs: Jane Rule Testifies at the Little Sister's Trial.* Vancouver: Lazarus, 1995. Print.

– "Jane Rule: The Woman behind *Lesbian Images*" (interview). *Body Politic* 21 (December 1975): 14–15. Print

– *Lesbian Images.* New York: Crossing Press, 1975. Print.

– *Loving the Difficult.* Sidney, BC: Hedgerow, 2008. Print.

– "Moving On." *Redbook* 131 (June 1968): 86–7. Print.

– "No More Bargains." *Redbook* 121 (September 1963): 68–9. Print.

– "Not an Ordinary Wife." *Redbook* 133 (August 1969): 70–1. Print.

– *This Is Not for You.* New York: McCall, 1970. Print.

– *The Young in One Another's Arms.* Garden City: Doubleday, 1977. Print.

Ryder, Bruce. "The Little Sisters Case, Administrative Censorship, and Obscenity Law." *Osgoode Hall Law Journal* 39.1 (2001): 207–27. Web. Accessed 10 October 2012. Print.

Salzani, Carlo. *Constellations of Reading: Walter Benjamin in Figures of Actuality.* New York: Peter Lang, 2008. Print.

Schur, Edwin M. *Labeling Women Deviant: Gender, Stigma, and Social Control.* Philadelphia: Temple UP, 1983. Print.

Schuster, Marilyn R. *Passionate Communities: Reading Lesbian Resistance in Jane Rule's Fiction.* New York: New York UP, 1999. Print.

Scobie, Stephen. *Sheila Watson and Her Works.* Toronto: ECW, 1984. Print.

Sellar, Don. "When the Facts Are in Dispute." *Toronto Star* 12 June 1993: D2. Print.

Seton, Ernest Thompson. Introduction. *The Shagganappi*. By E. Pauline Johnson. Toronto: Ryerson, 1913. 7–9. Print.

Shapiro, Michael J. *Methods and Nations: Cultural Governance and the Indigenous Subject*. Routledge: New York, 2004. Print.

Showalter, Elaine. *A Jury of Her Peers: American Women Writers from Anne Bradstreet to Annie Proulx*. New York: Alfred A. Knopf, 2009. Print.

Slinger, Joey. "Callwood's Picture Depends on Who Does the Painting." *Toronto Star* 4 April 1993: A2. Print.

Small, Peter. "Panel Calls for Probe of Radio Host's Remarks." *Toronto Star* 5 March 1996: A16. Print.

Smith, Michelle Denise. "Soup Cans and Love Slaves: National Politics and Cultural Authority in the Editing and Authorship of Canadian Pulp Magazines." *Book History* 9 (2006): 261–89. Print.

Smith, Sidonie. *Subjectivity, Identity, and the Body: Women's Autobiographical Practices in the Twentieth Century*. Bloomington: Indiana UP, 1993. Print.

Smith, Sidonie, and Julia Watson. *Reading Autobiography: A Guide for Interpreting Life Narratives*. Minneapolis: U of Minnesota P, 2001. Print.

Sonneborn, Liz. *An A to Z of American Indian Women*. Rev. ed. New York: Facts on File, 2007. Print.

Steedman, Carolyn. *Dust: The Archive and Cultural History*. New Brunswick: Rutgers UP, 2002. Print.

Stoffman, Judy. "Frum Family, Writers' Group at Odds over Comic's Remarks.' *Toronto Star* 29 April 1995: A28. Print.

Stoler, Ann Laura. *Along the Archival Grain: Epistemic Anxieties and Colonial Common Sense*. Princeton: Princeton UP, 2009. Print.

– "Colonial Archives and the Arts of Governance." *Archival Science* 2 (2002): 87–9. Print.

St. Onge, Anna. *Sheila Watson Fonds Finding Guide*. Toronto: John M. Kelly Library at the University of St Michael's College, 2009. Print.

Strong-Boag, Veronica Jane, and Carole Gerson. *Paddling Her Own Canoe: The Times and Texts of E. Pauline Johnson*. Toronto: U of Toronto P, 2000. Print.

Taylor, Chloe. *The Culture of Confession from Augustine to Foucault: A Genealogy of the Confessing Animal*. New York: Routledge, 2009. Print.

Taylor, Diana. *The Archive and the Repertoire: Performing Cultural Memory in the Americas*. Durham: Duke UP, 2003. Print.

Tebbel, John. "Harcourt Brace Jovanovich." *A History of Book Publishing in the United States*. Vol. 4, *The Great Change, 1940–1980*. New York: R.R. Bowker, 1981. 171–80. Print.

– *A History of Book Publishing in the United States*. Vol. 11, *The Expansion of the Industry, 1865–1919*. New York: R.R. Bowker, 1975. Print.

Tebbel, John, and Mary Ellen Zuckerman. *The Magazine in America: 1741–1990*. New York: Oxford UP, 1991. Print.

Thobani, Sunera. *Exalted Subjects: Studies in the Making of Race and Nation in Canada*. Toronto: U of Toronto P, 2007. Print.

Tiessen, Paul. "'I want my story told': The Sheila Watson Archive, the Reader, and the Search for Voice." *Basements and Attics, Closets and Cyberspace: Explorations in Canadian Women's Archives*. Ed. Linda M. Morra and Jessica Schagerl. Waterloo: Wilfrid Laurier UP, 2012. 263–80. Print.

Tippett, Maria. *By a Lady: Celebrating Three Centuries of Art by Canadian Women*. Toronto: Viking, 1992. Print.

– *Emily Carr: A Biography*. Toronto: Oxford UP, 1979. Print.

Turkel, William J. *The Archive of Place: Unearthing the Pasts of the Chilcotin Plateau*. Vancouver: UBC P, 2007. Print.

Vernon, Karina. "Invisibility Exhibit: The Limits of Library and Archives Canada's Multicultural Mandate." *Basements and Attics, Closets and Cyberspace: Explorations in Canadian Women's Archives*. Ed. Linda M. Morra and Jessica Schagerl. Waterloo: Wilfrid Laurier UP, 2012. 193–204. Print.

Walcott, Rinaldo. "By Way of a Brief Introduction – Insubordination: A Demand for a Different Canada." *Rude: Contemporary Black Canadian Cultural Criticism*. Ed. Rinaldo Walcott. Toronto: Insomniac, 2000. 7–10. Print.

Walker, Stephanie Kirkwood. *This Woman in Particular: Contexts for the Biographical Image of Emily Carr*. Waterloo: Wilfrid Laurier UP, 1996. Print.

Walters, Wendy W. *Archives of the Black Atlantic*. New York: Routledge, 2013. Print.

Watson, Sheila. *Deep Hollow Creek*. Toronto: McClelland & Stewart, 1992. Print.

– *The Double Hook*. Toronto: McClelland & Stewart, 1959; rpt. 1966. Print.

– *A Father's Kingdom*. Toronto: NCL, 2004. Print.

– *Five Stories*. Toronto: Coach House, 1984. Print.

– *Four Stories*. Toronto: Coach House, 1979. Print.

– "It's What You Say." [Interview with Sheila Watson.] *In Their Words: Interviews with Fourteen Canadian Writers*. By Bruce Meyer and Brian O'Riordan. Toronto: Anansi, 1984. 157–67. Print.

– Untitled interview (with Pierre Coupey, Roy Kiyooka, and Daphne Marlatt). *Capilano Review* 8/9 (1975–6): 351–60. Print.

– "What I'm Going to Do." *Sheila Watson: A Collection*. Special issue of *Open Letter* 3:1 (1974–5): 181–3. Print.

Watts-Dunton, Theodore. Introduction. *Flint and Feather: The Complete Poems of E. Pauline Johnson*. By Pauline Johnson. 1912. Repr: Toronto: Musson Book Company, 1913. vii–xvi. Print.

Willmott, Glenn. Afterword to *A Father's Kingdom*. By Sheila Watson. Toronto: NCL, 2004. 87–98. Print.
– "Modernism and Aboriginal Modernity: The Appropriation of Products of West Coast Native Heritage as National Goods." *Essays on Canadian Writing* 83 (2004): 75–139. Print.
– "The Nature of Modernism in *Deep Hollow Creek*." *Canadian Literature* 146 (1995): 30–48. Print.
– "Sheila Watson, Aboriginal Discourse, and Cosmopolitan Modernism." *The Canadian Modernists Meet*. Ed. Dean Irvine. Ottawa. U of Ottawa P, 2005. 101–16. Print.
Wood, Paul. *Varieties of Modernism*. New Haven: Yale UP, 2004. Print.
York, Lorraine. *Canadian Literary Celebrity in Canada*. Toronto: U of Toronto P, 2007. Print.
– "'Your Star': Pauline Johnson and the Tensions of Celebrity Discourse." *Canadian Poetry: Studies, Documents, Reviews* 51 (Fall/Winter 2002): 8–17. Print.

Index

www.ingramcontent.com/pod-product-compliance
Lightning Source LLC
LaVergne TN
LVHW090807070826
844660LV00022B/1102

* 9 7 8 1 4 4 2 6 2 6 4 2 3 *